Light Dragoons

"What is there like the army?" she interrupted . . . "I like the cavalry better than anything I know; and the dragoons the best of the cavalry!"

Thomas Hardy, *The Trumpet Major*

THE MAKING OF A REGIMENT

by
ALLAN MALLINSON

Pen & Sword
MILITARY

First published in Great Britain in 1993 by
Leo Cooper

Reprinted in 2006 and 2012 by
PEN & SWORD MILITARY
An imprint of
Pen & Sword Books Ltd
47 Church Street
Barnsley
South Yorkshire
S70 2AS

ISBN 978 1 84884 880 1

A CIP catalogue record for this book is
available from the British Library

Printed and bound in England
By CPI Group (UK) Ltd, Croydon, CR0 4YY

Pen & Sword Books Ltd incorporates the Imprints of Pen & Sword Aviation,
Pen & Sword Family History, Pen & Sword Maritime, Pen & Sword Military,
Pen & Sword Discovery, Wharncliffe Local History, Wharncliffe True Crime,
Wharncliffe Transport, Pen & Sword Select, Pen & Sword Military Classics,
Leo Cooper, The Praetorian Press, Remember When,
Seaforth Publishing and Frontline Publishing

For a complete list of Pen & Sword titles please contact
PEN & SWORD BOOKS LIMITED
47 Church Street, Barnsley, South Yorkshire, S70 2AS, England
E-mail: enquiries@pen-and-sword.co.uk
Website: www.pen-and-sword.co.uk

CONTENTS

MAPS

I am very pleased that after almost a decade and a half since the formation of The Light Dragoons, a second and updated edition of the Regimental history is being published. In the foreword to the first edition, my late predecessor, Her Royal Highness the Princess of Wales, declared the history to be a fitting way of expressing the determination of the serving and retired members of the 13th / 18th and 15th / 19th Hussars, that the amalgamation should be outstandingly happy and successful from the outset. Anyone who knows the Regiment knows that that determination has truly been rewarded.

In this history, the author draws together the many common threads of the six distinguished light cavalry regiments whose individual histories over nearly 300 years led to the formation of the new regiment on the 1st of December 1992. He also places the major events, campaigns and battles experienced by those regiments in a wider historical setting, so that we can understand clearly the important role played by our forebears in the challenges, triumphs and disasters of the British Nation. And, in the new chapter he does the same, for The Light Dragoons were involved from the outset in events that have shaped, and continue to shape, the world in the late-Twentieth and the Twenty-first Centuries.

We can all take pride in carrying forward the fine traditions and standards of our antecedent regiments, and in the achievements of The Light Dragoons. I, therefore, commend this book to all ranks and to the wider regimental family. I commend it, too, to those unconnected with the Regiment who would wish to see what it is that makes the British Army today such an effective and respected institution.

Abdullah II Ibn Al Hussein

Preface to the Second Edition

"A REGIMENT has two purposes. It is an administrative unit which, under the law, trains, disciplines and marshals men in arms for the preservation of a nation's peace and security . . . it has also to evoke from its members an habitual self-mastery and capacity for comradely selflessness and obedience which will enable them willingly to sacrifice their bodies and lives in the course of duty."

Sir ARTHUR BRYANT, *Jackets of Green*

That great, patriotic historian, Sir Arthur Bryant, wrote those words three decades ago in his glorious history of The Rifle Brigade. I quoted them in the preface to the first edition of Light Dragoons because I thought them singularly apt for a history of both the 13th/18th Royal Hussars (Queen Mary's Own) and 15th/19th The King's Royal Hussars, who on 1st December 1992 amalgamated to become The Light Dragoons – and in turn for the history of their forebear regiments, who had all at one time or another borne the separate numbers 13th, 15th, 18th and 19th Light Dragoons. I did not think, then, that the words could still be quite so apt a decade and a half into that amalgamation. Apt and poignant, as I trust the additional chapter in this new edition will show.

That first edition sparked considerable interest outside the Regiment. It was mainly, I think, through curiosity: no regiment had before – or has since – published a consolidated history for an amalgamation. The late Field-Marshal Lord Carver, a man of impeccable military and literary credentials, reviewed the book in *The Spectator* under the headline "Four Into One Will Go." For readers without the benefit of old-fashioned arithmetic, this refers to the first step in the process of division – a clever allusion, though amalgamation is of course the opposite of division. What it was saying was that the historical evidence suggested the amalgamation would be a good one. The Light Dragoons' first decade and a half has been a triumphant justification of that prediction. Indeed, the evidence speaks for itself, and could not be better summarized than in the words of General the Lord Guthrie, former Chief of the Defence Staff, which open the additional chapter of this new edition.

We may say with certainty now, therefore: "four into one will go." Indeed, they have gone – happily and in fine cavalry style.

ALLAN MALLINSON
The Cavalry and Guards Club
April, 2006

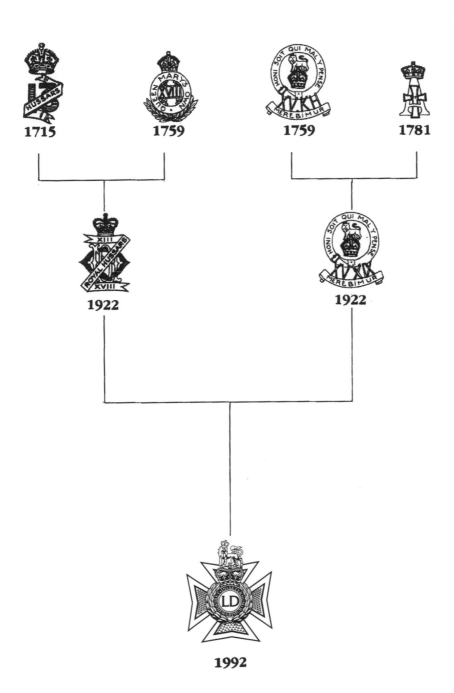

1715 **1759** **1759** **1781**

1922 **1922**

1992

CHAPTER 1

The Glorious Reinforcement

"It is right to have some cavalry to support and assist infantry, but not to look upon them as the main force of an army, for they are highly necessary to reconnoitre, to scour roads ... and to lay waste an enemy's country, and to cut off their convoys; but in the field battles which commonly decide the fate of nations, they are fitter to pursue an enemy that is routed and flying, than anything else."

MACHIAVELLI, *The Art of War*

Foundations of the Regular Army; Munden's Dragoons; Eliott's Light Horse: Emsdorf; Drogheda's Light Horse; 19LD.

When the Northern Light Horse swept up a hillside in France in 1544 in a demonstration of their speed and manoeuvrability, Charles V, the Holy Roman Emperor, was said to have cried out with honest delight. Three hundred years later another foreign observer, the French General Bosquet, said of the Light Brigade's advance towards the Russian guns at Balaklava, *"C'est magnifique"*. Light cavalry have always excited admiration, even if their exploits have sometimes justified Bosquet's qualification, *"mais ce n'est pas la guerre."*

Henry VIII's Northern Light Horse were formed from the bands of cattle reivers and drovers of the Scottish borders. They had served the King well in patrolling those wild parts and he took them with him to France as a reconnaissance and raiding force, where, in alliance with the Emperor Charles, he

1

sought to inflict a salutary defeat on the French King Francis I. These northern horsemen wore iron caps and cuirasses and carried lances and bucklers (small round shields), or occasionally bows. They rode sturdy little ponies of around 13 hands, native to the borders, and proved an invaluable component of Henry's 6,000-strong army.

When the King returned to England, successful, he stood-down the Light Horse from royal service. This followed the pattern of previous centuries whereby there was never a standing army, only armies improvised from various bodies of armed men at a time of crisis. One hundred years later, however, the English Civil War was to change this pattern for good.

Both Parliamentarians and Royalists entered the Civil War ill-equipped and ill-trained. The Royalist cavalry had the edge because Prince Rupert of the Rhine, King Charles I's German nephew, led the Cavaliers with dash and courage. Better-horsed and better horsemen than the Parliamentary forces for the most part, they had things largely their own way until the Roundheads raised the so-called New Model Army, the first to receive regular pay. The new army's cavalry consisted of eleven regiments of horse, each with six troops of 100 men, and one regiment of dragoons 1,000 strong. The regular cavalrymen of the Horse wore light iron helmets and, over leather coats, light iron cuirasses. The dragoons, or mounted infantrymen, wore no armour and usually fought on foot with a sword and musket. They also did the outpost and reconnaissance work for the army, although they were neither properly mounted nor equipped for the job.

When the Civil War ended, the Parliamentary army was largely kept in being, but when the experiment of the Commonwealth failed and Charles II was restored to the throne ten years later, in 1660, the army was hastily disbanded. This continued the pattern of not maintaining expensive standing forces in peacetime, but it was also hastened because of doubts as to the army's loyalty. The disbandment was short-lived, however, since a small uprising in London against the King in 1661 led him to decide that a regiment of horse was needed in addition to his

Life Guards and Foot. The Earl of Oxford raised, accordingly, a regiment from recently discharged Parliamentary troopers and, adopting his family colour as its uniform, it became known in time as 'The Blues'. The following year Charles married the daughter of the Queen Regent of Portugal, Princess Catherine of Braganza. It is said that the large dowry offered made the match irresistible in London: £800,000 in cash and the ports of Tangier and Bombay was the richest dowry any bride had brought to England. Tangier needed a large garrison, including mounted troops, so a third horse-regiment, later to become the 1st, or Royal, Dragoons, was raised.

And so, in the aftermath of the Civil War, the foundations of the regular, standing army, with its continuous history to the present day, were laid. It expanded frequently in the next hundred years as the situation at home and abroad became more threatening. The Duke of Monmouth's rebellion in 1685, on the accession of the Catholic King James II, gave cause to raise a further eight cavalry regiments, bringing the total to eleven. The Infantry meanwhile comprised sixteen regiments. After James was deposed these numbers increased steadily during King William III's campaigns in Ireland and on the Continent. The War of the Spanish Succession (1703-13), in Queen Anne's reign, saw further expansion, and at the accession of George I the Cavalry stood at seventeen regiments, of which two were Life Guards, eight true horse and the rest dragoons.

In 1715, at the prospect of the 'Jacobite' rising in Scotland to restore the Stuart monarchy, the Army was again hastily expanded and a further five regiments of dragoons were raised during July, including one under the colonelcy of Richard Munden. This was later to be given the number 'Thirteen'. Munden's Dragoons were raised in the Midlands and first quartered in Cheshire.

Dragoons were not intended for use as cavalry in the usual sense of the term: that was the rôle of the regiments of horse. Dragoons wore red, predominantly the colour of the Infantry, and were used to seize defiles or secure flanks, dismounting once in position to fight on foot. They wore a lighter boot than the long jacked boots of the Cavalry proper and periodically had to

3

be reminded of their primary function, the Duke of Cumberland (Commander-in-Chief of the Army) at one stage remonstrating that:

> "the Dragoon Officers are to remember that they are still Dragoons, and not Horse, that they are to march, and attack on Foot, if there is occasion when Dismounted, therefore, the Men's Boots are not to be encumbered with great Spur Leathers and Chains, to hinder them from getting over a Hedge, Ditch or Works when they are ordered to attack."

The term 'dragoon' itself derives from the French *dragon*, a short musket, or carbine, which suggested a fire-spouting dragon. It was carried in the middle of the sixteenth century by Marshal de Brissac's mounted foot, who seem to have been the first to be called dragoons.

The Thirteenth first went into action on 12 November, 1715, against Jacobite rebels who had advanced as far south as Preston and barricaded the streets of the town. The rebel piquets were quickly driven in, and a squadron of the regiment dismounted and stormed the street leading to Wigan. The other two squadrons likewise supported a party storming the Lancaster road. The rebels surrendered. The Thirteenth had been blooded. Only four men and twelve horses had been wounded and the regiment's conduct earned the praise of the general officer commanding. They then spent the next thirty years on quiet home service or on garrison duty in Ireland.

Their next taste of action was far less praiseworthy, however. The 'Old Pretender', Prince James Stuart, had been defeated in 1715 and was in lonely exile, but the Jacobite cause was again taken up in 1745 by his son, Charles Edward Stuart, 'Bonnie Prince Charlie'. The 13th Dragoons, under Colonel James Gardiner, were stationed in Scotland when the 'Young Pretender' landed on the west coast in July. When eventually he began making his way to Edinburgh with his Highland army, the Thirteenth, along with other forces, were ordered to Falkirk from their billets in Stirling in order to intercept him. The two armies met on 21 September at the village of Prestonpans, seven miles west of Edinburgh. In the thick mist of that autumn morning a strong column of highlanders advanced against the Royal army's right flank and captured a large part of the artillery. According to the Thirteenth's own historical records (published in 1847):

> "The dragoons, seeing the artillery lost, became disheartened . . . fired their carbines, and then advanced to charge a column of Highlanders, so numerous, that the dragoons were dismayed, and being seized with sudden panic, the greater part of them fled."

It was all over in less than ten minutes. Colonel Gardiner was killed trying to rally his, and other, troops: a highlander cut him down from his horse with a scythe fastened to a pole, and as he fell another highlander delivered a mortal blow to the head with a battle axe. The incident is commemorated in a fine silver centrepiece in the officers' mess.

This defeat allowed the Jacobite army to march south as far as Derby, but here they lost their nerve and turned for home to be decisively defeated at Culloden six months later. But before this battle, which sent Bonnie Prince Charlie fleeing for his life "over the sea to Skye", the Thirteenth were to lose another commanding officer, this time Colonel Francis Ligonier, brother of John Ligonier who was eventually to become a field marshal and commander in chief. Colonel Ligonier contracted pleurisy early in the new year of 1746. The Thirteenth were part of the force sent to relieve the siege of Stirling, and, when a general action looked likely, Ligonier left his sick bed since he was temporarily in command of the dragoon brigade. Pleurisy would have been bad enough, but a few days before the battle the surgeon had "bled and blistered" him. There was a strong wind and heavy rain throughout the day and night, and it was numbingly cold. The force retired to Linlithgow at last light, Ligonier's dragoons covering the withdrawal throughout the darkness, but a week later the heroic colonel was dead of pneumonia.

The Thirteenth had not distinguished themselves during this rebellion. It is said that the Duke of Cumberland considered the regiment to be so unreliable that he left them out of the order of battle for Culloden. It was to be nearly sixty years before they fully regained their reputation in action. Perhaps Dr Johnson, who began his famous dictionary two years after the rebellion, had this in mind when he made the following punning entry under *dragoon*: "a kind of soldier that serves indifferently either on foot or on horseback", 'indifferently' then used as much to mean 'equally, without difference' as 'not especially good'.

Notwithstanding the distractions of such rebellions, the British army was at this time beginning to take on some of the characteristics of the larger continental armies, but unlike them it had few light infantry and no light cavalry. The Austrian armies had always brought with them a host of savage creatures called pandours, Croats, Crabbates, Tolpatches and hussars, who were not strictly part of the order of battle. They were irregulars – a wild, thieving, plundering, murdering lot of rogues, dressed as outrageously as they sounded. They were little use for fighting but invaluable for reconnaissance and raiding.

The French had had their hussars since the seventeenth century, and under Marshal Saxe employed Polish scouts. The Russians, famously, had their Cossacks. Now it was the turn of the British to raise light cavalry. In 1756, at the outbreak of the Seven Years' War with France, and under threat of invasion, a light troop was added to eleven regiments of dragoons. Each man in the troop wore a jockey's cap and boots and was expected to carry out his task mounted, unlike the rest of the regiment.

The Seven Years' War was essentially a violent eruption of French and British colonial and trade rivalry. It was also another outbreak of French continental expansionism, though a less virulent one than that which had seen in the century with Louis XIV or was to see it out with Napoleon. Britain could not ignore it, however, because the British King was also Elector of Hanover. Two alliances therefore developed, on the one hand Britain and Prussia, on the other France, Austria and Russia. Three years later, in 1759, as the war intensified, six regiments of light dragoons were raised, of which the first was the Fifteenth, or 'Eliott's Light Horse' after their colonel, George Augustus Eliott.

Eliott was an exceptional and distinguished soldier. Born in 1717, he was educated at Leyden University in Holland and the French military college of La Fère. He served for two years as a volunteer in the Prussian army before becoming a cornet in the 2nd Life Guards in 1739, and was present at the battles of Dettingen and Fontenoy, becoming aide-de-camp to George II in 1755. In 1758 he led a 'brigade', formed from the light troops of nine dragoon regiments, in raids on the French coast. Three years after raising the Fifteenth he was promoted major general and gained renown fifteen years later in the protracted and heroic defence of Gibraltar as the colony's governor.

Under their commanding officer, the Earl of Pembroke, Eliott's Light Horse immediately became the focus of style and popularity. "There was much smartness in these light dragoons", writes Sir John Fortescue, the finest chronicler of the British Army: "They wore a helmet with all kinds of adornments and their horses were of the hunter type with nag-tails, contrasting much with the full tail which by that time had become the rule for the heavies." One of the reasons for the smartness in Eliott's was no doubt the fact that a large number of their recruits were taken from journeyman tailors on strike at the time, so many in fact that the regiment gained the nickname 'The Tabs'. In August 1760, needing replacements for the casualties sustained in Germany, the Secretary of War, Viscount Barrington, wrote to the Lord Chamberlain suggesting that the Fifteenth should be brought up to strength by drafts from one of the other light dragoon regiments still in England: "And I think those Draughts would be replaced here, with tolerable ease; there being still a great disposition in the people to enlist in the Light Cavalry."

But why did Eliott's need battle casualty replacements so soon after raising? The year 1759 was, after all, one of the most victorious in the nation's history: in Germany the allies had won a significant victory at Minden; at sea the French fleet was practically destroyed in the battles of Quiberon Bay and Lagos, and in

Canada Amherst took Ticonderoga and Wolfe took Quebec. The author Horace Walpole complained that the church bells were worn threadbare with ringing for victories. In Prussia, however, things were going badly, with Austria and Russia inflicting several defeats on Frederick the Great's armies, so in early 1760 Eliott's Light Horse, together with six other cavalry regiments, were sent out to Germany as part of what was to become known as 'The Glorious Reinforcement'. They were in action within three days of arriving but it was in July at Emsdorf, near Kassel, that this new regiment astonished the veterans by charging three times against formed French infantry, routing them completely. Eliott's captured six cannon and took prisoner no less than 177 officers and nearly 2,500 other ranks. They lost 125 men and 168 horses, however, about a quarter of their strength, and had to be sent back to Hanover to reorganize. But they had achieved a famous victory. At a stroke they had restored the Cavalry's reputation, lost almost irretrievably at Minden the previous year when the useless Lord George Sackville had sat idly by with his cavalry despite the protests of his second in command (the Marquess of Granby). The brilliant affair at Emsdorf confirmed the value of light dragoons. The precedent was also established, to be followed so often in the next century and a half by British light cavalry, of charging through and through without hesitation – though not always to advantage.

The battle also has unique significance in the history of the Army as a whole, for it was the first time an action was recognized as a battle honour: *Emsdorff* (the second 'f' was later dropped) was ordered to be engraved on the helmets of all ranks, and the reversed Lilies of France to be borne on all appointments. Battle honours for earlier actions such as Blenheim and Dettingen were authorized later following the Emsdorf precedent.

Their casualties replaced and remounts found, Eliott's were back in action by October and repeated their earlier exploits at the battle of Kloster Kampen on the Rhine above Cologne. Here the British and German infantry performed less than their usual best, and their retreat from the field would almost certainly have turned into a rout had it not been for a spirited charge by the 15th Light Dragoons. They undoubtedly saved the Crown Prince of Brunswick and his troops. Undoubtedly, that is, if the Fifteenth were in fact there: Fortescue says they were; Wylly, the regiment's weightiest historian, believes they were not. What is certain, however, is that King George II died in that same month and was succeeded by his grandson, George III. And, France's energy having been sapped, peace began to spread across the Continent, formally recognized in 1763 by the Treaty of Paris, a monument more to the *energy* of the Prime Minister, Pitt, than to his strategic thinking, of which more later.

Meanwhile in Ireland, one of the other five regiments of light dragoons was being raised at Moore Abbey, Kildare – seat of Charles Moore, Sixth Earl of Drogheda. They were numbered 'Nineteen', were known as Drogheda's Light Horse and they too wore red with much ornamentation to the uniform. In 1762 they were renumbered 'Eighteen'. There was much renumbering and renaming at this time as a result of the reductions at the end of the Seven Years' War. In 1765 George III honoured Eliott's with the title "15th The King's Light Dragoons" but they were also, for a few years, designated "1st (or The King's Royal) Light Dragoons" and the Eighteenth were also known as the Fourth. This numbering of light cavalry separately from the rest of the line was short-lived but reflected the general intention that light dragoons should be employed in the same way that irregulars were in continental armies; indeed they were known colloquially as 'hussars'. In some regiments the word was actually brought into the title, albeit unofficially, as early as the 1790s. The 25th Light Dragoons, who equally unofficially adopted the fur-trimmed jacket, or pelisse, were known for example as 'Gwyn's Hussars' after their colonel.

The word *hussar* itself was rather fancifully believed to derive from the Hungarian *husz*, 'twenty', because at one time in Hungary one cavalry soldier used to be levied from every twenty families. The word in fact entered the Hungarian language through Serbian from the Italian *Corsaro*, a pirate or freebooter. "Properly speaking," maintained one senior French officer, "hussars are little more than bandits on horseback."

There was really no difference, as far as the British army was concerned, between light dragoons and hussars although the Austrian army would not have expected to see hussars drilled in ranks as much as the British insisted, and the British notion of field discipline would certainly not have embraced the French definition of *hussar*. It boiled down essentially to a matter of style, dress and a certain *panache* which accompanied this – an independent spirit, an abhorrence of routine and a penchant for the daring. There was also more than an element of swagger, so that Conan Doyle's *Brigadier Gerard* could say that the hussar "always had the whole population running; the women towards us, and the men away".

Although the new regiments received special training in horsemanship and were taught to fire from the saddle even at the gallop, they received no instruction in scouting and reconnaissance, the true work of the hussar. Some commentators have remarked adversely on the Fifteenth's casualties at Emsdorf, many gained in the twenty-mile pursuit which followed. Comparing them with the accompanying Prussian hussars who sustained no casualties at all, Fortescue suggests that the Fifteenth did not yet know their business as light cavalry, notwithstanding their undoubted courage.

Another inconsistency was squadron guidons. Light troops, but especially those acting in the fashion of irregulars, strictly speaking never had to conform to a line nor rally to a point and therefore had no need of colours, standards or guidons (witness rifle troops who to this day do not have colours). They were also dressed in red, a colour wholly inappropriate for 'irregulars'. This changed in 1782 when all light dragoons were ordered into blue, only the farriers having been in blue previously.

After Emsdorf light dragoons became very much the mode with the War Office. Regiments were raised and then disbanded shortly afterwards when the immediate need was past. In 1779 the number 'Nineteen' was again seen in the line: the 19th Light Dragoons were raised, together with four other light dragoon regiments, largely because the revolutionary war in America was going badly for Britain. The Nineteenth saw only home service in southern England and East Anglia, however, and were disbanded four years later when Britain recognized American independence and concluded a peace. The 23rd Light Dragoons remained after this 1783 contraction because they had been raised specifically for service with the Honourable East India Company and had arrived in Madras only the previous year. In 1786 the War Office renumbered this regiment 'Nineteen'. So by this year, all the regiments of the present-day Light Dragoons were wearing the blue jackets and fur-fringed caps of the light cavalry because, in 1783, the Thirteenth were converted from heavy to light dragoons.

But what of the Thirteenth and the Eighteenth during the intervening period? In 1748 the Thirteenth had embarked for Ireland where they remained for nearly 50 years until the French revolutionary wars called for their service overseas. There can scarcely have been a corner of that island where the red coats and dark green facings of the 13th Dragoons, and then the dark blue coats and buff facings of the 13th Light Dragoons, were not seen. It was the same story with the Eighteenth: years of garrison duty throughout Ireland, so much so that 'Irish' came to be used unofficially in the regiment's title from time to time. There appears to have been much extended absence of officers, and general undermanning, during these years. Arthur Wellesley, later Duke of Wellington, was gazetted twice to the regiment, in 1791 and again in 1792, before exchanging into the 33rd Foot which he afterwards commanded in India. There is no record, however, of his ever having joined for duty.

In addition to the continuing problems in Ireland, Britain at this time was finding herself in an increasingly friendless state. The open rebellion which had broken out in America in 1775 had presented the European powers with an opportunity to challenge British power. France was trying to recapture the West Indies and India. Spain was raiding convoys and besieging Gibraltar whose defences were, as has been described, in the capable hands of Lieutenant-General Eliott. The Baltic powers, sensing Britain's impotency, looked likely at any time to challenge her naval supremacy. Prussia, usually a worthy ally, seemed to welcome this distraction of European power in order to be able to get on with internal reconstruction. Holland, too, joined in to get her share of the spoils. The American war was brought to an end early in 1783, not entirely conclusively as will be seen in Chapter Five, and the other threats never quite proved to be as bad as they had appeared, but when Britain went to war with revolutionary France in 1793 the situation looked bleak.

CHAPTER 2

Breaking More Windows with Guineas

"The English Army, under Pitt, was the laughing stock of all Europe. It could not boast of one single brilliant exploit. It had never shown itself on the continent but to be beaten, chased, forced to re-embark, or forced to capitulate. To take some sugar island in the West Indies, to scatter some mob of half naked Irish peasants, such were the most splendid victories won by the British troops under Pitt's auspices."

Lord MACAULAY

13LD and 18LD in the West Indies 1794–8; 15LD in the Netherlands expedition 1794–5: Villers-en-Cauchies; 15LD and 18LD in the Helder Campaign 1799: Willems, Egmont-op-Zee.

William Pitt, the chief minister during the time that most of the regiments of light dragoons were raised, had been widely criticized for his strategy of diversionary attacks on the French coast during the Seven Years' War. These operations were said to have consumed far more in resources than their results justified: his critics likened them to "breaking windows with guineas". His classic failure to concentrate forces to achieve decisive results meant that France's defeat, and the peace treaty of 1763, was more the result of French exhaustion than of British strategy.

Thirty years later there was another Pitt in the office of prime minister. 'Pitt the Younger', so-called to distinguish him from his father, had succeeded to that office in 1783 in his twenty-fifth year. His preoccupation during the decade which followed was the reduction of the national debt. Strict economy was his policy, and nowhere was this more sharply observed than in the Army. Pitt saw no need of a strong standing army. His problem was, however, that as one commitment disappeared, another grew: India in particular was beginning to demand significant numbers of British regular troops, including cavalry – as will be seen in Chapter 3. There was little chance of returning to a small peace establishment, and what little money there was for the Army was spread increasingly thinly.

The Army's strength in 1783 was set at 50,000 men, of which some 17,000 were for Britain, 12,000 for Ireland, 9,000 for the West Indies, 3,000 for Gibraltar and more than 6,000 for India, with artillery numbering 3,000. It was, arguably, the worst-recruited, poorest-equipped and worst-trained regular army in British history. It lacked organization and direction, but, thankfully, when it was well led, it had fighting spirit and endurance. Indeed, the historian Sir Arthur Bryant has called the 22 years of campaigning on which Britain embarked in 1793 *"The Years of Endurance"*.

In 1789 the French assembly, no longer able to tolerate the absolute monarchy of Louis XVI, forcibly introduced constitutional controls. The French Revolution had begun. The first two years saw an indecisive power struggle among various factions; it was not until the summer of 1792 that the institution of the monarchy itself was seriously threatened. Louis handled the crisis with total ineptness, however, and on 21 September the First Republic was proclaimed. Four months to the day later, the King was executed by guillotine and there soon followed the mass executions of the 'Reign of Terror'. The Revolutionary Council, having thus thrown caution to the wind, annexed Belgium and massed an army for the invasion of Holland. It was an act of national expansion masked by ideological crusading, and, knowing that such a course was bound to bring Britain to war, revolutionary France took the initiative and declared war on Britain on 1 February 1793. She was already nominally at war with Austria and Prussia.

Britain went to war most reluctantly. Pitt, who had sensed its inevitability, had called out two-thirds of the Militia in December 1792, and received Parliament's authority to strengthen the Army by 17,000 soldiers. He now made precisely the same faulty choice of strategy as his father. He believed that the French could be held and defeated in Europe by Austrian and Prussian armies financed by Britain. For her part, Britain would take the French possessions in the West Indies, thereby generating the wealth with which to subsidize the Austrians and Prussians. He failed to see that Flanders, astride the Belgian-Dutch border, was the vital theatre. In this flawed strategy of dispersion, which was soon to look like breaking more windows with guineas, The Light Dragoons' forebears played a significant part – the Fifteenth with great distinction in the Low Countries and again in the later campaign in north Holland, the Thirteenth in the West Indies with appalling losses, and the Eighteenth with quite staggering losses in the West Indies and with largely unrecognized achievements in north Holland. The Nineteenth enjoyed the most spectacular success, however, in India – of which more in the next chapter.

Despite Pitt's intention to pursue a 'blue water' strategy against the French and their possessions, Britain was forced almost immediately to assign some of her few uncommitted regiments to the defence of Holland. The Dutch Stadtholder, or president, was reduced to near panic at the prospect of a French invasion, and a British brigade of three battalions of footguards was sent to bolster both his and the Dutch army's spirits. It was not a useful gesture: many guardsmen became impossibly drunk during the embarkation and had to be carried to the ships on carts; reserves and supplies were not available, and the force was instructed not to move more than twenty-four hours' march from the coast in case a hasty evacuation became necessary. One month later, in April 1793, three weak battalions of the line were sent to join the Guards, and the Duke of York was sent to command the force which, although meant only for defensive operations, was to prove quite incapable of *any* effective action.

It became clear to Pitt that, in order to maintain the anti-French alliance, 'The First Coalition', he would have to take the offensive against the Austrians in south Holland and Belgium. This required the British to augment their expeditionary force, but at that moment there was scarcely an infantry battalion in any condition to be sent to the Netherlands. Dundas, Pitt's war minister, was therefore obliged to send cavalry instead – fourteen regiments including the 15th Light Dragoons, their combined strength numbering only 2,500. This cavalry force was to be augmented by some 13,000 of King George III's Hanoverian troops (he was also Elector of Hanover) and by hiring 8,000 Hessian mercenaries. The Duke of York, by the late summer of 1793, was to command an army of 17,000.

Two squadrons of the Fifteenth, a little over 200 men, under the command of Lieutenant-Colonel George Churchill, embarked at Blackwall and landed two days later, on May Day, at Ostend. Churchill, unusually for those times, had been commissioned as a cornet in the Fifteenth and had risen to the lieutenant-colonelcy within the regiment. More usually, officers advanced by transfer on purchase into regiments where a vacancy existed at least once during their service, and frequently at every rank. Opportunities were created, however, when war thinned the ranks of officers, leading to juniors being promoted 'in the field' without purchase. Churchill was a brave and able commander, rising eventually to lieutenant-general, and exercised a remarkably relaxed but effective discipline: the lash was a punishment very rarely used in the Fifteenth, whereas in many another regiment it was the usual form of punishment for even slight transgressions. This approach to discipline continued to be a regimental characteristic for many years until the practice elsewhere in the Army became the same. Nevertheless it does seem that the enlisted man was regarded more as an individual in the Fifteenth, and for that matter in the other light cavalry regiments, than he usually was elsewhere – as will be seen shortly in the story of Private Comberbache.

From Ostend, the Duke of York's Anglo-Hanoverian army, with the Austrian, Prussian and Dutch armies operating independently, embarked on a plodding campaign to evict the French from Flanders. The nursery rhyme sums up the campaign's

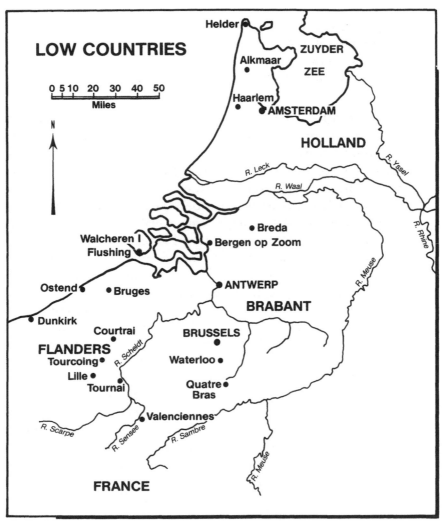

LOW COUNTRIES

0 5 10 20 30 40 50
Miles

N

Helder
ZUYDER
Alkmaar
ZEE
Haarlem
AMSTERDAM
HOLLAND
R. Leck
R. Yssel
R. Waal
• Breda
Walcheren I
Bergen op Zoom
Flushing
R. Meuse
Ostend
ANTWERP
Bruges
BRABANT
• Dunkirk
Courtrai
BRUSSELS
FLANDERS
R. Scheldt
Tourcoing
Waterloo •
Lille •
Quatre
Tournai
Bras
• Valenciennes
R. Scarpe
R. Sensee
R. Sambre
R. Meuse
FRANCE

character, if a little unfair to the commander in chief (he was
only thirty) and inaccurate as to the numbers involved:

"The grand old Duke of York;
He had ten thousand men;
He marched them up to the top of the hill,
And he marched them down again.

And when they were up, they were up;
And when they were down, they were down;
And when they were only halfway up,
They were neither up nor down."

The Fifteenth, however, were soon in action, notably at Famars near Valenciennes on 23 May, and were constantly called on for outpost work, on one occasion saving the Austrian cavalry leader, Prince von Schwarzenberg, from capture. Allied operations, though ponderous, had their successes, and by the late autumn of 1793 the French had been virtually ejected from the Low Countries. At this stage, with royalist risings against the revolution in southern and western France, and Spanish troops crossing the Pyrenees, a swift march on the revolutionaries' centre of gravity, Paris, could have brought about a French collapse. The campaign, however, under the overall command of the Austrian Duke of Coburg, petered out in a series of largely irrelevant sieges of unimportant border fortresses. The armies went into winter quarters in December, the Fifteenth employed by half-squadrons on outpost work on the Menin-Paris road from their quarters at Courtrai.

This respite for the French was their saving. The Committee of Public Safety took the opportunity to put the whole of France on a war footing – the *levée en masse*. Every man, woman and child, almost irrespective of age, was given a duty to perform. Young, single men were immediately enlisted into the army. Those who were older or married were stood-by for military service. The remainder were set to the running of depots and ordnance factories. Women and children made uniforms and medical dressings, and became nurses. Almost every public building was given a military use; private dwellings were subject to billeting and no house was free from the threat of requisitioning. When the allies emerged from their winter quarters they were to meet a formidable nation-in-arms.

The campaign of 1794 proved to be disastrous. It was brightened only by three British victories, in two of which the Fifteenth played their, by this time, customarily conspicuous part. At the battle of Villers-en-Cauchies (sometimes rendered *Villiers en Couche*) on 24 April, the Fifteenth and a regiment of Austrian hussars charged a large body of French cavalry which wheeled aside to reveal a 'masked battery' and an even larger body of infantry. The battery's guns, however, did little damage owing to faulty charges, and the French infantry was broken by the sheer momentum of the charge, but at some cost. It was said that there was scarcely a man nor a horse untouched "by steel or shot" that day. One charger, its tongue having been shattered by grapeshot, was famously nursed back to condition on a diet of milk and gruel.

The Fifteenth and the Austrians exploited for four miles. Their subsequent withdrawal was conducted not without some difficulty, since the infantry had not been entirely routed, and the French cavalry, augmented from a nearby garrison, were massing to cut off their line of retirement. Desperate fighting ensued, but the real losses were on the French side: 800 were killed and 400 wounded in this action. The Fifteenth and the Austrian Leopold Hussars, almost incredibly, lost less than thirty killed. One of the Fifteenth's farriers was said to have killed twenty-one of the enemy by his sword.

The Fifteenth earned praise from all quarters. Sir James Craig, the Duke of York's adjutant general, wrote to Secretary of State Dundas: "Yesterday was a glorious day for the 15th Light Dragoons, who distinguished themselves most honourably." The Austrian Emperor Francis II, who had himself been in a precarious situation near to the battle, ordered a gold medal to be struck and presented to each of the Fifteenth's officers who had taken part, admitting them two years later to the Order of Maria Theresa. The distinctive lace worn ever since by the regiment, and today by The Light Dragoons, is known as the 'Austrian Wave' and also dates from this combined feat of arms.

Only two weeks later, on 10 May, 1794, at Willems, the regiment was again in the thick of things, breaking several

French infantry squares (a novel formation for the French) and capturing several guns. The battle honours *Villers-en-Cauchies* and *Willems* were awarded to the Fifteenth, although the latter was not officially authorized until as late as 1909.

Eight days after Willems the allies suffered a severe defeat at Tourcoing, the battle being saved from complete disaster by, again, some spirited cavalry charges. Accolades from senior officers are expected after successful actions, but those from soldiers are sometimes more convincing: an infantryman, one Corporal Brown, wrote of the battle, "Our British Light Cavalry who were with us performed wonders of valour, charging the enemy with unexampled courage whenever they approached; it was no uncommon thing to see one of them attack three of the French dragoons at once, in order to rescue the prisoners they were carrying off."

The whole army possessed a remarkable fighting spirit, remarkable because the chaotic command and administrative arrangements hardly seem to have deserved it. Lieutenant-Colonel Arthur Wellesley, later Duke of Wellington, commanding a line battalion, saw what the British soldier was capable of if given only half a chance, and maintained that "seeing how not to do it" in this campaign was the foundation of his later success.

From June onwards allied cohesion began to falter as checks and defeats mounted. The armies were forced to retreat in diverging directions, the Austrians eastwards, the British and Dutch north to cover Holland. The Duke of York's army had to endure another harsh winter, this time rarely in the comfort of winter quarters. The sickness rate mounted, at one time a third of the army being non-effective. Indiscipline increased markedly, usually the result of alcohol. The Fifteenth were spared this, no doubt because of good regimental organization but also because they were at continuous duty covering the retreat. And what a retreat it was. Sir John Fortescue writes:

"Far as the eye could reach over the whitened plain were scattered gun-limbers, wagons full of baggage, stores or sick men, sutlers' carts and private carriages. Beside them lay the horses, dead; here a straggler who had staggered on to the bivouac and dropped to sleep in the arms of the frost; there a group of British and Germans round an empty rum cask; here forty English Guardsmen huddled together about a plundered wagon; there a pack-horse with a woman lying alongside it, and a baby swaddled in rags peering out of the pack with his mother's milk turned to ice upon its lips – one and all stark, frozen dead. Had the retreat lasted but three or four days longer, not a man would have escaped."

The Light Dragoons' forebears were to see more than they would wish of such retreats over the next 150 years.

The Duke of York was recalled to England to account for the campaign's failure, and soon afterwards Pitt's war council decided to evacuate the remaining force, reduced to around 6,000, via Bremen. The infantry and artillery were embarked in April, 1795, but the cavalry remained in Germany until the following winter. There was little for them to do, and they appear to have been very hospitably treated. Over 400 all ranks, as many horses, and a couple of dozen dependants embarked in early December, the bulk of them disembarking at North Shields just after Christmas.

* * *

Operations had not been going very well, either, in the Caribbean. In February, 1794, a British force of 7,000 men arrived in the region and, with the aid of French settlers loyal to the old royal regime, succeeded in capturing Guadeloupe, St Lucia, Marie Galante and the Saints, and gaining a foothold on Haiti, the western part of the island of Hispaniola (the eastern part being the Spanish colony Santo Domingo). French reinforcement across the Atlantic was largely, but not entirely, prevented by the Royal Navy, but two stronger forces were at work in the Caribbean: revolution among the black native population and yellow fever. In Guadeloupe, for instance, the garrison of 1,800 men was quickly reduced to 125 by sickness.

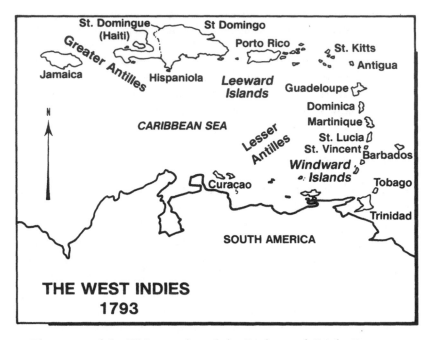

Elements of the Thirteenth and the Eighteenth Light Dragoons were pitched early into this fever trap. From their garrison duties in Ireland the Thirteenth had started sending detachments to the West Indies as early as 1790 until, by degrees, both regiments were fully committed there in 1796. The first to sail after war had broken out was a detachment of the Eighteenth, which left Cork and landed in Jamaica in July, 1794, while the following year the remainder of the regiment, numbering a little over 450 men, handed over their horses and sailed for Southampton and thence to Haiti. Remounts were to be bought for them from America but there is no evidence as to how effective this plan was. In 1796 the remainder of the Thirteenth left Ireland for Haiti via Barbados and Jamaica, a hundred of them remaining in Jamaica. After six months' campaigning in Haiti the regiment's losses were over 250 men, including twenty officers; they were withdrawn to Jamaica at the end of the year.

Late in 1795 the Maroon population of Jamaica began violent marauding from their strongholds in the central mountains. The

Maroons had been black slaves of the Spanish, who had fled their plantations in 1655 when the British conquered the island. They had been continually troublesome but after a treaty in 1738 they had been quiet in their reservations in the mountains. These reservations were deep broad ravines, easily defended because the approaches were so narrow as to prevent entry more than two abreast. They were known as 'cockpits'.

The situation in Jamaica had become serious by the middle of 1796, but by good fortune, in July that year, some 400 light dragoons (including troops from both the Thirteenth and Eighteenth) and an infantry battalion landed in Jamaica *en route* to reinforce Haiti. This force was immediately sequestered by the governor, Major-General The Lord Balcarres, to suppress the rebellion. Using them and the other troops on the island (a little over 500), he threw a cordon round the cockpits – a cordon of some forty miles in the most difficult country. This provoked the Maroons into open hostility and a successful attack was made on one of the cordon's outposts, the rebels concentrating their strength and at once exposing the weakness of the strategy. Balcarres ordered an immediate general attack, but it was so general that it achieved nothing. During the operation, however, a troop of the Eighteenth was caught in ambush. Thirty men were killed, half as many again were wounded and five officers and 102 men were taken prisoner. The prisoners were taken to Guadeloupe and were not released until the following year.

Angry at the failure of this attack, Balcarres strengthened his cordon with Jamaica militia. The Maroons, however, masters of fieldcraft and extremely good shots, systematically picked off cordon outposts and passed between them to ravage the plantations. When the rainy season came, at the end of August, the Militia melted away to their plantations leaving the cordon much weakened, its numbers of regulars already reduced by fever. The climax of disasters occurred a few weeks later when the ground commander, General Fitch, was killed in an ambush along with two other officers. In a little over a month the cordon strategy had cost seventy killed, numerous wounded, over 200 captured and many on the sick list. There was no evidence that a single Maroon had been touched.

Fitch was succeeded as ground commander by Colonel The Honourable George Walpole of the Thirteenth, who was promoted local major-general. Walpole saw immediately that a passive cordon strategy was doomed to failure. He therefore withdrew the Seventeenth Light Dragoons from the cordon and trained them intensively in skirmishing on foot. He also succeeded in positioning a howitzer in the mountains with which he harassed the Maroons in the cockpits. In the space of three months his offensive strategy, combining cordon and skilful assault on each cockpit in turn, supported by the howitzer, drove the Maroons into their final stronghold, where they surrendered on Walpole's assurance that they would be allowed to remain on the island.

Unfortunately, Balcarres and the Assembly of Jamaica repudiated this assurance, and the Maroons were shipped to Nova Scotia. Walpole was furious. He refused a reward of a ceremonial sword of the value of 500 guineas voted to him by the Assembly, and resigned his commission soon afterwards. In the words of Fortescue's history,

> "Small though was the scale of operations, the spirit with which he inspired his troops to a service of extreme danger and exceptional hardship mark him as something more than an ordinary officer; and it cannot be doubted that he was a loss to the Army."

Having succeeded in quietening Jamaica, Balcarres released the troops originally bound for Haiti, less the Thirteenth who were so weakened by sickness as to be almost non-effective. Thus, by December, 1796, the Thirteenth, numbering less than 200 men in all, had become part of the Jamaica garrison.

The French had been relatively easily subdued in Haiti: many were in any case royalists not revolutionaries. The slave and native population was, however, in total revolt, having had their liberty and equality declared by the revolutionary council in France, but at the end of 1795, by a curious turn of luck, the British gained unexpected support. Spain, fearing British intentions towards her own possessions in the Caribbean, ceded to France the other half of the island of which Haiti formed a part. This so enraged the Spanish settlers, who were vehemently anti-French, that they to all intents threw in their lot with the British occupying Haiti. The advantage did not last long, however, for late in the following year Spain declared war on Britain and this diverted even more troops from the Caribbean. By 1797 there was little prospect therefore of any strong, decisive offensive. Fighting with French republicans, Spanish loyalists and revolutionary blacks wore down the British forces for the next two years. They were evacuated in October, 1798, after some intriguing with one of the Black leaders to secure British trading supremacy and immunity from attacks on Jamaica.

The Thirteenth had been worse than decimated by the campaigns in the West Indies, the overwhelming cause being yellow fever. In July, 1798, the regiment handed over a few of the remaining able-bodied men to the Twentieth Light Dragoons and the rest, amounting to only fifty-two, sailed for home. The Eighteenth, who in the end had all been fed into the garrison in Haiti, sailed from there in October 1798, in the words of the regimental digest of service, "a skeleton". The two regiments had between them lost over 800 men.

Though the capture of the West Indian islands destroyed French Caribbean trade, Pitt's government had miscalculated: never having expected to fight the French, the negro population *and* the fever, the government had nearly destroyed the British Army too. Forty thousand British soldiers died in the West Indies during this campaign, and as many again were made permanently unfit for service. There was no discernible effect on revolutionary France. As J. S. Watson's *The Reign of George III* puts it: "France, like Attila, did not fight on a book-keeping system. She could be reduced by a blow at Paris, but not at Port-au-Prince [Haiti]."

* * *

On return to England both regiments' priority was to reconstitute themselves by recruiting. They did so relatively quickly, the Eighteenth in particular due to the strenuous efforts of their new commanding officer, the twenty-one-year-old Lieutenant-Colonel The Honourable Charles William Stewart, later Marquess of Londonderry, of whom more later.

Recruiting in the Eighteenth century was a haphazard affair to say the least: bribery, coercion, an alternative to imprisonment – these were as much a feature of recruiting as any heroic impulses. Nevertheless cavalry service could seem attractive to the recruit, especially if he knew nothing about horses and therefore nothing of the work involved in tending them. There were many who enlisted for noble reasons during the threat of invasion and some high-grade citizens found their way into the ranks. One such was Private Silas Tomkyn Comberbache, youngest son of the Vicar of Ottery St. Mary in Devon. He was a Classics scholar at Cambridge but after adopting extreme views on religion and politics he went to London in 1793 and enlisted in the Fifteenth.

S.T. Comberbache was, however, an alias: he was in fact Samuel Taylor Coleridge, later one of the giants of English literature, composer of the narrative poems *The Rime of the Ancient Mariner* and *Kubla Khan*. Comberbache was not, it seems, a natural soldier, to say the least. He became, in his own mocking phrase, "a very indocile Equestrian" and suffered greatly from boils, "dreadfully troublesome eruptions, which so grimly constellated my Posteriors". A cavalryman's boils are an even greater handicap than an infantryman's blisters: Comberbache was declared temporarily unfit to ride and instead was put in charge of a fellow dragoon suffering from smallpox in the 'Pest House' of the Henley workhouse. The experience of nursing him for a fortnight, alone, is said to have contributed something to the hallucinations in the *Ancient Mariner*. Fancy has it too that Comberbache's unusually cultured origins for a trooper were discovered when he could not resist correcting the orderly officer's Greek quotation from

Euripides at guard mounting. Once he was 'outed' he appears to have been treated with even more kindness by all ranks, sharing gentlemanly conversation and bottles of wine with the adjutant, and composing love-letters on behalf of those fellow troopers who were illiterate. After four months his brother was allowed to 'buy him out'. The Regimental Muster Roll records succinctly, and not entirely without foundation: "discharged S.T. Comberbache, Insane; 10 April 1794."

But the Fifteenth had another soldier at this time, Sergeant William Roberts, whose story is really quite remarkable. In 1750 one Hannah Snell had gained fame, or notoriety, by the publication of her memoirs as an enlisted 'man'. She had served for five years and had been invalided out of the Army with a pension after receiving wounds at the Battle of Pondicherry in India. Sergeant William Roberts served for twenty-one years with the 15th Light Dragoons, having enlisted in 1779 at the age of fourteen and having been marked out for early promotion during recruit training. But Roberts was in fact *Elizabeth* Roberts, the daughter of a Manchester bricklayer, who had been used to dressing as a boy in order to labour for her father. At the end of her colour service, during which she had been twice wounded in action – once by a sabre cut to the head, the second time by a musket ball in the leg – and with her sex still not discovered, she asked to prolong her engagement and accepted a transfer to the 37th Foot who were in the West Indies. It was not long before she contracted yellow fever and, from her supposed death bed, she 'confessed' to the wife of a sergeant. Quite what the 37th Foot made of the 15th Light Dragoons when this bombshell burst can only be imagined. Certainly the story is illuminating as to social conditions in the Army at the time, though it ultimately begs more questions than it answers. Nor it seems was Elizabeth Roberts any sort of physical freak, for soon after her unexpected recovery from the fever she married another sergeant in the 37th by whom she had three children!

The Fifteenth, since their evacuation from Bremen in 1795, had been re-training in southern England along the lines laid out in the new cavalry drill manuals written by General Sir

David Dundas, who had served for five years as a major with the regiment and was one of the Army's early tactical innovators. Dundas's manuals placed particular emphasis on the charge at a regulated speed with rapid rallying and recalling. A full establishment and good training were of vital importance, for two of the three regiments would soon be committed to action: in January, 1799, the fragile truce with France came to an end with the formation of Pitt's 'Second Coalition' consisting of Britain, Russia, Austria and Prussia.

Pitt immediately decided to mount a combined operation from north Holland with the Russians in order to recapture the Dutch and Belgian arsenals and the Dutch fleet. These were in the hands of the French and French-sympathizers in the so-called Batavian Republic (formerly Holland), one of the several new 'puppet' republics created by revolutionary France, and in Belgium which had been fully annexed by France. The campaign was also expected to stimulate a Dutch royalist rebellion which would assist the ejection of the French and restore the pro-British Prince of Orange to the Dutch throne.

The Fifteenth and the Eighteenth were ordered to muster in the force being assembled for this expedition under the command of General Sir Ralph Abercromby, an exceptionally able general who had done well in the West Indies despite the difficulties. The overall command of the allied army was again to be the Duke of York's.

The landing in Holland was made on 27 August, 1799, at the Helder peninsula against stiff resistance from the republican Dutch. Three days later the entire Dutch fleet surrendered under the guns of the Royal Navy, but the land operations proved less successful. Cooperation between the allies was not good and logistics were wretched. The popular Dutch royalist uprising failed to materialize. Some indecisive skirmishing took place for a month or so and then the Duke ordered a general attack at Bergen-op-Zoom in which both regiments took part, Stewart of the Eighteenth particularly distinguishing himself in spite of being wounded. The battle was equally indecisive, however, since the Russians failed to hold their initial gains.

Two weeks later, in pouring rain which persisted throughout September and October, Abercromby renewed the attack at Bergen. In this action the Fifteenth skirmished with French hussars along the sandy coastline for six miles, finally assisting in the repulse of a French counter-attack in front of the town of Egmont-op-Zee, which became their fourth battle honour. Although the attack at Bergen was much more successful, the allies were again checked by the French four days later while following up. At this point, as Watson's history puts it, "The armies stuck in the mud and sickened." The Duke of York decided that further campaigning was pointless: after a treaty with the French, hostilities ceased on 18 October and evacuation to England took place soon afterwards. Napoleon Bonaparte seized power in France the following month.

And so ended the most dismal period in the Army's history, although courage, endurance and low-level tactical success had been far from uncommon, as the conduct of the 13th, 15th and 18th Light Dragoons demonstrates. Being chased off the continent, struggling to take and subdue sugar islands in the West Indies, scattering unruly mobs of Irish peasants, this indeed seemed to be the Army's fate. Fortunately for the esteem of the Army, for the prosperity of the country and to the greatest pride of The Light Dragoons, some truly remarkable military feats were being seen elsewhere . . . in India.

CHAPTER 3

The Elephant, Superscribed 'Assaye'

"The Duke of Wellington always thought of Assaye – all his victories and Waterloo notwithstanding – as the best thing he had done in the way of fighting."

Earl STANHOPE

19LD in India: Seringapatam; Mysore; Assaye.

For much of history, India has been ruled by invaders. Greeks, Persians, Turks and others have come and gone. Early in the sixteenth century a descendant of Genghis Khan, Zahir-ud-Din Mohammad, better known as Babur, led a Mongol army into India from Afghanistan. Occupying Delhi and Agra, he extended his power eastward and founded the Moghul dynasty.

The dynasty was still in place when, on 31 December, 1600, Queen Elizabeth I incorporated the remarkable establishment which became the Honourable East India Company. The royal charter, for "The Governor and Company of Merchants of London trading into the East Indies", granted the exclusive right to trade with all countries beyond the Cape of Good Hope. In 1609 King James I renewed the Company's charter in perpetuity and in the next two years trading stations, or 'factories', were established along the coastline of Bengal.

From the outset, Dutch, Portuguese and French competition was intense. At times this developed into open warfare, particularly with the Dutch. In 1634 the Great Moghul granted the English permission to trade throughout Bengal, the original agreement having confined them to the coast. The Company's size and strength began to increase rapidly. It acquired almost sovereign powers when Charles II gave it the right to coin money, exercise criminal and civil jurisdiction, raise an army, form alliances and make war and peace. In 1668 he presented it with the port of Bombay which his bride, Catherine of Braganza, had brought in her dowry along with Tangier.

After the death in 1707 of Aurungzeb, the sixth Moghul Emperor of Hindustan, India began to slide into anarchy. Many provincial governors seized the opportunity to create their own independent states and to turn themselves into rajahs, and the Company took the same opportunity to acquire as much of the old empire as it conveniently could. This entangled the Company in Indian politics, and warning bells began to sound in Britain over its growing power. When a Company employee, Robert Clive – 'Clive of India' – set loose the European captives from the infamous 'Black Hole of Calcutta' and went on to defeat the French-backed Nawab of Bengal at Plassey in 1757 with company troops, Parliament began to demand closer control. It was not for another hundred years, however, in the aftermath of the Great Mutiny, that the rule of the Honourable East India Company ended and its domain passed to Her Majesty's Government.

Thus it became the custom from Plassey onwards for a small number of British regiments to be stationed in India under the command of the Governor General of Bengal, the senior of the three divisions, or 'presidencies', of the Company's territory. They were meant to be both a symbol of the British Government's interest in India and a reliable nucleus for operations. The first cavalry to be sent there arrived in October, 1782. These were the 23rd Light Dragoons, renumbered '19' in 1786, who had been raised specifically for Indian service. Until their arrival the only armed horsemen at the Company's disposal had been those recruited from Europeans in India, or native cavalry hired from local nawabs. In the several battles against Hyder Ali of Mysore, this lack of cavalry had been a severe limitation, especially since Hyder Ali's use of his own horsemen had been extremely skilful: as Sir John Fortescue writes, "They veiled the movement of their own army in a cloud of mystery; they hung about the enemy like rooks about a heron, hustling, threatening, swooping, always too far away to receive injury, always near enough to inflict it." In consequence, the commander-in-chief in India, Sir Eyre Coote, had written to the Company's court of directors to obtain a regular cavalry regiment from Britain.

By the time the Nineteenth arrived in Madras the war with Hyder Ali was nearly over, though it was not until 1794 that his death and a peace treaty, of sorts, brought an end to all fighting. In order that the Company was not to be found wanting in the mounted arm again, however, the regiment was set to the task of raising and training the first regular native cavalry in India.

The Nineteenth's commanding officer was a remarkable man called John Floyd. He had obtained a cornetcy in Eliott's Light Dragoons and was their riding master at the age of fifteen, charging with them at Emsdorf. He became something of a legend in India, rose to the rank of general and was created baronet in 1816, but in the immediate years following the Nineteenth's arrival he used his considerable talents in the task of raising Company cavalry. Officers and men of the Nineteenth, not only in Madras but also in the two other presidencies of Bengal and Bombay, began to form native horseman into disciplined, well-trained units under British officers. It is no exaggeration to say that Floyd was the father of the Indian Cavalry – yet, on his arrival in India, he was only 33 years old.

* * *

Seringapatam may be one of the Nineteenth's bloodiest victories, and *Assaye* its most glorious, but there could hardly be a harder-won honour than *Mysore*. Although operations in India were against native rulers hostile to Britain, there was invariably an element of French intrigue and often active support, especially along the Coromandel coast where French trading stations operated. Clearly it was in France's interest to divert British resources from Europe irrespective of whether there would be any direct French gains on the sub-continent. And so it was with the continuing trouble in Mysore, for Hyder Ali's son, Tipu Sultan, proved every bit as cunning as his father. War broke out again in 1790. The Nineteenth were in action throughout this two-year campaign, and the native cavalry, which they had been training so assiduously in the previous years, proved themselves worthy allies. Under Floyd's overall command this small cavalry force inflicted defeat after defeat on Tipu along the Coromandel coast. Peace was concluded in 1792 but it remained a fragile one.

When Napoleon invaded Egypt, six years later, he intended it to be a stepping-stone to India. Tipu Sultan immediately saw the possibilities. In the following year, after again canvassing French support, he attempted once more to evict the British from Mysore. The new Governor General of Bengal was Richard Wellesley, Lord Mornington – Arthur Wellesley's elder brother. He immediately sent two armies into Mysore. These consisted of forces from all three presidencies, stiffened by British regiments (including the Nineteenth), plus a strong contingent from the Nizam of Hyderabad. They were under the overall command of Major-General George Harris, but the second in command and cavalry commander was John Floyd, by this time a major-general too. Floyd's handling of his cavalry, comprising the Nineteenth, the 25th Light Dragoons and two native regiments, was again masterly. This was the first cavalry force of any appreciable size to be used in India and the charges he led were instrumental in winning the key battle of Malavelly. The confidence this instilled in the native cavalry had an important and lasting effect.

Also on this campaign was Arthur Wellesley himself. A thirty-year-old colonel, he was commanding both a division and his regiment, the 33rd Foot (later called The Duke of Wellington's Regiment). His division faced almost certain annihilation at Malavelly had it not been for Floyd's cavalry charges. Wellesley was soon to gain lasting fame in several battles in India, but he

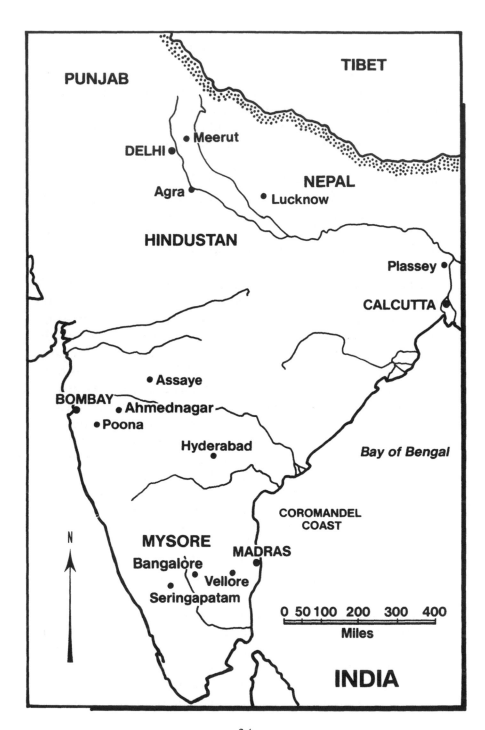

never forgot the Nineteenth's feats of arms at this time – as will be seen.

Tipu's headquarters were in the city of Seringapatam in the heart of Mysore. By 1 May, 1799, after three months' hard fighting and marching, the Company's forces had closed on the city. During the bombardment the magazine was blown up and the fortress fell to a determined and bloody assault. Tipu was killed, fighting bravely as befitted 'The Tiger of Mysore', and with his death the war ended. The Nineteenth were awarded the battle honour *Seringapatam* for this action, and *Mysore* for the three campaigns in which they had been so deeply involved.

There was to be little respite for the regiment, however. A particularly troublesome dacoit (bandit), Doondia Wao, had been exploiting the Company's distraction in Mysore. After the Battle of Seringapatam Arthur Wellesley had been appointed the city's governor and the military and civil administrator of Mysore, and it therefore fell to him to check Doondia Wao's depredations in the province. This was to be his first independent command and it comprised Company forces with, in addition, the British 73rd and 77th Foot and the Nineteenth and 25th Light Dragoons, the 25th being one of only two other British cavalry regiments in India. Although operations against Doondia began in May, 1799, it was not until 10 September that he was decisively engaged. Wellesley himself led a charge by the Nineteenth against the dacoits, scattering them and killing Doondia.

* * *

Three years of relative peace followed, but the legacy of Floyd's spectacular handling of his cavalry in the Mysore campaigns was soon to be drawn on. In 1803 the Second Maratha War erupted, although by this time Floyd himself had returned to England on promotion to lieutenant-general. Though the French adventure in Egypt had failed, Bonaparte still had an eye to expelling the British from India. With the death of Tipu and the destruction of his army at Seringapatam, there was only the loose alliance of Maratha princes preventing total British control of central and southern India. Napoleon therefore supplied the Maratha chiefs with both officers and arms: their forces already included tens of thousands of horsemen and large quantities of artillery.

One of the most able Maratha leaders, Doulat Rao Sindhia, had based himself in Poona in the Deccan. Wellesley, by now a major-general, was placed in command of one of two armies which were to conduct operations and destroy both Maratha power and French influence. One army under General Lake was launched into Hindustan in the north while Wellesley's, which included only three British regiments (the 19th Light Dragoons and the 74th and 78th Foot) pushed into the Deccan. The remainder of his force consisted of some Company troops, a 9,000-strong Hyderabad contingent plus loyal Mysore and Maratha horse.

Wellesley's small force recaptured Poona, quite easily, on 20 March, 1803, but Sindhia's army withdrew intact to Ahmednagar, a key hill fortress on the north-west frontier of the Nizam of Hyderabad's territory. Between 8 and 11 August Wellesley besieged, then stormed, this fortress with almost contemptuous ease. Gooklah, another Maratha chief, afterwards summed up his despair of fighting the English, "who were a strange people, and their general a wonderful man; they came here in the morning, looked at the fortress's wall, walked over it, killed all the garrison and returned to breakfast! What can withstand them?" But again the main forces had evaded a decisive engagement, and this time had withdrawn north-east.

In pursuit Wellesley found, rather unexpectedly, Sindhia's army at Assaye on 23 September. They numbered around 50,000, including a host of cavalry, European-led infantry and over 100 guns. Wellesley, having split his force, had but 7,000 men. These odds were not unusual in the two-hundred-year history of the British in India but they nevertheless posed a tricky tactical problem. The tactic of the time was to make an immediate attack to gain the initiative rather than to await what would probably prove an overwhelming onslaught by the enemy. Wellesley, in his first large-scale action as a major-general, applied the same principle on this occasion. Though his situation was made even more precarious by rivers on either flank, restricting his scope for manoeuvre, he led his British and Company troops against the first position while his Maratha and Mysore cavalry guarded the southern flank.

The British 74th Foot, on the right of the line, soon found themselves in a potentially fatal situation facing an impending attack by a mass of Sindhia's cavalry. The Nineteenth, and a Madrasi cavalry regiment, charged the threatening enemy cavalry, routing them, then cut through the first line of infantry and on to the guns. After pursuing, rallying and returning with some difficulty they were immediately called on to charge a second enemy brigade. In doing so, the commanding officer, Colonel Maxwell, was killed at the moment of contact. As he died he involuntarily checked his charger and, interpreting this as a signal to hold, the squadrons behind him swerved crying "Halt, halt!" Confusion followed for a time, during which they would have been destroyed had Sindhia's cavalry attacked. Without cavalry Wellesley's position would have been fatal; fortunately they just managed to rally in time and get away.

Slowly but surely, sheer hard fighting by Wellesley's troops began to overcome the numerical superiority of Sindhia, whose army began to melt away as evening approached. The casualties on both sides were fearful and there was much heroism. Lieutenant Nathan Wilson of the Nineteenth took part in both charges though his arm had been smashed by grape-shot early in the battle: his mangled limb hung by his side, his good arm wielded a sabre and he held the reins between his teeth! Sergeant Strange, though pierced through the lungs by a pike, remained in the saddle to the end of the action.

Wellesley's exhausted infantry bivouacked that night where they had fought, the dead unburied and the wounded in many cases untended. The cavalry were sent to escort the army's equipment forward which had been left for safekeeping some six miles back. They were so exhausted that it took them all night to do so, and it was to be a whole week before the wounds of all the injured were dressed and Wellesley's force, now reduced to 5,500, was ready to follow up the broken Maratha army.

The campaign continued until November, but it was largely one of pursuit. Though there was sporadic resistance over the next two years, the task of pacifying central and southern India was complete; indeed there was no other major campaign in India until the Nepal War of 1814-16.

There was always a reluctance to award distinctions to regiments in the Company's service. It was over three years before the Nineteenth's action at Assaye was recognized, and it is evident that it was the result of recommendations at the highest level – as this letter from the Horse Guards to the Nineteenth's Colonel indicates:

> Horse Guards,
> 15th April 1807.
>
> My Lord
> I have received the Commander in Chief's directions to inform you, that the Marquis of Wellesley and Major General the Honble. Sir Arthur Wellesley have represented to H.R.H. the distinguished services of the 19th Light Dragoons in the course of the arduous Campaigns which occurred during the period of his Lordship's Government in India, and have earnestly solicited permission, that the Regiment may be distinguished by some emblematical Badge.
>
> The Commander in Chief has with great satisfaction submitted this representation to the King, and His Majesty has in consequence thereof been most graciously pleased to approve of the "Elephant" being used in Colours and Appointments of the 19th Light Dragoons with the word "Assaye" superscribed, in Commemoration of the Gallantry and good Conduct displayed in the Action fought at that place on the 23rd September 1803.
>
> I have the honour to be &c.
> HARRY CALVERT,
> A.G.
>
> General Visct. HOWE, K.B.
>   or O.C. 19th Light Dragoons.

And so it was that the Nineteenth were awarded the singular battle honour *Assaye*, the only British cavalry to bear it. The Elephant, superscribed *Assaye*, was a proud device borne by the 19th, and subsequently the 15th/19th, Hussars. In later years it was worn as a collar badge and is today borne by The Light Dragoons on the crossbelt pouch and on the guidon.

❋ ❋ ❋

Postscript

Although India was relatively peaceful for over ten years following Assaye, there occurred in 1806 another event which should be regarded with the greatest pride by The Light Dragoons. It is a shining example of prompt, decisive action and personal courage, the essence of light cavalry work. It arose from a mutiny in a native infantry battalion at Vellore, near Madras. One of those needless and insensitive orders which punctuated the Company's history had been issued to the army of Madras by its newly arrived commander in chief. The order forbade caste marks on the face and required the shaving-off of beards, both things offensive to these sepoys' religion. In the heat of a July night the battalion attacked the practically unarmed officers and men of the British 69th Foot, killing many of them as they slept in bed. A message was somehow got to the Nineteenth who were in barracks about 14 miles away. The commanding officer, Lieutenant-Colonel Rollo Gillespie, at once set off with a squadron of the regiment and a troop of the 7th Madras Native Cavalry, leaving orders for the rest to follow.

He arrived to find the 69th down to their last few rounds making a stand on the walls of the fort, mutineers both inside and outside. Unable to get through one of the fort's gates, Gillespie had himself hoisted up by a rope under intense fire to join the dwindling band of infantrymen. This action renewed the defenders' spirits and they were able, just, to keep the mutineers at bay until two galloper guns arrived with the rest of the Nineteenth. The guns did their work against the gate, at which moment Gillespie led a bayonet charge to clear the way for his squadrons to enter the fort. Over 400 mutineers were slaughtered in the fight which followed.

By this prompt action any wider mutiny in the Madras army was nipped in the bud, though the governor and commander-in-chief were recalled to England and an extra 4,000 troops sent to India. Gillespie, by this time widely regarded as the bravest man in the Army, was awarded £2,500 by the Company, and all ranks of the cavalry present were given additions to their pay. Gillespie remained in the east after the Nineteenth left India in 1806, seeing continual action and rising to major-general. He was killed in 1814 in the attack on Kalunga during the Nepal War, the news of his being named KCB reaching India only after his death. He is buried at Meerut.

CHAPTER 4

To Cooperate with the Spanish Armies

"I am thinking of the French that I am going to fight: I have not seen them since the campaign in Flanders, when they were capital soldiers, and a dozen years of victory under Bonaparte must have made them better still. They have besides, it seems, a new system of strategy which has out-manoeuvred and overwhelmed all the armies of Europe. 'Tis enough to make one thoughtful; but no matter."

The Duke of WELLINGTON

15H and 18H in the first Peninsular campaign 1808–9; Sahagun; 13LD, 15H, 18H in the second expedition: Albuhera, Vittoria, Orthès, Toulouse.

After the Duke of York's army had been ejected from northern Holland in 1799 (the year of the Nineteenth's battle at Seringapatam), the 'Second Coalition' began to disintegrate. It had been forged by Pitt in the afterglow of Nelson's destruction of the French fleet at the mouth of the Nile in 1798, which had marooned the French expeditionary army in Egypt. This victory showed Pitt what sea power could really achieve. Instead of continuing the small-scale tip-and-run raids on enemy coasts and islands, he despatched a new fleet to Egypt towards the end of 1800. On board was a substantial army under General Abercromby, the man who had held things together in the West Indies and northern Holland. This army utterly defeated the French at Aboukir (Alexandria) in March, 1801.

Although the action was perhaps of no great importance in Pitt's grand strategy, because by that time Egypt had become a strategic backwater, it was significant in terms of national morale because it was a complete defeat of French forces by superior training, tactics and fighting spirit. The Duke of York may have been a poor field commander in Flanders and Holland, but he had set in motion a number of reforms which were beginning to pay dividends by this time. Commanders of high ability were also coming to the fore who were to put the lessons of the earlier disasters to good use. It is significant that the field commander at Aboukir was Major-General John Moore (of whom more later) who had been with Abercromby in the West Indies and the Helder campaign. The success at Aboukir boosted the country's confidence in the Army enormously.

Despite the collapse of the Second Coalition, therefore, it would seem that by 1802 the British had the measure of their enemy, and Pitt now realized that Britain could no longer take a secondary role in fighting the French armies. There could be no simple trade war of the old kind. The Royal Navy guarded the country against immediate invasion but to break the threatening French armies Britain would need a continental strategy, and to have a continental strategy she would need a continental army – a large and well-found army.

Meanwhile there was what Correlli Barnett has described as a delusory pause in hostilities between Britain and France, brought about by the Treaty of Amiens (March, 1802), what the dramatist and parliamentary orator Richard Brinsley Sheridan called "a peace which all men are glad of, but no man can be proud of". Pitt had fallen from office a year earlier after seventeen years' premiership.

The peace did not last long. It foundered in 1803 because even the new administration, desperate though it was to cut back defence spending, could not trust Napoleon. But Britain stood alone. The whole weight of French arms, which had not ceased growing in power since revolution erupted twelve years earlier, was now turned by Napoleon to the immediate destruction of the British – by direct invasion.

The English Channel stood, as it always has, between the Nation's survival and disaster. The Royal Navy was hastily expanded, as were the Army and Militia. The whole national effort was directed towards repelling a clearly imminent invasion. Martello towers and forts were built along the coast. Signalling beacons were set up across the country for the first time since the Spanish Armada. The Thirteenth, Fifteenth and Eighteenth, their establishments swelled to nearly 900 each, and occasionally augmented to over 1,000, were dispersed throughout Britain and Ireland to await and prepare for a French landing. Napoleon's *Grande Armée* assembled at Boulogne while plans were made to lure the Royal Navy away from the Channel so that his invasion fleet of flat-bottomed boats could cross the thirty miles or so of water to the beaches of Kent and Sussex.

As preparations for war intensified in 1804, the new Prime Minister, Addington, was swept from office and Pitt was returned to power. Still only forty-five, Pitt threw himself at his task and soon encouraged Russia and Austria to re-enter into alliance, the 'Third Coalition'. This threat from the east put paid to Napoleon's immediate plans for invasion, for by September, 1805, his *Grande Armée* was making a forced march eastward to destroy the resurgent Austrians. The following month, on 21 October, Nelson's Mediterranean fleet destroyed the combined French and Spanish fleet at Trafalgar and removed any remaining possibility of invasion. Britain had been saved, but on the continent first Austria, then Prussia, then Russia were crushed in a series of the bloodiest battles to date, followed by humiliating peace terms. Britain once more stood alone.

The next two years were uncertain ones: Pitt died in January, 1806, it is said from exhaustion, and the hotch-potch government which followed could see no way of coming to grips with the French on land on reasonable terms. The navies of both sides, or rather what was left of the French navy, maintained a sort of mutual blockade, but a miscalculation by Napoleon in 1808 gave Britain her chance. In 1806 he had issued the 'Berlin Decrees' forbidding any country to trade with Britain. The Portuguese refused to comply, so in 1807 France and Spain agreed to the partition of Portugal. In October French forces crossed Spain, and by November had captured Lisbon. The Portuguese royal family was embarked in His Majesty's ships and taken to Brazil. Then, despite their treaty, French forces began to occupy Spain. The Spanish King was deposed and Napoleon placed his brother, Joseph Bonaparte, on the throne. The Spaniards rose spontaneously in outraged revolt and at last the British had their opportunity to intervene effectively in continental Europe – and in a region where their sea power gave them more secure lines of communication than the French enjoyed on land.

* * *

Command of the expeditionary force of 13,000 men (including the Eighteenth) was given to Sir Arthur Wellesley, the victor of Assaye, and his instructions were to ensure "the final and absolute evacuation of the Peninsula by the troops of France". His main force landed north of Lisbon in late July, 1808, and the Eighteenth arrived a few weeks later. Because of difficulties with unloading which the main force had experienced, they remained embarked until 1 September when their transports could safely enter the River Tagus, further south. Wellesley had gone on to the offensive immediately, however, and by 22 August in two infantry battles, Rolica and Vimeiro, had utterly defeated the French under Marshal Junot.

At this point Wellesley was superseded by two senior generals, Dalrymple and Burrard, who, though recently arrived, had promptly given the French such generous terms of surrender (though Portugal was to be evacuated, the French were to be shipped home with their arms by the Royal Navy) that when news of it reached England both they and Wellesley were recalled to answer to Parliament. Command of all operations in the Peninsula was then given to Sir John Moore, of Aboukir fame. The expeditionary force was considerably strengthened: with 20,000 men he was to enter Spain from Portugal and then join forces at Valladolid with Sir David Baird who was to land

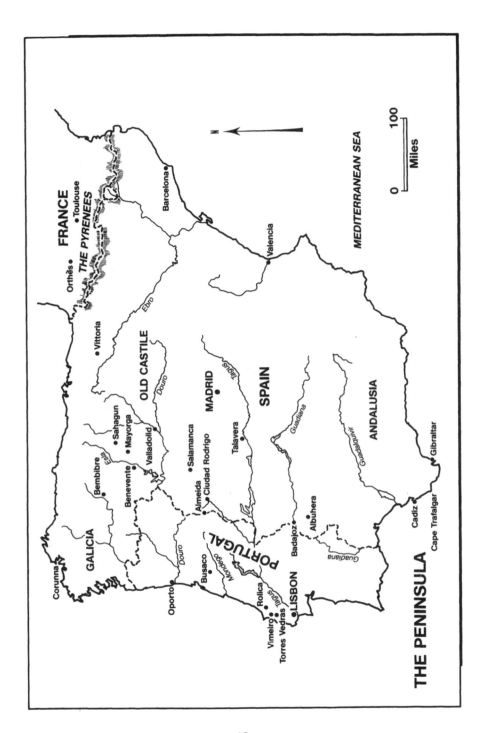

45

at Corunna with up to 17,000 men. It was the largest army to be sent abroad since the days of Marlborough.

With Baird was Lord Paget (later Earl of Uxbridge and 1st Marquess of Anglesey), who had handled his cavalry with distinction in the Helder Campaign nine years earlier. Paget was to command the cavalry division comprising two brigades. The first, known as the Hussar Brigade, consisted of the Eighteenth and the 3rd Hussars of The King's German Legion under the command of Brigadier-General Charles Stewart who had commanded the Eighteenth with such ability and courage in the Helder. They were already consolidating at Lisbon. The other brigade, which included the Fifteenth, was to land with Baird's force. Both regiments were a little over 650-strong and dressed and styled 'Hussars' though they were not officially titled so in the Army List for several more years.

Moore's instructions from the Secretary at War, Lord Castlereagh, were more specific about cooperation with Spanish forces than Wellesley's had been, enjoining him "to cooperate with the Spanish armies in the expulsion of the French from that Kingdom". Nor was there any doubt about the gravity of the commitment: the Foreign Secretary, Canning, wrote, "The army . . . is not merely a considerable part of the dispensable force of this country. It is in fact *the* British army. . . Another army it has not to send."

While Moore and Baird were marching to link up at Valladolid, Napoleon was reinforcing his armies in Spain and taking personal command. He rapidly defeated two of the three Spanish armies on whose cooperation the whole British strategy depended and occupied Moore's and Baird's rendezvous, Valladolid. By the last week of November, 1808, although having advanced as far as Salamanca, Moore had no option but to retreat. Napoleon, however, made a surprising move: instead of pressing westwards to engage the British, he turned south to Madrid. When Moore then learned that the whole population of the capital had risen to defend it he felt obliged to lend his support. His plan was to mount a diversionary attack on Marshal Soult's 20,000-strong army which had been left as a containing force in the north-west. He halted the retreat and ordered a general advance towards Valladolid on 11 December.

Stewart's cavalry, scouting well ahead, learned through captured documents and prisoners that Soult had, however, evacuated Valladolid, believing the British still to be retreating westwards. Soult's force was now entirely unsupported only some fifty miles north. This information, a significant part of which was acquired and verified by the Eighteenth, caused Moore to change his plan radically. He halted the eastward advance and turned his axis north, ordering Baird's force to rendezvous with him at Mayorga.

The junction of Moore's and Baird's forces was brilliantly screened by Stewart's brigade, the Eighteenth scouting deep on Moore's right flank as far east as Valladolid itself. The diary of the Eighteenth's senior major, Loftus William Otway, describes the action:

> "Rueda is 24 miles from Valladolid where Genl Francesca was with 400 French chasseurs and 100 infantry. Understanding that he did not keep a good look out I determined to surprise him and applied to the Alcalde of Rueda for 200 Spaniards to assist; with difficulty he got me about forty men, mounted on mules and asses – we arrived within 2 miles of Valladolid at 12 of night when I sent my interpreter and a Spaniard forward to the town for intelligence.
>
> They soon returned with information that the French had retired with precipitation a few hours before, leaving some men and horses and their sick behind. At 2 o'clock I entered the town and an Officer and 22 privates surrendered. I arrested the French Indentant General (Dr Zavier D'Urbina) and left Valladolid at 9 o'clock being then 40 miles in advance of the outposts."

Baird's force was led into the rendezvous at Mayorga by the Fifteenth on the evening of 19 December in driving snow. The following morning Moore's force entered the town from the south through deep snowdrifts and the remainder of that day was spent resting and regrouping.

Early the next morning, 21 December, there followed what the great chronicler of the Peninsular War, Sir Charles Oman, described as "perhaps the most brilliant exploit of the British cavalry during the whole six years of the war. When the Peninsular medals were distributed, nearly forty years after, a special clasp was very rightly given for it." This brilliant exploit took place at Sahagun, some eighteen miles north-east of Mayorga, and was carried out by just 400 men of the 15th Hussars.

Moore's force had begun its march towards Sahagun in the early hours of 21 December, the snow still falling. In front of them were Paget's cavalry which reached the town just before dawn. Paget ordered his senior brigadier, Slade, to mount a frontal attack with the 10th Hussars, the other regiment of the brigade, while he himself took the Fifteenth round the town to cut off the French retreat. By the time the Fifteenth were in position on the far side, Slade had still not made his attack. He was a slow, deliberate officer and this was his first battle: while he was still issuing lengthy, detailed orders the Fifteenth were confronted by 600 French dragoons trying to withdraw. As this heavy cavalry force began to deploy for the charge, a little over 400 yards away, the Fifteenth watched them in silence, hands and feet so numb with cold that they could hardly feel their reins or stirrups. Paget felt he could wait no longer for the 10th Hussars to show, so he ordered the Fifteenth to charge, whereupon they took off cheering and shouting "Emsdorf and Victory!"

It was not an easy manoeuvre, uphill, over a ditch and across broken, snow-covered ground. It is not clear why, but the charge was received virtually at the halt. The French dragoons managed to fire only a few shots from their carbines before the hussars were on them.

> "The shock of impact at Sahagun, one officer said, 'was terrible; horses and men were overthrown and a shriek of terror, intermixed with oaths, groans, and prayers for mercy issued from the whole extent of their front.' The struggle lasted only a few minutes before the French broke and fled with the regiment in

pursuit. Of the 600 dragoons, only 200 escaped death or capture; only two hussars were killed and twenty-three wounded."

Some light may be shed on the French Cavalry's inactivity by an entry in Otway's diary for ten days later:

"It may be right here to observe, that the French did not in the course of this morning advance to the charge. They always waited our attack and I think to advantage except in the final instance when I attacked them on hard ground, but all the other charges we made were in very deep ground, wheatland, the horses above fetlock deep, and in consequence the horses always came up blown and feeble."

Sahagun became the principal battle honour of the 15th, and then the 15th/19th, Hussars and has been faithfully celebrated on 21 December every year, beginning with the officers serving the soldiers with rum and coffee at dawn, the band having woken them with 'The Sahagun Song'. The Song is possibly unique in that it was composed by one of the troopers soon afterwards and sung at the first anniversary of the battle in the presence of the Colonel, the Duke of Cumberland:

'Twas in quarters we lay, as you quickly shall hear,
Lord Paget came to us and bade us prepare,
Saying "Saddle your horses – by the light of the moon,
For the French they are lying in the town of Sahagun."

And while no doubt Private 'Comberbache' would have composed something of more literary merit, the song's ten verses recount in soldierly style what happened:

With our glittering broadswords right at them we sped,
They turned threes about and away they all fled.

We soon overtook them as frightened they fled,
Cut through the brass helmets they wore on their head;

49

The reward was immediate:

> The Spaniards turned out of the town of Sahagun
> To welcome the Fifteenth, the "King's Light Dragoons",
> With jugs full of wine, our thirst for to quench,
> Crying, "Long live the English and down with the French."

The Spaniards' celebrations were premature, however. Two days after Sahagun, before he could launch his attack against Soult's main force, Moore learned that the object of his diversionary movement had been achieved: Napoleon was marching north-west from Madrid with an army of over 200,000. But this also placed Moore's army in the perilous position which he had long feared. On Christmas Eve, therefore, he ordered a rapid withdrawal towards Corunna. His escape route was nearly 200 miles as the crow flies, over some of the most mountainous country in Europe and in the depths of a hard winter. The retreat was to become, as is well known, an epic.

A vivid impression of the nature and hard conditions of this retreat can be gained from J.P. Beadle's celebrated painting *The Rear Guard*: into the distance, up a rutted track into the snow-covered mountains of Galicia, march weary and dishevelled-looking redcoats and struggling gun-teams of horse artillery; in the foreground, in the intense cold, without great-coats, stands a company of the 95th Rifles – later The Rifle Brigade – grim-faced, determined. With them is Major-General Robert Crauford, 'Black Bob', commander of the Light Division, and an ADC of the Fifteenth.

The scene is chilling but there is an orderliness, an indication that this was a controlled and measured withdrawal. Yet before the Army could reach the stage of orderly withdrawal it had to disengage and put some distance between itself and the enemy, especially in order to cross the rivers along the first part of the line of retreat. To do this, the cavalry had to buy the infantry time, their classic role in such an operation.

For two days after Moore ordered the retreat on Christmas Eve, Paget's five cavalry regiments harassed the French outposts

1. *"Another highlander delivered a mortal blow"*. (*p. 5*) Colonel James Gardiner at the Battle of Prestonpans. The Commanding Officer of the 13th Dragoons was killed near his own house by highlanders of Bonnie Prince Charlie's rebel army 21 September, 1745.

2. *"There was much smartness in these light dragoons."(p.7)* A vedette (mounted sentry) of Eliott's Light Horse about 1760. Oil, C R Beavis.

3. *"A great disposition in the people to enlist in the Light Cavalry."(p.7)* One of the Fifteenth's most illustrious recruits was the poet Samuel Taylor Coleridge, who described himself as *"a very indocile equestrian"*. Oil, Peter Vandyke.

4. *"The strenuous efforts of their new Commanding Officer, the twenty-one-year-old Lieutenant-Colonel the Honourable Charles William Stewart, later Marquess of Londonderry."*(p.26) The 18th Light Dragoons were decimated by yellow fever in the West Indies and returned to England in 1798. They were ready for service in Holland within a year thanks largely to Stewart's zeal and energy. Oil, Sir Thomas Lawrence, (original is in the National Portrait Gallery; the regiment has a full-size studio replica).

5. *"Without cavalry Wellesley's position would have been fatal."(p. 37) The 19th Light Dragoons were the only British cavalry*

6. *"Nearly 200 miles as the crow flies, over some of the most mountainous country in Europe and in the depths of a hard winter."(p.50)* The withdrawal to Corunna was a severe test of the Cavalry's discipline, a test they passed with distinction. Oil, C R Beavis.

7. *"For one man the action at Campo Mayor brought regimental fame - and a little money."(p.58)* Corporal Logan, 13th Light Dragoons, slaying Colonel Count Chamorin, 25 March, 1811. (Artist unknown).

8. *"The horses had great difficulty recovering themselves due to the infantrymen . . . hanging on to the stirrups."(p.61)* The 15th and the 18th Hussars, and 51st foot, almost came to grief crossing the River Esla, May, 1813. Oil, Gilbert Holiday.

9. *"Sparing of praise for his cavalry."(p.53)* Wellington had been gazetted captain in the 18th Light Dragoons in 1791 but never joined for duty, transferring subsequently to the 33rd Foot which was later to bear his name. Both the Thirteenth and the Eighteenth, indeed the Cavalry in general, were to receive his sharp rebuke in the Peninsula for, amongst other things, gallant but, in his view, improvident charges. Oil by Sir Thomas Lawrence.

10. *"Ten squadrons of French lancers advanced to threaten the right flank near Hougoumont. Uxbridge immediately sent Grant's brigade to deal with them."(p.76)* Denis Dighton's dramatic painting showing the Earl of Uxbridge, later Marquess of Anglesey, urging on the Fifteenth. The painting is in the possession of the 7th Marquess.

11. *"Now come on, drive them back Thirteenth!"(p.78)* Lord Hill directs the 13th Light Dragoons to a final charge to break Napoleon's *Garde* in the closing moments of the Battle of Waterloo. The parade-ground smartness in this painting by Harry Payne is fanciful: by this stage the regiment had charged so many times that the survivors were smoke-blackened and tattered.

Massacre at St Peters or "BRITONS STRIKE HOME"!!!

12. *"A cotton-weaver saw ten or twelve of the Yeomanry Cavalry and two of the Hussars cutting at the people".(p.86)* Cruikshank's cartoon of what became known as 'The Peterloo Massacre', 16 August, 1819, at St Peter's Fields, Manchester. An officer of the Manchester and Salford Yeomanry is urging on his Yeomen: *"Down with 'em! Chop 'em down my brave boys . . . the more you kill the less poor rates you'll have to pay . . ."* The truth is more prosaic: the Yeomanry could not control their horses in the crowd, and panicked. The Fifteenth were ordered by the magistrates to restore the situation and generally earned praise for their skill and restraint.

13. *"Sailors should wear blue and soldiers should wear red."(p.87)* King William IV's strong views on uniform derived from his active naval career prior to his unexpected accession to the throne in 1830 on the death of his brother, George IV. In consequence all the light cavalry changed their predominant blue to red, reverting to blue after William's death. Watercolour by Orlando Norie, 13th Light Dragoons

14. *"This fine old Waterloo soldier defending his honour against his aristocratic persecutor."* (p.89) The trial of Captain Augustus Wathen led to Lord Brudenell (later the Earl of Cardigan) being dismissed with disgrace from command of the 15th Hussars. Etching by William Heath.

15. *"'He writes books,' said Lord George Paget . . . with evident distaste."(p.106)*
Captain Louis Edward Nolan, 15th Hussars, had written textbooks on military
equitation and cavalry tactics. The grandson of a trooper in the 13th Light Dragoons,
and an 'India man', Nolan returned Cardigan's contempt with fierce passion. He
delivered the fateful order for the Charge of the Light Brigade. (Artist unknown).

16. *"Lucan adjusted his positions slightly, placing the Light Brigade at the western end of the North Valley."(p.104)* Orlando Norie's watercolour of the Thirteenth before the charge at Balaklava is a more faithful portrayal of the look of the regiment than many of the romanticized versions which appeared on the subsequent wave of Victorian sentimentality.

17. *"Lance-Sergeant Joseph Malone won the newly-instituted Victoria Cross for rescuing a wounded officer of the 17th Lancers under fire, the first VC to be won by The Light Dragoons' forebears."(p.109)* Harry Payne's sentimental *Boy's Own*-style painting is in fact a faithful portrait of the four men and was obviously undertaken from photographs. The other two NCOs, both of the Seventeenth, also received VCs.

18 "*In the final hundred years the momentum was terrific.*" (p109) 13LD overrun the Russian battery at Balaklava: "*the Charge of the Light Brigade*" (from the painting by Peter Archer.)

so effectively that Soult had no idea that the retreat had begun, believing instead that a major assault was about to begin. Soult made an encircling movement but found the trap empty when sprung: by their 48 hours of exertion the cavalry had allowed the infantry to steal three vital marches on the enemy.

With a vengeance the French then began their pursuit. The whole weight of their attacks fell on Paget's five regiments, which numbered in all not many more than 2,000 sabres. For four wearying days every man was in action from dawn until dusk, scarcely resting even at night, in order to keep the enemy advance guards at bay. Oman's history is fulsome in describing the zeal of this covering action:

> "The 18LD turned back to clear their rear six times on Dec 27, and on each occasion drove in the leading squadrons of their pursuers with such effect that they secured themselves an unmolested retreat for the next few miles. At one charge, near Valencia de Don Juan, a troop of 38 sabres of this regiment charged a French squadron of 105 men, and broke through them, killing 12 and capturing 20."

A most critical time was the crossing of the River Esla. By 29 December all the infantry had got safely over its few bridges and Paget's cavalry retired across, blowing the bridges in the enemy's sight. There is another fine painting by Beadle which portrays the Tenth guarding the fords on the Esla. General Lefebvre-Desnouettes, commanding Napoleon's guard cavalry, found one of these fords near the village of Benavente and led his regiments across. These were held in check by the Eighteenth's outposts long enough for Stewart to bring up the rest of his brigade to cut off or drive back those who had crossed. Paget brought up the other brigade to complete the destruction. The Eighteenth captured Lefebvre-Desnouettes and were congratulated by Paget, but Slade criticized them for having acted initially too vigorously in driving the advance guards back. He complained that, "Had the picquet shown less gallantry and a little more address we could have got between them and the river and have taken them all"! Slade was a difficult man and, though he had influential supporters, was considered by many to be dangerously incompetent: on one occasion Paget, after giving his orders, sent an aide after him with instructions in an inexcusably loud voice to "ride after that damned stupid fellow" to see there was no mistake. The French did not attempt to cross the Esla again that day, however: Moore's infantry had once more been bought precious hours by the cavalry.

Benavente was the last major cavalry action of the retreat to Corunna. For the rest of the retreat the rearguard was conducted largely by the infantry, the mountain passes being too steep and narrow for cavalry in formed bodies. The reserve division under Lord Paget's brother, Edward Paget, handled the rearguards with skill and harsh discipline. He had the Fifteenth under command and they did some excellent outpost work.

By the time Moore's army reached Corunna discipline in many parts of it had broken down. Accounts of the retreat record with shame the drunken indiscipline of many regiments: in one small town in particular (Bembibre) several hundred soldiers, comatose through gorging on the wine in its cellars, were surprised and slaughtered where they lay by French cavalry. In contrast, in all Moore's cavalry regiments discipline was maintained. But at Corunna, where the bulk of the force was to embark for England, they were appalled to learn that there was only enough shipping to take 1,000 horses: those remaining of the cavalry and artillery, and the draft animals, were to be destroyed to prevent their being taken by the enemy. The manner in which this was carried out, ineptly rather than deliberately cruelly, made many a hardened trooper weep.

Sir John Moore was killed on 16 January, 1809, in the final battle outside Corunna, but his expeditionary force was safely taken off by the Royal Navy. So ended the campaign which had started with such high hopes of success. There was subsequently much criticism of Moore's conduct of the campaign, and in particular of the retreat, but Paget's cavalry had undoubtedly earned their laurels.

Sir Arthur Wellesley was re-appointed to command in the

Peninsula. Much has been made of the contrast between him and Moore. Correlli Barnett describes Wellesley as the iron disciplinarian while Moore was something of the scoutmaster, that Wellesley was an altogether stronger character and had a cooler nerve than Moore. Moore was a Scot, prim and prickly sometimes, and without political acumen. Wellesley, by contrast, was of the Irish aristocracy, urbane and with considerable political sense and influence. Perhaps of greater significance was their relative experience: Moore was a distinguished fighting general, a superb and imaginative trainer; Wellington's arguable superiority lay perhaps in his complete understanding of the problems of supply and movement, particularly over long distances in a barren country. This he acknowledged he had learned in India, and it was this mastery of logistic difficulties, and apparently instinctive understanding of 'time and space', which was to contribute so much to his success in Spain.

As for the cavalry in the coming campaign, the 7th Marquess of Anglesey, the pre-eminent historian of the British cavalry, perfectly sums up their fortunes:

> "The ascendancy which the British cavalry had established over the French in the Corunna campaign was largely maintained through the five remaining years of the Peninsular War. Wellington made skilful use of the mounted arm for reconnaissance and deception, and for covering withdrawals, but tended to distrust the 'cavalry spirit' as manifested by gallant but improvident charges."

It should be remembered that this ascendancy was achieved by just four British regiments, and the 3rd Hussars of the King's German Legion, and that two of these were forebears of The Light Dragoons. Wellington (created Viscount Wellesley in 1810 and Duke of Wellington in 1814, and so henceforward referred to as 'Wellington') was, as Anglesey implies, sparing of praise for his cavalry, however, and was to deliver some withering rebukes to the Thirteenth and Eighteenth in particular. As will be seen, on the whole his criticisms were not justified.

* * *

Wellington landed at Lisbon in April, 1809, in advance of his army of 20,000 British and 3,000 of the King's German Legion but without any of the Corunna veterans. Subordinate to him was the Portuguese army of 16,000 men under the British general, Beresford. He faced several French armies, Soult's of 20,000 men at Oporto to the north, Victor's of 25,000 at Medellin, 50 miles east of the Spanish border fortress of Badajoz and on the direct route to Madrid, and Lapisse's of 6,000 at Ciudad Rodrigo, another border fortress on the northerly route to Madrid and on the lines of communication with France. Scattered elsewhere in Spain the French armies totalled 200,000.

Wellington's task was to defend Portugal but not to enter Spain without the British Government's express permission. Although much of Spain was in arms against the French, the Spanish armies were poor quality and their leaders unreliable. The Government had little faith in the early prospect of being able to cooperate with them. But the beginnings of guerrilla warfare by Spanish irregulars, armed peasants and semi-independent regulars were promising. There is little doubt that their activities proved to be a decisive factor in the eventual defeat of the French, whose armies were bled white by constant guerrilla attacks. Of more immediate value to Wellington, however, was the effect which Spanish resistance had on communication and cooperation between the French armies: without a large cavalry escort, messengers simply did not get through a countryside in which these savage Spanish bands ranged. The effect of this on French operations was often crippling. Knowing this, Wellington was content to pursue a campaign of advance and withdrawal, between firm bases, while the French armies which pursued him suffered the opposite conditions.

His troops quickly defeated Soult's army at Oporto, driving them out of Portugal and so harrying them in a ten-day pursuit that they lost over 4,500 men and all their guns and baggage. He then turned towards Victor's army near Badajoz. Receiving permission to enter Spain, he hoped to be able to cooperate effectively with the Spanish General Cuesta's Army of Castile which appeared to have been invigorated by the early British victory. The two armies united on 20 July, 1809, and planned a joint attack on Victor, now reduced to 22,000. Wellington's 21,000 (the remainder covering Lisbon) and Cuesta's 33,000 should have been more than enough to despatch Victor in the same way as Soult, but Cuesta proved unreliable. The result was the close-fought battle of Talavera, Wellington's army losing nearly five and a half thousand men.

Wellington then began the first of his tactical withdrawals, the understanding being that he would continue the defence of Portugal while leaving the Spanish armies to concentrate on holding Andalusia in southern Spain. His intention was to maintain a forward defence of Portugal, but his base at Lisbon had to be guaranteed. He therefore ordered the construction, in great secrecy, of the massive defensive lines of Torres Vedras astride the Lisbon peninsula. This was excellent foresight, since in November, 1809, the remaining Spanish field armies were defeated, leaving Wellington effectively isolated, although Andalusia held out, the Spanish *Junta* installing itself at Cadiz as the capital of free Spain.

Throughout the winter of 1809–10 Wellington's army maintained its watch on the Portuguese border and continued the construction of the defences of Torres Vedras. A small force was sent to stiffen the defences of Cadiz, but the winter saw only light skirmishes there. The Thirteenth sailed from Portsmouth for Lisbon in February, 1810, as reinforcements (900 all ranks), and joined General Rowland Hill's 2nd Division. One squadron was detached to Cadiz, though it soon rejoined the regiment.

As the Thirteenth arrived, Marshal Massena was taking command of the French 'Army of Portugal'. He lost no time in going on to the offensive and began a seemingly irresistible march on Lisbon. The Thirteenth moved quickly to the frontier and were in continual action throughout the summer of 1810, skirmishing with Massena's cavalry patrols and covering the movements of the 2nd Division. On 27 September at Busaco, one hundred miles north-east of Lisbon on the northern approach from Ciudad Rodrigo, Wellington inflicted a sharp check on Massena. The Thirteenth, brigaded with the Portuguese Cavalry Brigade under Sir Henry Fane, were posted on the far right flank of Wellington's strong defensive position at Busaco to watch for enemy cavalry trying to outflank the line by crossing the River Mondego. No outflanking movement developed, however, for Massena threw his two corps, numbering nearly 60,000, in a frontal assault of Busaco ridge without a preliminary reconnaissance, believing the position to be held only by a rearguard. Rarely can the words of that noted Thirteenth officer of a later generation, the great proponent of scouting, Lord Baden-Powell, have been more apt than on this occasion: "There is scarcely a battle in history which has not been won or lost in proportion to the value of the previous reconnaissance." Massena's army stumbled on to 27,000 British, 25,000 Portuguese, and 60 guns on the reverse slope of this long ridge. He suffered nearly 5,000 casualties, finally withdrawing on 29 September.

Wellington withdrew the army, drawing Massena towards the prepared positions at Torres Vedras, all the while covered by his cavalry as Moore's cavalry had covered *his* withdrawal two years earlier. When the French closed up to the lines in October, Massena was truly astonished at what he saw, and rapidly became appalled. He knew he could not break through what *The Times* described as "an impenetrable blend of geography and fortification". Wellington had evacuated the area to the front of the lines and stripped it of all resources, yet Massena was loth to retreat. He therefore sat outside the lines for four months, while his army, isolated from support and harried by Portuguese guerrillas, slowly starved. 65,000 Frenchmen had entered Portugal in the summer of 1810 and by early March, 1811, this number was reduced to around 40,000; meanwhile Wellington's (British) army was reinforced through Lisbon and increased from 34,000 to 43,000. More importantly, his army was tolerably comfortable and well-fed in their winter quarters behind the lines.

Massena gave up the struggle in March, 1811, and began to withdraw. The lines of Torres Vedras had finally wrecked

French plans and saved Portugal. Further, they had increased the disillusionment with the war which was already growing in the French army. In this the Thirteenth had played a small but important part, as the Fifteenth and Eighteenth had done in the Corunna campaign.

✻ ✻ ✻

As Massena retired, Wellington pursued. He did not yet judge the situation right, though, for a general offensive. The fortress of Badajoz, the southern gateway to Portugal, had again fallen into French hands, Soult having gone on to the offensive on the Portuguese border. Massena, withdrawing north towards his fortress at Almeida, was still dangerous too. Wellington therefore divided his force, taking one half north towards Almeida and sending the other under General William Beresford towards Badajoz. With Beresford went the Thirteenth and on 25 March, 1811, there occurred the celebrated action at Campo Mayor, north of Badajoz.

The town of Campo Mayor was occupied by a French force of 1,200 infantry, over 800 cavalry with horse artillery, and a siege train of sixteen heavy guns. On Beresford's approach this force withdrew towards Badajoz. He told General Long, commanding two brigades of cavalry, one light, one heavy, to pursue. What followed has been variously described as "an affair", "a fiasco" and several other things too. Anglesey, the most thorough and impartial of historians, writes:

> "Five troops (about 200 men) of the 13th Light Dragoons by a series of truly brilliant charges, against three times their number of French cavalry, had captured all the French guns, rallied admirably, and were pursuing, in excellent order, when Beresford, thinking them destroyed, withheld the heavy brigade on which Long was depending. Left on their own [with two squadrons of Portuguese cavalry under Otway of the Eighteenth], the Thirteenth first chased the enemy cavalry for nearly ten miles, then returned, still in good order, having suffered no very great losses. But for lack of support they had to relinquish all their

prisoners, guns and other trophies just at the moment when the whole French force was on the point of surrender."

Anglesey has no doubt where the blame lay for this lost opportunity: it had resulted from "the incompetence of that astonishing man, Marshal Beresford. . . By interfering, on incomplete information, with a plan put into operation by General Long . . . he prevented the annihilation of 2,400 Frenchmen and sixteen heavy guns." Wellington did not see it that way, however. After receiving Beresford's despatches, which can be most charitably described as incomplete, he wrote in his own despatch:

> "Their conduct was that of a rabble, galloping as fast as their horses could carry them over a plain after an enemy to which they could do no mischief after they were broken. . . If the Thirteenth Dragoons are again guilty of this conduct, I shall take their horses from them and send the officers and men to do duty at Lisbon."

Sir Charles Napier, the definitive historian of the campaign, in his *History of the Peninsular War*, says, "the unsparing admiration of the whole army consoled them". They would also have been consoled by Fortescue's conclusion that: "Indeed I know of nothing finer in the history of the British cavalry." When Wellington discovered something of the truth he made what unofficial amends his pride permitted, and Beresford gave the regiment overwhelming praise when they performed a similar feat and brought in 150 prisoners three weeks later. The rebuke had cut the regiment to the quick, however, though not so badly as a similar one for the 4th Foot (King's Own) with Wellington himself in the north, where the commanding officer shot himself, so deeply did he feel the insult.

For one man, though, the action at Campo Mayor brought regimental fame – and a little money: Corporal William Logan slew the commanding officer of the French 26th Heavy Dragoons, Colonel The Count Chamorin, in single combat. Logan had sabred one of Chamorin's dragoons and the Count had seemingly singled out the corporal to avenge the death. Those who witnessed it spoke of the skilful swordsmanship of both combatants, of Logan cutting at the Count's helmet, which eventually came off, and how with a following stroke he virtually cleaved his skull in two. Logan acquired the Count's helmet and sword, presenting the sword to his commanding officer and selling the helmet to the paymaster!

In the following month, on 16 May, 1811, almost a hundred years after being raised, the Thirteenth gained their first battle honour. Soult, marching to relieve the siege of Badajoz, was intercepted by Beresford at Albuhera. The bloodiest of battles to date in the Peninsula ensued. The British and Portuguese numbered over 20,000, equally divided, and there were 15,000 Spaniards under one of their best generals. Soult's army was 26,000-strong. The allied divisions were not at all well-handled by Beresford, however, and at the end of the day's fighting both sides left the field believing the other to have gained the victory. The French lost around 8,000, but Beresford lost over a third of his British troops. The battle has been described as being perhaps the most heroic day in the annals of the British army, but Wellington observed that "another such battle would ruin us".

The Thirteenth's role in the battle was to guard the bridge and fords over the River Guadiana near Albuhera village. This, on Beresford's appreciation, would be the route for the principal French attack. In the event they feinted and made a deep hook to the left. Thus the Thirteenth found themselves on what turned out to be the allied left flank. During the day they made some successful charges against French cavalry attempting to cross but it appears that the French would not allow themselves to be closely engaged.

The regiment sustained only one fatality that day – a horse. How it came about that the Thirteenth were awarded the battle honour *Albuhera*, whereas others present were not, is something of a mystery: the 4th Dragoons had been in the thick of the fighting and had over twenty men killed or wounded, but were not awarded the distinction; other cases seem even more unfair, such as the 28th Foot, later The Gloucestershire Regiment, who lost 164 killed and wounded. Perhaps it is too fanciful to imagine that it was by way of recompense for the Campo Mayor affair? Certainly the Thirteenth's bold actions up to this time had contributed much to the British cavalry's continuing ascendancy, which might account for the standing-off of the French cavalry on the left flank at Albuhera. But it also high-lights the haphazard, almost capricious, way in which honours were bestowed at that time – as will be seen later with the 18th Hussars.

There were no further major actions in 1811, but the war had begun to slip away from Napoleon. Wellington started preparing for the following campaigning season, setting in hand the sieges of the French garrisons in the key fortresses of Ciudad Rodrigo and Badajoz. Overcoming these led to two of the bloodiest battles of the war. Nevertheless, by the end of January, 1812, Ciudad Rodrigo had been taken, and Badajoz had fallen by the middle of April.

The capture of these frontier fortresses not only secured the forward defence of Portugal but also allowed Wellington to ad-vance into Spain, to which the Prime Minister, Lord Liverpool, now agreed. The situation for the French was deteriorating rapidly, not helped by Napoleon's withdrawing troops in prep-aration for his attack on Russia, nor by his placing his brother Joseph, King of Spain, in overall command in the Peninsula, for Joseph Bonaparte had neither the ability for this command nor the confidence of his subordinates.

The Thirteenth took part in the general advance towards Madrid, which was entered on 12 August, 1812, after the Battle of Salamanca in July, Wellington's largest battle to that date. The capital was not long occupied, however, for Wellington had overreached himself and counter moves now threatened his lines of communication with Lisbon. His subsequent retreat to Ciudad Rodrigo was, in the opinion of many, more arduous than the retreat to Corunna: the Thirteenth's loss of horses for want of forage, for instance, was appalling. The French armies were equally exhausted, however, and abandoned the pursuit near the

·border, allowing Wellington to replenish and reinforce his army during the remaining winter months.

In 1813 the situation became critical for the French in Spain. Not only had troops been diverted to Russia, a campaign which itself had been disastrous, but they were by this time being withdrawn for the war in Germany too. Soult and 20,000 men were recalled. Wellington now determined that his real chance of ejecting the French from Spain was at hand. He therefore asked for further reinforcements. Not many could be spared, but they did include the Hussar brigade comprising the Tenth, Fifteenth and Eighteenth under the temporary command of Colonel Colquhoun Grant, who had led the Fifteenth throughout the Corunna campaign. These numbered in all some 1,500 sabres. Wellington was, however, desperately short of cavalry for much of the campaign and although he had built up to sixteen regiments by the campaign of 1812, that, to quote Sir Charles Oman, was "almost the highest figure he was to own. For although during the campaign of 1812 he was sent four new Hussar regiments, yet at the same time four depleted corps were sent home."

They arrived in time to take part in Wellington's general advance which began in late May, but they nearly came to early grief, not at the hands of the French but of the elements. Protecting the army's northern flank during the advance towards Salamanca, the brigade came up to the River Esla, so familiar to them from the Corunna campaign. At daybreak they attempted to cross the ford at Almendra, the accompanying infantry holding on by the stirrups, but the river was swollen due to the heavy rain and was running fast. Many of the Fifteenth's and Eighteenth's horses stumbled during the crossing, throwing their riders. The horses had great difficulty recovering themselves due to the infantrymen of the 51st Foot (later The King's Own Yorkshire Light Infantry) hanging on to the stirrups. The Eighteenth's commanding officer was so badly injured when his horse came down on top of him that he had to be invalided home. Over twenty infantrymen drowned that morning under the weight of their equipment. Two ensigns (second lieutenants) of the 51st would also have died had it not been for the exertions of a sergeant of the Eighteenth and another sergeant with some privates of the Fifteenth. At a dinner given in Bangalore, India, by the 51st in 1849, where the Fifteenth were then stationed, several of the Regiment were guests including their ex-commanding officer, Colonel Lovell, then in command of the Bangalore brigade. Lovell, replying to some toast, mentioned that it was not the first time that the two regiments had met, and recounted the incidents at the Esla, in particular that one of the 51st's officers would surely have drowned without the prompt assistance of some of the Fifteenth's men. At this, one of the 51st's officers rose to his feet, a Major Mainwaring, who, much moved, said that *he* was the ensign who owed his life to the Fifteenth some thirty-six years earlier.

The 15th/19th Hussars and the 2nd Battalion The Light Infantry (the lineal descendants of the 51st) commemorated these events whenever in the same theatre by what is known as the Esla competition, one of the customs carried over into The Light Dragoons. It is an all-ranks sporting challenge of which the trophy is a painting of the crossing. The holders of the trophy specify the challenge and thus have a considerable advantage, which is probably why the painting has been in 15th/19th's possession since 1960.

By the beginning of June, 1813, the French had begun a general withdrawal towards the Pyrenees. Pushed hard by Wellington, with the Thirteenth, Fifteenth and Eighteenth always to the fore, Joseph Bonaparte, against the advice of his principal military adviser Marshal Jourdan, decided to make a stand, however, at Vittoria. The city contained a vast accumulation of war material and other stores, besides a convoy of treasure recently arrived from France for payment of the troops. On 21 June, 80,000 of Wellington's men (including 20,000 Portuguese) fell on 62,000 French in the valley of the Zadorra River west of the town. A furious battle began but it proved impossible to resist the British onslaught and, despite desperate fighting and a magnificently conducted withdrawal, the French retreat rapidly turned into a rout. Wellington loosed all his cavalry at both the town and the fleeing enemy who managed to save only two of their 153 guns.

The Thirteenth, and several other regiments, fell upon King Joseph's baggage train just outside the town. The disposal of this booty occupied some time, the 14th Light Dragoons acquiring, famously, Joseph's silver chamberpot which they have used ever since as a loving cup. The Thirteenth captured the bulk of the royal carriages but left them in the charge of a sergeant and a small guard while they continued the pursuit of the enemy cavalry. When they returned, they found the gullible sergeant had handed the prize to an unidentified officer who had persuaded him that he had orders to take possession. Partial amends were made when the Fourteenth went to India in 1840 and presented Joseph's magnificent dining table to the Thirteenth. The table is still in the officers' mess and there is a full inscription of the details of its provenance and renovation on a silver plate on one of its supports.

The Fifteenth were ordered to bypass Vittoria to intercept the fleeing French cavalry. This they did with some success, though not without loss, but since they were without support they could not press home the attacks. They spent the night in a wood to the east of the town and were lucky, as things turned out, to be away from the temptations of plunder in the town itself.

The Eighteenth did not wholly escape temptation and paid for it dearly. They were among the first troops to enter the town and some savage street fighting followed during which a dozen or so men of the regiment were killed and twice that number wounded. The town having been cleared, some of the men found wine and spirits. As one of the squadron leaders, Captain Kennedy, records: "In such a situation it is not to be wondered at that the men, after a long and fatiguing day in warm weather, should instantly drink and consequently get drunk."

By one of those strokes of outrageous fortune, the first person to come onto the scene was Wellington himself. His reaction was predictable: some days later he had the regiment paraded and berated them for neglect of duty, pillaging and drunkenness. He referred to them later in a despatch as "a disgrace to the name of soldier, in action as well as elsewhere".

There is no doubt that the regiment deserved the parade-ground rebuke, but the despatch was, to say the least, less than even-handed. Virtually the whole army had a hand in the looting of Vittoria: "our vagabond soldiers have got among them about a million sterling in money," complained Wellington, and, "instead of getting rest and food to prepare them for the pursuit," he went on, "they spent the night in looking for plunder."

As a footnote to the sorry tale of the Eighteenth, an obvious attempt to placate the General was made when the ornamental endpiece of Marshal Jourdan's baton was sent to him by the regiment. The baton had been taken from the Marshal's baggage by a corporal of the Eighteenth (a drummer of the 87th Foot had stolen the stick part!). Wellington acknowledged the gift and sent it on to the Prince Regent with a letter saying that it had been captured by a private of the 87th, a statement which some have said reflected the General's animus towards the regiment. If so, then Wellington's conscience might have been pricked by the Prince Regent's reply: "You have sent me among the trophies of your unrivalled fame the staff of a French Marshal, and I send you in return that of England." It could not have been deeply pricked, however, since the Eighteenth were excluded from the battle honour, which was awarded to almost every other regiment present, though they sustained twice as many casualties (thirty-four, including eleven killed) as any cavalry regiment save the Fifteenth.

Whatever the rights and wrongs of the accolades for Vittoria, the battle was the end of the French in Spain. Napoleon was so angry with his brother's incompetence that he replaced him in overall command by Soult, who was then ordered to bar the way to southern France over the Pyrenees. With Austrian, Russian, Prussian and Swedish armies pressing on France from the east, there were few men and little *materiel* to be spared for this task. Despite Soult's prodigious efforts at reorganizing the remains of his field forces and lines of communication troops into one army, Wellington's pressure was inexorable. Soult mounted some determined rearguard actions and sharp counter-attacks, but Wellington managed to cross the rugged

Pyrenees and get into winter quarters in the villages in the French foothills before the severest weather set in. All three regiments continued their screening role during the crossing and did outpost duty during winter quarters.

The weather improved enough for Wellington to take up the advance again in early February, 1814, and on the 27th the first battle on French soil was fought at Orthès. Though all three regiments were present, only the Thirteenth were awarded the battle honour. The regiment was in the thick of this fighting from the outset, at one stage the commanding officer, Lieutenant-Colonel Patrick Doherty, leading a charge against the French cavalry with his two sons, one a captain and the other a lieutenant, on either side of him. The Fifteenth lost several men wounded during the battle and the Eighteenth were in general reserve in the centre, seeing everything but not being required to support. It appears that the Eighteenth's commanding officer was taking no chances with discipline that day: for reasons not recorded, he had seven men flogged first thing that morning!

Wellington continued his advance with increasing momentum towards Bordeaux and Toulouse, his cavalry leading. On 8 April, 1814, the Eighteenth were in a sharp action at a key bridge over the River Ers at Croix d'Orade, which went some way to restoring their reputation with the Field Marshal (whom, it will be remembered, had at one time been gazetted a captain in the regiment). In a despatch made four days after the action he writes that they

"had an opportunity of making a most gallant attack upon a superior body of the enemy's cavalry, which they drove through the village of Croix d'Orade, and took about 100 prisoners, and gave us the possession of an important bridge over the river Ers, by which it was necessary to pass in order to attack the enemy's position."

Later, in July, having received a letter from Lord Drogheda, Colonel of the Regiment, pressing for some formal recognition of the action, he was even more magnanimous:

"It would have been impossible for any regiment to have behaved better than the 18th Hussars did at the affair of Croix d'Orade, and I hope what passed on that occasion, and my report to the Secretary of State, showed that I was as ready to applaud good conduct, when I observed it, as I was to find fault."

Possession of the bridge at Croix d'Orade opened the way to Toulouse, into whose defences Soult's army had withdrawn. Meanwhile, Paris had fallen to the allied offensive from the east and Napoleon had abdicated on 6 April, 1814. The news took a week to reach the southern front, however, and so on 10 April the last great battle of the war was fought unnecessarily at Toulouse, all three regiments taking a part, though again only the Thirteenth were awarded the battle honour. Soult concluded an armistice on 27 April and, quite remarkably for those times, the three regiments were back in England by the middle of July having marched the 650 miles to Boulogne.

* * *

Any attempt to sum up the five and a half years of the Peninsular campaigns would be inadequate, but it was undoubtedly an epic period in the annals of The Light Dragoons. Napier reminds his readers that Moore's and Wellington's armies had "won nineteen pitched battles and innumerable combats; had made or sustained ten sieges and taken four great fortresses; had twice expelled the French from Portugal, once from Spain; had penetrated France, and killed, wounded or captured 200,000 enemies – leaving of their own number 40,000 dead, whose bones whiten the plains and mountains of the Peninsula."

The three regiments had not been involved in all these actions, but one or other had been there at almost every one, and as light cavalry had seen numerous "affairs, many of which were sharp and contested, besides the general actions", as the Thirteenth's digest relates. A good many whitened bones were those of The Light Dragoons' forebears. The Thirteenth's losses, though the regiment had not taken part in the Corunna campaign, are illustrative: landing at Lisbon some 800-strong in early 1810 and thereafter receiving only occasional drafts of battle casualty replacements, the regiment covered some 6,000 miles, sustained 280 casualties, a quarter of which were fatal, and lost 1,009 horses.

All three regiments were promptly awarded the campaign honour *Peninsula*, but although they had fought together frequently, sometimes side by side, they had yet to be awarded a common battle honour. As the regiments landed at Ramsgate and Dover that July, 1814, the prospect of ever being engaged together again to win such an honour must have appeared remote. Yet in under twelve months from landing that is exactly what occurred – at Waterloo.

CHAPTER 5

Waterloo

"I see the English papers say '*The Light Dragoons could make no impression on the French Cuirassiers.*' Now our Regiment actually rode over them."

Captain CHARLES WOOD, 10th Light Dragoons

19LD in the American War of 1812: Niagara; 13LD, 15H and 18H at Quatre Bras and Waterloo.

The 13th/18th and 15th/19th Hussars never made much of Waterloo. Other, minor battles seemed more important to the regiments because their forebears appeared to have played a greater part in them. Certainly their casualties were comparatively light, but the 13th Light Dragoons and the 15th and 18th Hussars played a significant part in one of the most decisive battles in history – and Waterloo was the first battle (as opposed to campaign) honour which all three shared.

It might have been that all *four* regiments shared the honour, for 19LD had left India and returned to England in 1807. Throughout most of the Peninsular War the Nineteenth were retained for home service, including Ireland. The reason was not the threat of invasion, but industrial unrest – and, to an extent, the shortage of suitable horses. In 1812, however, another conflict erupted which threatened to divert even more resources from the Peninsula: the United States declared war on Britain. The ostensible reason for this was the Royal Navy's boarding and searching American merchantmen in order to maintain the blockade of Napoleonic Europe. The real reason was almost certainly to annex Canada which was weakly defended and difficult to reinforce. Her defences comprised four regular battalions of infantry, a 'veteran' battalion and a locally-raised unit of regulars (the Newfoundland Regiment) plus a few companies of artillery, in all about 4,500 men to defend a 1,600-mile frontier.

The United States' declaration of war reached the British Government on 30 July, 1812, hence it is called the 'War of 1812', but the formal declaration of war by Britain was not made until the following January. In the intervening six months there was some small-scale but effective skirmishing around the Great Lakes settlements, and the US Navy operated against opportunity targets as distant as the Bay of Biscay: in early January, for instance, a man-of-war captured one of the ships transporting the Eighteenth to Portugal. The transport and its men, disarmed, were later released in exchange for a £3,000 ransom. In March, 1813, the 19th Light Dragoons, who were in Ireland, received orders for embarkation for Canada. Taking only officers', sergeants' and corporals' horses, the regiment landed at Quebec in May, among the first reinforcements to arrive. The conditions in which the Nineteenth were to operate are best summarized by a passage from Biddulph's *The Nineteenth And Their Times*:

"The war in which the regiment was about to engage was one in which cavalry could play only a subordinate part. The country in which they were to operate was a vast expanse of forest and swamp, with a few sparsely inhabited . . . clearings. The chief mode of communication was by boat. The war was to be fought out by small bodies of men far from their supports, wielding the axe and the oar as much as the rifle: forage was hard to get and there was little place for mounted men. Under these conditions, the 19th Light Dragoons were only engaged in small detachments, never more than a squadron, seldom more than a troop. Their duties were of a most harassing kind, on outpost and reconnaissance duty. Never once did they have an opportunity of crossing swords with the enemy's cavalry."

Nevertheless, the regiment played an active part in the operations around the Great Lakes and remained in the Province for some time after peace was concluded (signed formally at Ghent in December, 1814, though the news did not reach the combatants until the following March). In these operations the Nineteenth gained their fourth honour, *Niagara*. One squadron had taken part in the skilful attack on the fort there and, in the words of the Horse Guards' letter of 19 May, 1815:

> "His Royal Highness the Prince Regent has been pleased, in the name and on behalf of His Majesty, to approve of the Regiments named in the Margin, being permitted to bear on their Colors and Appointments in addition to any other Badges or Devices, which may have been heretofore permitted to be borne by those regiments the Word "Niagara", in consequence of the distinguished Conduct of those Corps in the Capture of Fort Niagara by Assault on the 19th December 1813, and in the Battle at Lundy's Lane, in North America, on 25th July, 1814."

The Nineteenth were the only regular cavalry regiment to take part in this campaign, continuing their tradition of lonely service in distant parts, and thus *Niagara* is another cavalry battle honour unique to The Light Dragoons. They remained in Canada for a full two years after the Battle of Waterloo had been fought.

* * *

After Napoleon had abdicated, in April, 1814, he was exiled to the island of Elba, which lies between Corsica, his birthplace, and the Italian mainland. The French monarchy had been restored, though it quickly provoked disenchantment amongst both the civil and military, and the statesmen of Europe assembled in Vienna to determine the shape of post-Napoleonic Europe. The Congress of Vienna had barely settled to its serious business when, in early 1815, news reached it that Napoleon had escaped and had landed in France. His probable intention was no more than to inflict sufficient damage on the allies to persuade them to accept a negotiated peace. The allies, however, declared him an outlaw, formed the Seventh Coalition and determined to dethrone him permanently.

They agreed to assemble an army of over half a million men, financed largely by Britain, but this was going to take time. Meanwhile all that was available to oppose Napoleon's new *Armée du Nord*, some 128,000-strong, were the forces in the Netherlands comprising Wellington's Anglo-Dutch-Belgian army of 95,000 and the Prussians numbering 124,000 under Marshal Blücher. Wellington's army was not his battle-hardened Peninsular one, however, an army with which he said he "could have gone anywhere and done anything", although it did include a few veteran corps. Reinforcement was obviously required and amongst the additional troops rushed to Belgium were the Thirteenth and Eighteenth, who landed in April, and the Fifteenth who landed the following month, having been stationed in Ireland.

Wellington and Blücher concentrated their armies south of Brussels in anticipation of Napoleon's advance. They were aware of his usual tactical procedure for dealing with two opponents: he would interpose his own army, 'pin' one of the opponents with the minimum force necessary, destroy the other with the major part of his army and then return to finish off the first. It was therefore going to be essential for Wellington and Blücher to cooperate closely.

Napoleon achieved a large measure of tactical surprise when he crossed the border on 15 June, 1815, earlier than Wellington himself expected (the Duke was at the Duchess of Richmond's ball in Brussels). The Duke had done his reconnaissance thoroughly, however, and was able to set his army in motion to occupy a good defensive position on the ridge of Mont St Jean, south of the village of Waterloo on the Charleroi–Brussels road, with a covering position some nine miles further south at the crossroads at Quatre Bras.

The allied cavalry, excluding the Prussians, numbered nearly 12,500, of which 7,400 were British. This was a much larger number than had taken part in the Peninsular War. During the weeks before Waterloo when it should have been concentrated for training, however, it had been dispersed across the Belgian countryside for administrative reasons, mainly forage supply. Wellington had placed all the cavalry under the Earl of Uxbridge (Lord Paget, of Corunna fame) who was widely regarded as the finest allied cavalry leader. Captain Jones of the 15th Hussars confided in his journal: "He is not only the cleverest cavalry officer in the British Empire, but unfortunately he is almost the only one with cavalry genius." Uxbridge's intention had been to form his brigades into divisions but the difficulties of doing so in the circumstances proved insurmountable. Had he been able to do so it is probable that their casualties at Waterloo would have been lighter, on the old principle of 'the more you use, the less you lose'. Lieutenant William Turner, 13th Light Dragoons, in a letter home, alludes to the practical problems which this dispersion caused as they were summoned to Quatre Bras: "At 7 next morning 15th instant was rousted out of my bed by a Sergeant to say we were to march immediately, soon turned out but owing to the Regiment being so distributed about the country we were not able to march before 11 a.m."

While the cavalry and the rest of the army were thus hastening to their positions, the Prussians were taking up theirs at Ligny, five miles to the south-east of Quatre Bras, covering a parallel road to Brussels. Napoleon fell on them in strength on 16 July and, after sustaining many casualties, Blücher (who himself had been badly injured) began a general retirement towards Wavre. From here they could still block the French approach to Brussels whilst being close enough to support Wellington at Waterloo. Meanwhile, Marshal Ney had been given the task of pinning the Anglo-Dutch at Quatre Bras, but his approach was so hesitant, and the covering action by Prince Bernhard of Saxe-Weimar's 8,000 Nassauers and Netherlanders so resolute, that he failed to achieve his aim. Uxbridge's cavalry made desperate forced marches, in some cases of up to fifty miles, to get up to Bernhard in front of Quatre Bras, but battle was joined before they could do so. "We marched by Enghein, Braiñale, Cante and Nivelle," wrote Turner, "and arrived on the field of battle near Genappe about 10 p.m. just as the battle ended, (nothing to eat all day)."

Once news of the Prussians' reverse at Ligny had reached Wellington, he decided that the advanced position at Quatre Bras was untenable and ordered the withdrawal of its battalions to the main position at Waterloo. Throughout the day of 17 June, in torrential rain which soaked everyone to the skin, this withdrawal was covered by Uxbridge's cavalry in three columns, the Thirteenth and Fifteenth together in Grant's 5th Brigade west of the main road, the Eighteenth in Vivian's Hussar Brigade to the east, and the 'heavies' covering the *chaussée* itself. There was some brisk skirmishing for most of the nine-mile retirement, French lancers following up very boldly, but all three regiments managed to join the main position that evening for a total of one officer wounded and one soldier killed.

The rain continued while the army bedded down in the open as best it could. Thomas Hardy, better known for his 'Wessex' novels, described the scene poetically in *The Eve of Waterloo*:

"And what of those who tonight have come?
–The young sleep sound; but the weather awakes
In the veterans, pains from the past that numb;

Old stabs of Ind, old Peninsular aches,
Old Friedland chills, haunt their moist mud bed,
Cramps from Austerlitz; till their slumber breaks.

And each soul shivers as sinks his head
On the loam he's to lease with the other dead
From tomorrow's mist-fall till Time be sped!"

Lieutenant Turner's letter adds hunger to the discomfort:

"It was a dreadful rainy night, every man in the Cavalry wet to the skin and nearly all the Infantry as bad; nothing to eat all day, being without rations and our baggage at Brussels. At 4 a.m. on the memorable 18th June turned out and formed on the field of battle in wet corn and a cold morning without

anything to eat, nothing but some gin, which I purchased from
a German woman, saved and enabled me and three other officers
to stand the fatigues of the day."

The position Wellington had chosen for the main battle was
a low ridge which crossed the Charleroi-Brussels *chaussée* at
right angles. It allowed the bulk of his troops to occupy reverse slopes. To the west, his right flank was protected by a
weak British brigade. His left rested on the fortified villages of
Papelotte, La Haye and Frischermont, garrisoned by Nassauers.
These villages, together with the farm-strongpoint of La Haye-
Sainte on the forward slope astride the *chaussée* (2nd King's
German Legion Light Battalion and the 95th Rifles) and the
strongly built, walled château of Hougoumont forward of the
right flank (held by the light companies of the Guards Brigade),
provided 'anchors' for the main line.

Between ten and eleven o'clock on the morning of Sunday
18 June, 1815, the cavalry took up their positions for the great
battle. The 'Heavies' were placed centrally, just behind the crest,
astride the *chaussée*. Vivian's brigade was posted to cover the
left flank; Grant's brigade was sent to cover the right and to
help stiffen the resolve of the Dutch-Belgian batteries near that
flank. Wellington must have felt a certain confidence at having
these two experienced Peninsular brigade commanders watching
his flanks, and all three regiments could share that confidence,
having served under these very men for much of the second
campaign.

The battle opened at about 11.50 am with a colossal bombardment by Napoleon's massed artillery batteries, and an assault on
Hougoumont. This assault was a diversion, aimed at drawing in
Wellington's reserves and leaving his army vulnerable to assault
through the centre. The tables were turned by the Guards, however, who defended the château so successfully throughout the
day that Hougoumont drew in instead more and more French,
fatally weakening Napoleon's own reserves.

Just before launching his first main attack on Wellington's
centre Napoleon learned that the Prussians had *not* retreated

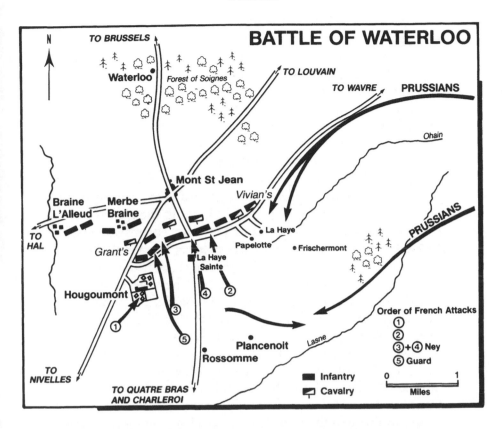

beyond supporting distance, as he had supposed, and were advancing on Waterloo from the east. He therefore ordered a defensive right flank to be formed and this further consumed troops from his reserve throughout the day.

The French attack astride the *chaussée* began at 1.30 pm. After great slaughter by the disciplined volleys of British musketry the densely packed columns of infantry were thrown back, at which point Uxbridge's Heavies counter-attacked. This famous charge was at first spectacularly successful but the brigades ran on too far, the Scots Greys in particular, and were subjected to a devastating counter-charge by French lancers. Vandeleur's light brigade charged to help extricate them and to cover their withdrawal, but Vivian's was told to remain covering the left flank of the line. With so much happening at the centre, and the neighbouring brigade charging dramatically, guarding a quiet left flank was desperately frustrating for many. Sergeant Mathew Coglan of the Eighteenth, in his reminiscences of the day, writes, "It was painfully apparent, from the groans which escaped from some, and the agonized expressions on the countenances of others, how greatly we were tried, waiting so long for the striking point, and how much our courage was taxed." But the precaution was necessary not only because a flank must be protected: many of the Dutch-Belgian troops, and some of the Hanoverians too, were unsteady, requiring the physical proximity of British troops to keep them on the position. Later in the afternoon, for instance, the Duke of Cumberland's Hussars (Brunswickers) left the field *en masse* and made for Brussels, adding insult to injury by looting the Eighteenth's officers' baggage on the way!

The Heavies had been extricated but they were exhausted. There was then a fortuitous lull in the battle, but it was soon broken by a bombardment even greater than the opening one. Next, to Wellington's astonishment, Marshal Ney, to whom Napoleon had entrusted all his cavalry save that of his *Garde*, began a series of costly and utterly futile attacks against the unbroken squares of the British infantry in the centre. As a diversion, ten squadrons of French lancers and twelve guns advanced to threaten the right flank near Hougoumont. Uxbridge immediately sent Grant's brigade to deal with them, whereupon the squadrons and guns began to retire. As Grant was about to charge them at the head of the Thirteenth and the Fifteenth, he heard the French lancers cheering the attack of the *cuirassiers* on their right. With great good judgement he abandoned his move against the *lanciers* and moved the brigade back into position ready to assist in the counter-attacks against the heavy cavalry. Both regiments then took part in several counter-charges and counter-moves against the *cuirassiers*, whose attacks seemed to continue for many hours. Indeed, some observers have said that Ney made as many as twelve separate assaults. By 6.00 pm all Uxbridge's cavalry, except Vandeleur's and Vivian's brigades on the left flank, were exhausted. The strongpoint of

La Haye-Sainte farm fell soon afterwards because its defenders simply ran out of ammunition.

The situation was, for a time, critical, but Ney failed to reinforce his success strongly enough. It would have been difficult for him to find reinforcements, however, for at this time the Prussians, who had made slow progress through the mud and the heath and forest fires, appeared on the extreme left of Wellington's position. Their appearance so shook Napoleon that he spread the word that they were in fact Marshal Grouchy's men arriving from Ligny. To Wellington and the British troops who could see them, the Prussians appeared as their deliverers:

> "What a delightful sight;" writes Sergeant Coglan, "nothing ever appeared to me to equal it, good and imposing as it really was. Grand and imposing was the sight, and what a spirit did it infuse into our minds on beholding their formation, and on seeing them open their fire on the enemy, although I thought they were not within range at the time."

Indeed they were *not* within range, but the fire had a signal effect: *why were Grouchy's men firing on their fellows* demanded Napoleon's soldiers? Treason: *"nous sommes trahis!"*

Blücher's cavalry had already made a junction with the British line enabling Uxbridge to move Vandeleur's and Vivian's brigades, the only British cavalry by then capable of sustained effort, to the centre. They got there in the nick of time. Napoleon was making his last desperate fling by ordering the Imperial Guard to attack, and several allied regiments, including Halket's British brigade, were again beginning to give way. It was not surprising, for the carnage to their front was horrific. Vivian relates what he saw on getting to the centre: "never did I witness anything so terrific [terrifying] – the ground actually covered with dead and dying, cannon shot and shells flying thicker than I ever heard even musketry before". He wheeled his brigade into line behind the wavering infantry and brought them to a halt "with our horses' heads almost resting on their rear ranks," in Coglan's words. Vivian's intention was to charge the attacking French columns the instant the infantry had retreated through the intervals between his squadrons, but it was not necessary: the cavalry's arrival steadied them, particularly the Dutch-Belgians, and the line held.

The *Garde's* attack was made with astonishing courage: they had, after all, never been beaten. But as the allied centre held firm, and momentarily checked what the French might have presumed was irresistible, Wellington personally directed a devastating counter-attack by fire. Major-General Peregrine Maitland's Guards brigade was lying concealed in the standing corn and behind the banks of the road on the centre right: "Now, Maitland, now's your time!" called out Wellington: "Stand up, Guards!" As if from nowhere 1,500 guardsmen appeared in the face of two densely-packed battalion columns and at forty yards' range poured volley after volley of musketry into them. The 1st/52nd Light Infantry at this moment wheeled to their left and began a furious enfilading fire. The Imperial Guard's assault was over. A general retirement began: the cry "*La Garde recule!*" went up from the rest of the French army. Mixed with cries already of "*Nous somme trahis*", it was enough to break their will.

Now was the time for vigorous counter-attacks to deny the *Garde* any opportunity to re-form. Maitland's Guards charged; so did the 52nd. "Go on, go on! They won't stand," shouted the Duke to their commanding officer. Vivian needed no urging: he launched his brigade at the supporting cavalry, the *Chasseurs* and *Grenadiers à Cheval*, who resisted desperately at first and then broke. The Eighteenth overran and silenced the last two active batteries and set about the *Garde's* squares which were in the process of being hurriedly formed. A third cry was now heard throughout Napoleon's army – "*sauve qui peut*" – as more and more Frenchmen began to run for their lives. Wellington gave the signal for the whole line to advance.

On the right Lord Hill, commanding the 2nd Corps, was heard to call, "Now come on, drive them back Thirteenth!", and the much-depleted regiments of Grant's brigade surged forward, though they could manage no more than a trot, so numerous were the bodies of dead and dying French soldiers and the lines of allied infantry delighting in this turning of tables.

The Prussians conducted the pursuit, for Wellington's army was utterly exhausted, not least his cavalry. Even the final numbers of dead and injured do not give the full picture. At the close of the battle, "When the regiment mustered at 10 p.m., that night," writes William Turner of the Thirteenth, "we had only 65 men left out of 260 who went into the field in the morning, the rest were either killed, wounded or missing, the 15th also suffered most dreadfully." The loss of horses throughout the day had thinned the ranks too; Grant himself had had no less than five horses shot from under him. The Thirteenth's commanding officer, Shapland Boyse, had been severely injured when his horse was brought down by a cannon ball, and was removed from the field at about midday. The Fifteenth's commanding officer, Leighton Dalrymple, lost a leg by a cannon ball which then killed Grant's horse. Command devolved to the regiment's major, Edwin Griffith, who was then killed whilst leading one of the counter-charges. Joseph Thackwell, senior captain, led the regiment in the final charges but he too was wounded. Captain Skinner Hancox brought them out of action.

Between them the 13th Light Dragoons and the 15th and the 18th Hussars had lost forty-seven officers and men killed and nearly 200 wounded. That night, on the two square miles over which the day's fighting had taken place, some 40,000 men and 10,000 horses lay dead or wounded. "Darkness at 9 p.m. put an end to the slaughter. The last charge was literally riding over men and horses who lay in heaps," writes the Thirteenth's Lieutenant Turner. "I assure you our Regiment had been without rations since Thursday, and it was not till Monday evening June 19th that we got our meat. I luckily had one fowl and some mouldy bread in four days."

If logistics were creaking, casualty evacuation and treatment had all but broken down. Countless numbers died of wounds as they lay out that night. Thackwell managed to survive the night despite much loss of blood and had his arm amputated after being brought in the following morning. Some of the wounded were helped to their deaths by marauding peasants and allied soldiers alike, mainly the latter, who were intent on plundering the dead and wounded. It was a situation virtually incomprehensible to the modern, professional soldier and is worth analysing. David Howarth, in *A Near Run Thing*, does so:

> "The paralysis of the army in the dark seems strange in retrospect. Wellington, who rode back across the battlefield, and then sat down to his dinner and went to sleep, gave no order and made no suggestion about the wounded until the following evening. Nor did any other senior officer, so far as can be known. The army medical service was overwhelmed, and it was nobody else's business even to give first aid. Everyone was distressed by the groans and shrieks he could hear, but nobody walked a yard from his bivouac to fetch water or to help to bandage men who needed it. Everyone, of course, was tired, and that was some excuse. And the dark field, where friends and mortal enemies were lying mixed together, was genuinely terrifying. Above all, it was an unfamiliar situation, for which there were no standing orders. Battles seldom ended so suddenly, so conclusively, or so exactly at dusk: more often both armies had moved before nightfall, one in retreat and the other in pursuit, and both had to be ready to fight again the next morning. So active soldiers were accustomed to leaving their wounded companions behind with their dead and quickly forgetting them all. The idea of halting among them was unfamiliar, and nobody liked it. Some British regiments at Waterloo moved off the field before they bivouacked, simply in order to spend a quiet night. And the rest of them slept, compact little groups of healthy men among the sea of suffering, waiting like armies everywhere for somebody to tell them what to do."

Howarth is misleading in one respect. Wellington did not, as is suggested, simply go to sleep after dinner. He did not turn in until he had completed a long and detailed despatch to London. It was in many respects, however, a somewhat terse despatch, depending on viewpoint and taste: at least one cavalryman, Sergeant-Major Edward Cotton of the 7th Hussars (the third regiment in Grant's brigade that day) praised "its noble simplicity, perfect calmness and exemplary modesty", but, predictably perhaps, the Eighteenth were not happy. One of its senior captains, Arthur Kennedy, complained that it was "a lame account, giving offence to the whole army, especially to the cavalry". It does seem to have had a mixed reception and Wellington himself later admitted that he should have given more praise. He was always chary of giving it, though. He had been heard to remark, however, "Well done the Tenth and Eighteenth," as he watched Vivian's brigade cut through the *Garde*. It was obviously not enough to assuage the regiment's hurt pride after Vittoria.

There were no recriminations for the Eighteenth, or for any other regiment for that matter, so far as looting was concerned after this battle. Following in the wake of the Prussians towards Paris, it seems there was nothing left to loot: "This war cannot possibly last long," suggested Turner, "for every town and village is completely ransacked, and pillaged by the Prussians and neither wine, spirits or bread are to be found. The whole country from the frontier to Paris has been laid to waste." While Turner's letter rather relishes the destruction – "We are waiting for the Prussians when that infernal City Paris will be attacked and no doubt pillaged, for it is a debt we owe to the whole of Europe" – the Eighteenth's accounts seem much more magnanimous, and are certainly chivalrous:

> "We passed one fair Château, where we found all doors and windows broken open, and on entering released the old master and his two handsome young daughters, who we found shut in one of the rooms, the latter having suffered the greatest indignity and shame at the hands of our allies."

There was prize money to be divided, but not a great deal – field officers received a little over £433, captains a little over £90; a sergeant received £19.4s.4d. (£19.22p), and troopers £2.11s.4d. (£2.57p) – the equivalent of a month and a half's pay. The regiments had their own prize money too: the Eighteenth bought a silver trumpet for the Trumpet Major from the proceeds of the sale of captured horses. It is now on display in the museum at Cannon Hall near Barnsley.

British troops were also awarded a medal bearing the effigy of the Prince Regent, the first medal ever to be given to all ranks by the British Government. More important to the average soldier than prize money or medals, however, was the grant of two years' reckonable service towards their pension. A popular rhyme sums up the place of this battle in the minds of the British public at that time:

> "Were *you* at Waterloo?
> I have been at Waterloo.
> 'Tis no matter what you do,
> If you were at *Waterloo*."

Though the three regiments' successors in later years may have made little of the battle as a whole, the three had nevertheless played an important part in its outcome. They had, by their presence and bearing, put heart throughout the day into a good many unsteady allied troops (who comprised over a third of Wellington's force) and later in the day had likewise steadied some badly battered British regiments. The Thirteenth and Fifteenth had materially helped to thwart the French plan to divert troops from the centre to strengthen Hougoumont and the right flank. And the Eighteenth, together with the Tenth, kept relatively fresh all day guarding the key left flank onto which the Prussians were to come, sealed the *Garde*'s fate in the closing stages: Napoleon himself acknowledged the role of Vivian's brigade in determining the outcome. The commanding officer of the 2ème Chasseurs, who were overcome in the charge, said quite simply, "Two regiments of the British Hussars decided the affair."

The matter is, of course, less straightforward than that. But though the honours for Waterloo are frequently given to the Infantry, whose sheer tenacity undoubtedly frustrated Napoleon's attritional battle plan, or occasionally to the Prussians' arriving, it is not as straightforward as that either, for

19. "At the rally the regiment could muster mounted only two officers and eight men." (p. 110) The Thirteenth on the morning after the Charge - one of Roger Fenton's pioneering photographs of the campaign.

20. *"Britain groaned at the disaster of Majuba Hill."(p.124)* The 15th Hussars retire after the humiliating defeat at the hands of the Boers in February, 1881. Contemporary pencil drawing by Melton Prior.

21. *"Some desperate hand-to-hand fighting developed."(p.130)* Quartermaster-Sergeant William Marshall, 19th Hussars, rescuing the severely wounded second-in-command at the Battle of El Teb, 29 February, 1884. Marshall's outstanding courage won him the regiment's first VC. Contemporary sketch for the *Illustrated London News*.

The Unkindest Cut of All.

22. *"To Pretoria by train in open trucks."*(p.136) The capture of over half of the 18th Hussars, including the commanding officer, on the first day of fighting in Natal during the second Boer War had a profound effect on morale throughout the Army in South Africa and with the public at home. Cartoon by J M Staniforth, *Western Mail*, 28 October, 1899.

23. *"They were soon to regain their reputation during the prolonged defence of Ladysmith."*(p.141) A group of the Eighteenth's officers during the famous siege.

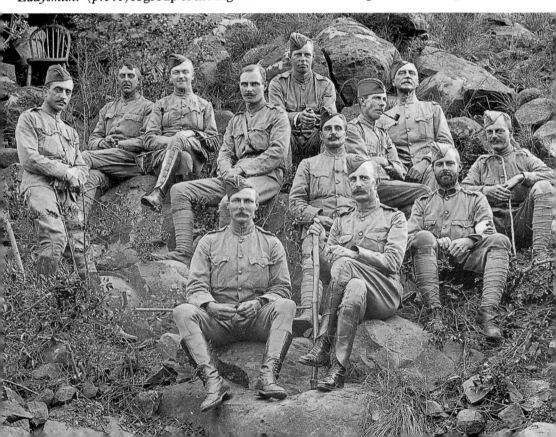

24. *"The Cavalry was trained first of all for attack, but only insufficiently in the use of the carbine"*(p.156), concluded the German General Staff's report on the Boer War. Both the Cavalry and Infantry were shocked to find their fieldcraft and marksmanship no match for the Boers. This photograph shows a trooper of the 13th Hussars and his mount in field service order in Natal, 1900. Note the 'flash' on the side of the helmet, known today as the 'South Africa Flash', and worn by The Light Dragoons on the upper left arm of No 2 Dress.

25. *"At this time the VC was not awarded posthumously."*(p.151) A watercolour by Baden-Powell depicting the rescue of a 13th Hussar officer. The trooper died in the course of the rescue but no decoration could be forthcoming. A similar rescue the previous year won the VC for the Eighteenth's Private Harry Crandon.

Wellington himself never underestimated how close a contest it was. He is said to have remarked that it was "a near-run thing", or similar words, and later, "By God, I don't think it would have done if I had not been there." The regiments' role at Waterloo should be viewed in light of that judgement.

CHAPTER 6

Retrenchment at Home, Mixed Fortunes in India

"Soldiers in peace are like chimneys in summer."
WILLIAM CECIL,(Lord BURGHLEY)
Advice to His Son, 1555

19LD become lancers; 18H and 19L disbanded; 13LD and 15H in aid of Civil Powers in England and Ireland; 13LD and 15H in India.

It was only to be expected that as soon as peace in Europe was firmly secured the Army would be drastically reduced. The process began almost immediately after Waterloo with the Infantry. The Cavalry were largely spared for a few years because of growing civil unrest throughout the Kingdom. The war had stimulated the economy, but peace brought a general depression. There were widespread disturbances over both the price of corn and the unemployment resulting from increasing mechanization in industry and agriculture. Demands for reform of the electoral system (voting for an MP required, in the main, a man to own property) fed on the economic unrest. There were no properly constituted police forces, so when violence erupted the local magistrates' only recourse was to call out the Yeomanry or, if at hand, the regulars. Light cavalry, mobile and often able to quell a disturbance by just appearing, were regarded by the Government as the best insurance policy during these dangerous years, though their establishments were reduced considerably. Regiments were therefore dispersed around Britain and Ireland in aid of the civil authorities, and especially His Majesty's Customs and Excise.

The Nineteenth returned from Canada in 1817 and were immediately converted to lancers, together with the 9th, 12th and 16th Light Dragoons. The French had used lancers to good effect during the war, and Wellington himself had witnessed their effectiveness at Waterloo. After two years in the south of England the 19th Lancers were sent to Ireland, as were the Eighteenth. Inevitably, the reduction in the overall establishment of the Army caught up with the more junior cavalry regiments and, on 10 September, 1821, both the Eighteenth and the Nineteenth were disbanded. By coincidence, both were quartered in the same barracks at Newbridge outside Dublin.

Meanwhile, the Thirteenth and the Fifteenth were kept busy by the demands made by the general unrest, particularly in northern England. The Thirteenth spent the whole of the summer and autumn of 1818 quelling disturbances in Lancashire. In the following spring, however, they received orders to embark for India. They arrived in Madras in June, 1819, to begin a period of garrison duties on the sub-continent which was to last twenty-one years.

The Fifteenth relieved them in India in 1840 but until then they continued the routine of home service in England and Ireland. In 1819 they took part in one of the most celebrated, or infamous, incidents in English social history, the so-called 'Peterloo Massacre'. On 16 August, at St Peter's Fields in Manchester, a crowd of about 60,000 gathered under the auspices of the Reform Movement to hear the fiery orator Henry Hunt. Two years earlier another large crowd on St Peter's Fields had been peacefully dispersed by the King's Dragoon Guards. Afterwards the authorities, alarmed at what might have been had regular troops not been available, hastily formed the Manchester and Salford Yeomanry. They were an ill-chosen and ill-trained unit, to say the least.

Six troops of the Fifteenth, under 300 men, were in support of the magistrates that day in addition to a troop of the

Yeomanry, about 50-strong. The chief magistrate decided to arrest 'Orator' Hunt at the start of the meeting and brought the Yeomanry troop forward to assist. Worthy city tradesmen though they were, skilled horsemen they were not. Their horses soon got out of hand and the Yeomanry themselves became frightened, though the crowd was good-natured and included many women and children. The troop drew their swords. It appeared to the magistrates that the Yeomanry were in trouble and needed rescuing, so the Fifteenth were ordered to disperse the meeting. The regiment extended their line and charged the crowd. Cornet Joliffe records:

> "The charge ... swept this mingled mass of human beings before it: people, yeomen and constables, in their confused attempts to escape, ran over the other... The hussars drove the people forward with the flats of their swords; but sometimes, as is almost inevitably the case when men are placed in such situations, the edge was used."

A cotton-weaver saw:

> "ten or twelve of the Yeomanry Cavalry and two of the Hussars cutting at the people, who were wedged close together, when an officer of the Hussars rode up to his own men, and knocking up their swords, said 'Damn you, what do you mean by this work?' He then called out to the Yeomanry, 'For shame, gentlemen; what are you about? The people cannot get away.' They desisted for a time, but no sooner had the officer rode to another part of the field, than they fell to their work again."

The exact number of casualties was never determined but it appears unlikely that more than eleven were killed, and these probably from crushing or trampling. The Yeomanry were roundly condemned, rightly, and the affair was dubbed 'Peterloo' by the press in ironic reference to the charges at Waterloo. The Fifteenth escaped serious criticism since it was generally acknowledged that they had conducted themselves with skill and restraint.

* * *

In India the Thirteenth spent a remarkably peaceful time, mainly in Bangalore, Mysore. In 1832 they were involved in the prompt, and relatively bloodless, prevention of a mutiny of sepoys and in 1839 they took part in operations against the Nawab of Kurnool, losing thirty-two men during the campaign, mainly from cholera. In 1831 their uniform changed from blue to red, along with the rest of the Cavalry (except the Royal Horse Guards). King William IV, who had ascended to the throne the previous year on the death of his brother, George IV, had strong views on uniform. He had been an active naval officer for much of his life and believed, simply, that sailors should wear blue and soldiers should wear red. Accordingly, the light cavalry had to change although, for simplicity and economy, hussars retained their blue tunics but changed the colour of the pelisse to scarlet. The light cavalry reverted to blue in 1841, four years after William's death.

The Fifteenth sailed for India in 1839 and took over the Thirteenth's horses and a hundred of their men who had volunteered to stay on in Bangalore. They must have been relieved in a way to see India because during the preceding decade they had been dispersed a good deal. But worse, they had become so notorious in the popular press and the music halls and alehouses because of the antics of their commanding officer that the situation at times resembled a comic opera.

Lord Brudenell, later Earl of Cardigan, had bought command of the regiment in 1832. Obstinate, vain, snobbish, jealous and extremely rich, he set about correcting what he judged to be the slovenly standards which had crept into the Fifteenth during the easy-going command of his predecessor, the Waterloo veteran Joseph Thackwell. Parades and field days were ordered with unprecedented frequency. The horses and men could hardly keep up. Leave was curtailed and there were constant rows and arrests. When the regiment went to Dublin in 1833, a very fashionable posting, Cardigan became a veritable martinet so keen was he to show them off to perfection. He pounced on 'malingerers' whatever their rank and, as Fortescue says, behaved in general more like a sergeant-major than a command-ing officer.

The second in command was Major Walter Scott, eldest son of the 'Waverley' novelist. His father sums up his dismay at his son's situation and prospects in the Fifteenth in a letter to a friend:

> "Everyone grumbles at his own profession, but here is the devil of a calling for you, where a man pays £5,000 for an annuity of £400 a year and less – renounces his free-will in almost every respect – must rise at five every morning to see horses curried – dare not sleep out of town without the leave of a cross colonel, who is often disposed to refuse it merely because he has the power to do so; and, last of all, may be sent to the most unhealthy climates to die of the rot, or be shot like a blackcock. There is a per contra, to be sure – fine clothes and fame; but the first must be paid for and the other is not come by, by one out of the hundred."

Things were certainly not happy, and rumours of this began circulating later that year. Captain Augustus Wathen, one of the five troop captains, seemed to attract Cardigan's particular attention. Wathen was older than Cardigan by ten years (Cardigan was thirty-six) and, like Thackwell, whose easy-going ways Cardigan disdained, was a Waterloo veteran. That alone was enough to rouse the commanding officer's vanities and jealousies, but Wathen was also a pauper in comparison with Cardigan's wealth, and this brought out the worst in his lord-ship's snobbishness.

As is often the case, the regiment's unhappiness was first manifested among the wives. Bitchiness soon reached aston-ishing levels and was eagerly reported by the press, Wathen's wife usually managing to get her side into print before Lady Brudenell, Cardigan's wife. Later generations, though accus-tomed to the explicit approach of the 'tabloids', might still be surprised at the *New Weekly Despatch's* potted account of Lady Brudenell's earlier sexual escapades: "the wife of a gallant Major

– the friend of another – the attaché of a third – and, at last, the lady of the Lieutenant-Colonel."

Dress has always been important in a cavalry regiment. Unkind critics would say pre-eminently important. But it was a matter of dress which finally brought Wathen to court martial, turned the Fifteenth's squabbles into a national scandal and precipitated Cardigan's flight, like a scalded cat, from Dublin to London and half-pay. The appearance of his regiment naturally meant a great deal to the commanding officer, but the men in Captain Wathen's troop began complaining that Cardigan was making them buy replacement stable jackets on the slightest pretext. These were the days when troopers were placed under stoppages of pay for the routine wear and tear of their uniforms: today's soldier would sign the beloved Army Form P1954 only for losses or 'negligent misuse and damage' – *P1954 him S'arnt-Major*!

A particular row developed when Wathen took something of a stand on the issue, throwing Cardigan into apoplexies of rage. He sneered at Wathen for seeming not to be able to afford to pay off his troop's clothing debt from his own pocket: he had no right to be in this smart and expensive regiment was Cardigan's view. The officers of the regiment divided into two camps – those who considered that Cardigan's conduct was unbecoming (of an officer and a gentleman), and those who thought he was merely insane. It was not long before there were charges of insubordination against Wathen, and a general court martial.

The court martial itself was a masterpiece of drama, resembling alternately the trial in Herman Wouk's *The Caine Mutiny* and the case of Pickwick vs Bardell. The press had a field day. Captain Wathen himself addressed the court for two hours in the closing submission and tears were reportedly rolling down the cheeks of old soldiers in the Cork barracks courtroom at the sight of this fine old Waterloo soldier defending his honour against his aristocratic persecutor.

It was not perhaps surprising therefore, although there is evidence that Wathen was not quite so innocent as was made out (and Wathen's wife is said to have written his speech), that the court martial's findings went against Cardigan. But the censure which accompanied them was, for the times, really quite remarkable. Cardigan was at dinner in the mess when the findings arrived from the Horse Guards at the beginning of February, 1834, promulgation of court martial proceedings not being immediate at that time (harking back to the Restoration settlement when feeling against Cromwell's military government ran so strong that court martial findings were made conditional on civil review). Not only was Captain Wathen *honourably* acquitted but Cardigan himself was censured by the Adjutant General for conduct "revolting to every proper and honourable feeling of a gentleman". And then the unthinkable – by the command of King William IV himself, Cardigan was dismissed from the 15th Hussars.

At this point Cardigan's connexion with the regiment ends, but the very manner of his leaving sheds light on the later happenings in the Crimea. As he studied the document at the dinner table those present saw his face turn ashen-white. The words, "His Majesty has been pleased to order, that Lieutenant-Colonel Lord Brudenell shall be removed from command of the 15th Hussars" were bad enough, but the Commander in Chief had added an order that the details of his disgrace were to be read out to the regiment on parade, *and* to every other regiment in the Service.

He sprang to his feet and, after issuing a few orders from regimental headquarters recalling the second in command from duty in a nearby town, and cancelling the following day's field training, he mounted his horse and at midnight in the cold, heavy rain, galloped out of the barracks. The roads of that part of southern Ireland were virtually impassable, but through the rain and total darkness of the country lanes and tracks he crossed the hills and rode down into the town of Fermoy. From here he crossed another range of hills and stopped the morning coach for Dublin near Clonmel. He had covered a distance of sixty miles, and to do so at night and in such conditions was, if nothing else, a remarkable feat of horsemanship. It would be mirrored twenty years later by a similar prodigious feat when at last he experienced the active service he was so jealous of having missed.

From Dublin, Cardigan sailed for London, and the Fifteenth could begin to return to normality. He was succeeded in command by Lieutenant-Colonel Benjamin Lovell, the Peninsular veteran who had been on half-pay since 1828, and Lovell seems to have brought the regiment back to its former equable ways very quickly.

There were two other officers in the Fifteenth at this time whose names are of interest, one of regimental significance, the other of much greater repute. Captain Robert Rollo Gillespie, the son of the Nineteenth's famous commanding officer, had been commissioned in 1814, the year of his father's death in action in Nepal. He died in 1843 at the Cape. The other was Captain Louis Edward Nolan, whose grandfather had served as a trooper with the Thirteenth in Jamaica and whose father had become British assistant consul in Milan. Nolan was to become one of the most talked-about men in the Army. It was Nolan who carried the fateful order for the Light Brigade's charge at Balaklava, of which more in the next chapter, but even before then he was well known as an authority on military equitation and cavalry tactics.

During their time in India, which was spent entirely at Bangalore and which was even less eventful than the Thirteenth's, the Fifteenth took part at Nolan's initiative in extensive trials to determine whether or not stallions were better than geldings on arduous service. A hundred of each were trialled and the details are recorded in his book *Cavalry; its History and Tactics*. They show that there was no difference in performance between the two, although the geldings were universally preferred because of their better manageability.

Soldiering in India, however, was generally becoming dangerously slack and corrupt, even dissolute. The officers of the East India Company's army were too often below par and insensitive to the effect of their excesses. Their discipline was often particularly poor. Parts of the Company army were veritable powder kegs of increasing, but largely unnoticed, sepoy discontent. Although the royal army regiments were distanced from much of this, the malaise could be infectious, especially where regiments spent long years in the same garrison with officers who had exchanged into the regiment because they could not afford to soldier in England – 'Hindoos' as they were derisively dubbed by the 'elegant extracts' who would exchange into a home-posted regiment at the first rumours of Indian service. In February, 1837 a correspondent of the *Naval and Military Gazette* maintained that:

> "At the present moment such is the degraded state of the army in India, and the feeling against serving in that country, that none but needy adventurers and seedy boys can be procured for the King's regiments there."

The native press began to be openly critical too, one paper reporting a dance in tones of moral outrage:

> "Having stuffed themselves with unclean food and many sorts of flesh, taking plenty of wine, they made for some time a great noise, which doubtless arose from drunkenness. After dinner they danced in their licentious manner, pulling about each other's wives. . . Captain ——————— who is staying with Mr ———————, went away with the latter's lady (arm in arm), the palanquins following behind, and they proceeded by themselves into the bungalow; the wittol remained at table, guzzling red wine."

For a country with the most pornographic carvings on public display in its temples it seems a little rich to carp at such 'goings-on', but they were clearly offensive to many Indians. And if the officers' behaviour was considered censorious then so was the soldiery's: the *Madras Conservative* reported in September, 1836, that regimental life had deteriorated still further with "the introduction of gambling houses to which the soldier eagerly resorts", adding that in some regiments courts martial were running at the rate of a dozen every month.

But it wasn't just in India that things were going awry. The 1830s and 1840s were a time when the Radical press and the

Reform Movement saw the Army as little more than a decadent society of Tory drones. In August, 1840, the *Examiner*, in an article entitled "Military Licentiousness", declared that after Waterloo men who had been good enough to fight Bonaparte but were not ornamental on parade or able to meet the expenses of a fashionable mess were weeded out. The paper specified the Hussars and Lancers, and exhorted the Commander-in-Chief to clean up the act:

> "We specify Hussars and Lancers because ... we find that the greater number of offences against the peace and decency of society have been committed by individuals of those rich and generally aristocratic bodies."

This then was the state of things at home and in India when the Thirteenth exchanged with the Fifteenth in Bangalore. The Thirteenth, almost as fashionable as the Fifteenth, soon settled to the routine of English garrison life but there were still not enough permanent barracks, even by this time, so billeting was common and there were frequent changes of scene. Long marches were still common too, but the railways were expanding rapidly and troop movements by train began to be the rule. The 1840s were a relatively peaceful and prosperous time in Great Britain although there was the occasional scare of war with France. In Ireland there was growing unrest associated with Home Rule, exacerbated by bad landlords and crop failure. In Europe there was revolution, of sorts, in 1848, and in India there was ferocious fighting in the north, particularly the Punjab. None of this touched the Thirteenth or the Fifteenth, however.

In Britain the results of the progressive neglect of the Army after Waterloo, particularly in the quality of enlisted men, was becoming evident. Though all this was ultimately the fault of the politicians and their policies of financial retrenchment, things were not helped by the Army's being presided over by old heroes with an aversion to anything new: the Duke of York, Hill and Wellington served as Commanders-in-Chief into old age, Wellington until he was seventy-seven, and only death wrested office from the Duke of York. When in 1854 the requirement arose to send an expeditionary force to Turkey, and thence to the Crimea, in the words of Correlli Barnett: "all preparations – material, organizational and psychological – started once again from nothing". It was as if the campaign in the Peninsula had never taken place.

CHAPTER 7

The Crimea

"We marched that day [29 May 1856] into Cork barracks, and the next day to Ballancollig. That night I slept in a bed, for the first time since we left England on 10th May, 1854. During the campaign it was my great fortune and privilege to be permitted to pass through it all without a day's sickness in any shape or form. I hardly think there was a dozen men in the whole regiment so highly favoured."

Sergeant ALBERT MITCHELL, 13LD
Recollections of One of the Light Brigade

13LD in the Crimea: Alma; Balaklava; Inkerman; Sevastopol.

Sergeant Mitchell was a lucky man. Fifty-seven of the 13th Light Dragoons had died in Bulgaria and the Crimea, no more than thirty falling dead to the Russian cannon in the "valley of death" at Balaklava. The rest fell to disease and privation. A further twenty-eight had to be invalided out of the Army as a result of illness. The embarkation strength had been less than 300 and, though several drafts reached the regiment over the next eighteen months, the Thirteenth's parade strength never exceeded 400 and was frequently less than 200. The horses fared even worse: of the original 298 which left England with the regiment, only eight returned.

The causes of the Crimean War were simple enough. Russia, more specifically Tsar Nicholas I, had taken to the arrogant bullying of Turkey, the so-called 'sick man of Europe'. The ostensible reason for this was the issue of the protection of the 'holy places' – Christian sites in the Holy Land, tended by the Greek Orthodox church but under Turkish suzerainty. The real reason was expansionism. Any expansion of Russian power in the east, however, immediately alarmed Britain because of the implications for India. The maintenance of Turkish independence was therefore an important foreign policy objective. France's interests were purely self-aggrandizing. Having deposed King Louis Philippe in the revolution of 1848, Bonaparte's nephew, Louis Napoleon, was made president of the Second Republic. It was not long before he became thoroughly authoritarian and appointed himself, with the aid of a military coup, Emperor Napoleon III. He then hoped to strengthen his regime by military triumphs, so he threw in his lot with Britain and Turkey, attempting to justify this by championing the Roman Catholics' claim to custody of the Holy Places over that of the Greek Orthodox church.

In June, 1853, Russia invaded Turkey's neighbours, the Balkan principalities of Moldavia and Wallachia, the present-day Romania. Turkey declared war on Russia in October. Britain and France declared war on her too in March the following year, and by the end of May there were allied troops in Turkey. The commander-in-chief of the British force was Lord Fitzroy James Henry Somerset, first Baron Raglan, youngest son of the fifth Duke of Beaufort, and of whom more later. The force included a division of cavalry, comprising a light and a heavy brigade, under the command of Major-General George Charles Bingham, third Earl of Lucan, lately commanding the 17th Lancers – 'Bingham's Dandies'. In fact Lucan had hardly been at military duty since relinquishing regimental command because of his duties as an Irish peer; nevertheless the description of him as "a military maniac" does not seem unjust. He was conscientious and brave, certainly, but he was also prejudiced, vindictive, narrow-minded – and violently unpopular. Commanding the Light Brigade was James Thomas Brudenell, seventh Earl of Cardigan, who had galloped out of the Fifteenth's barracks in Cork some twenty years earlier. Such was the power of money and aristocratic leverage at this time, however, that the dramatic disgrace lasted for less than two years, for he bought command of the 11th Hussars in 1836 – and managed to hold on to it, despite such further celebrated affairs as 'the black bottle', for over fifteen years. These three appointments astonished the Army and much of the Press and public. Many officers said it would end in disaster.

The principal base was at Scutari, which soon achieved notoriety through the appalling conditions of its hospital until Florence Nightingale arrived to put things in order. Between May and August the armies moved on to the port of Varna, in the Turkish province of Bulgaria, to deal with the Russians in Moldavia and Wallachia. They were soon to discover that this was one of the unhealthiest places in the Black Sea, for malaria and cholera struck almost at once, the Thirteenth losing five men in one week. The Russians had by this time crossed the Danube and laid siege to the Turkish fortress of Silistria, seventy miles north of Varna. Raglan immediately ordered the Light Brigade's commander to make an extensive reconnaissance in order to determine the scale of the Russian penetration. Cardigan took with him a squadron of the 8th Hussars and another of the Thirteenth, numbering in all about 200 men. For seventeen days, from dawn to dusk, in great heat, this force scoured the country between Varna and the Danube. None of those taking part, including Cardigan, had much experience of protracted field conditions, let alone active service, and it was therefore not surprising that the state of both men and horses began to deteriorate alarmingly. The operation became known throughout the army as "the Sore-back Reconnaissance", for of the seventy-five horses of the Thirteenth which took part, only forty were fit for anything other than light work again.

It was, however, an invaluable operation, as Raglan told Cardigan. It confirmed that the Russians had withdrawn. The worst of Cardigan's nature has been described in the preceding chapter but it is interesting to balance this by noting the remarks in a letter home from one of the Thirteenth's officers, Captain Jenyns, at the end of the reconnaissance: "We got tremendous praise from Lord Cardigan, who is a capital fellow to be under at this work."

After the Russians had evacuated the lower Danube their remaining troops in this area were routed by the Turks, without the allies' aid, and by the middle of July, 1854, were in full retreat north-eastwards, abandoning Moldavia and Wallachia soon afterwards. The ostensible allied war aim had thus been achieved. The British cabinet and the French, however, decided that the reduction of the great Russian naval base at Sevastopol had become an essential political and military objective, so, despite the misgivings of Raglan and the French commander, Marshal St Arnaud, the armies re-embarked in August and sailed for the Crimea.

The regiments were pleased enough to leave Varna where the mounting death and sickness was truly alarming. Sergeant Mitchell, at this time still a trooper (though his rank was *Private*, since *Trooper* as a rank was not adopted in the Line Cavalry until after the Great War) recalls:

> "The sick, of whom there were many, were placed in arabas (small four-wheeled wagons), drawn by two bullocks or water buffaloes. There were a few poor fellows who were past recovery, yet not dead. These were left behind to die, a party of hospital orderlies being left with them to see the last of them and bury them. A surgeon was also left in charge of them."

The armies landed unopposed in Kalamita Bay, twenty miles north of Sevastopol, in the middle of September. To many the countryside resembled Salisbury Plain and promised to be wonderful for cavalry. But Raglan knew the advantage here lay with the Russians, for he had only two brigades, now numbering less than a thousand sabres, and the French even less. He concluded that he would need to keep them, in his words, "in a band-box".

The approach to Sevastopol required the crossing of four rivers, none of them any great obstacle, but each commanded by significant heights. The first river, the Bulganek, was not much

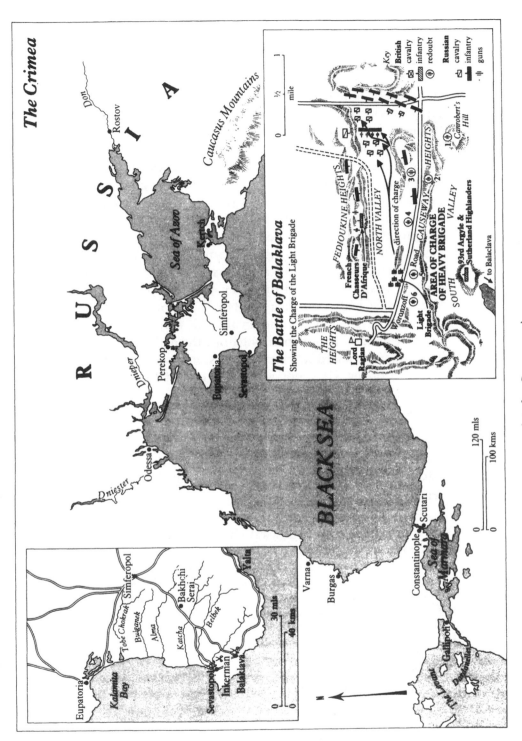

The Crimea

The Battle of Balaklava
Showing the Charge of the Light Brigade

Key
British
cavalry ⊠ infantry ⊞ redoubt
Russian
cavalry ▬ infantry ⚬ guns

BLACK SEA

Sea of Azov

Caucasus Mountains

Sea of Marmara

(reproduced with permission from *Beggars in Red*, John Strawson) more than a stream when Cardigan's brigade, as advance guard, crossed and ascended the ridge on the south side. About a mile and a half beyond they caught sight of about 1,500 Russian horse, many of which were Cossacks. Cardigan threw out 'skirmishers' from the Thirteenth but Raglan recalled them, having seen from his position an even larger force of infantry beyond. The Russian horse artillery opened up during the Thirteenth's retirement and were in turn silenced by a troop of Cardigan's gunners, though not before Paymaster-Sergeant Priestley of the Thirteenth was hit. He thereby gained the distinction of being the first British casualty in the Crimea, although as a paymaster sergeant he had absolutely no business being in the firing line! The retirement exasperated the Thirteenth and caused much anger, especially since it was accompanied by much jeering from the Russians. Few people had seen what Raglan had, nor knew it was he who had ordered the withdrawal. The cavalry blamed Lord Lucan who rapidly but unfairly gained the nickname 'Look-on'. The infantry viewed it with their customary contempt, Private Williams of the 41st Foot writing in one of his letters: "Serve them bloody right, silly peacock bastards!"

The armies resumed their march the following day. At the second river, the Alma, they found the Russians were defending in strength on commanding ground. Major-General John Strawson, in his study of the British Army during the century following the French Revolution, *Beggars in Red*, says of the action here:

> "The battle of Alma . . . was characteristic of most Crimean encounters so far as the Allies were concerned – no proper reconnaissance, no clear plan, poor coordination, those who were supposed to be directing the troops in the wrong place, exercising very little control, and the outcome determined by the sheer courage and endurance of the British infantry."

Nothing more need be said of the battle because the Thirteenth, along with the rest of the cavalry, were mere onlookers. An immediate follow-up by the whole of the cavalry division might have turned the Russian withdrawal into a rout and led to the fall of Sevastopol. Lucan wanted to follow up; Raglan probably did but allowed himself to be dissuaded by the French. Thus a major opportunity to end the war rapidly was lost and the armies were consigned to further slogging matches.

The Russians retired in reasonable order into the defences of Sevastopol and the allies crossed the two remaining rivers unopposed. They laid siege to the great naval base in late September, taking the small port of Balaklava, a few miles to the south-east, as their logistic base (if the haphazard system of supply could be dignified by such a term). On 25 October, 1854, the Russians made a sortie in strength from Sevastopol with the object of capturing Balaklava, and it was this offensive which gave rise to the three celebrated engagements including the charges of both the Heavies and the Light Brigade.

First, however, was the remarkable stand by the 93rd Highlanders. The road to Balaklava was commanded by several redoubts in which Turkish gunners and infantry had been posted. The main part of the allied army was involved in the siege operation outside Sevastopol itself, leaving the cavalry division and a few infantry to support the redoubts. Greater support was available from the infantry divisions resting from their turn in the siege trenches, but they were not at any short notice to move that day.

Soon after first light a large force of Russian cavalry advanced on the redoubts. The defenders, massively outnumbered, initially fought stubbornly, but soon they abandoned the earthworks and guns and fled in panic towards Balaklava. The 93rd took up a blocking position in extended line only two ranks deep – the famous "thin red line tipped with steel" – astride the road running from the Woronzoff Road and Causeway Heights, near the village of Kadikoi. Lucan's cavalry division, which had turned out before dawn as usual in case of just such a development, took post well to the left of the 93rd in order to be able to attack the Russian cavalry in the flank.

At this point Lucan received the first of the famous four orders from Lord Raglan which, in succession, led to one of the most celebrated military disasters. It read:

"Cavalry to take ground to left of second line of Redoubts occupied by the Turks."

Although Lucan complied, he did so with anger and dismay – anger because it appeared the cavalry were being tied to a static role, and dismay because, to his mind, from his position on the field, such a movement would leave the 93rd wholly unsupported. Neither officer's view of the battlefield was the same as the other's, nor was there any mutual comprehension of the difference. Thus, from the outset, Lucan could not understand the tactical purpose behind Raglan's instruction.

There then occurred an extraordinary event which should have alerted Raglan to the problem of perspectives. From his position on the Sapouné Heights he saw a large body of Russian cavalry pass within a few hundred yards of where he had positioned the Cavalry Division, yet Lucan did not attack them in their flank as Raglan had expected he would – as indeed was the purpose in positioning them there. The reason was simple: Lucan could not see them because of intervening high ground. Thus the Russian cavalry bore down unmolested on the 'Thin Red Line', but their successive charges against the Highlanders were repulsed by impressive steadiness. Seemingly bemused, the enemy withdrew and stationed themselves at the eastern end of the North Valley where their gunners unlimbered the guns.

On the other side of the Causeway Heights, however, a much larger force of Russian cavalry was still advancing. Trotting eastwards on a collision course with them was the Heavy Brigade (though neither side knew it owing to the intervening heights) because Raglan had sent the *second* order earlier to Lucan for eight heavy squadrons to move to the support of the Turks in the redoubts. The Heavies, commanded by Major-General Sir James Scarlett, suddenly found themselves overlooked by a large force of heavy cavalry and lancers. Scarlett was fifty-five and this was his first battle. He had been commissioned into the 18th Hussars in 1818, transferring to the 5th Dragoon Guards when the Eighteenth disbanded. His great virtue, so far as this command was concerned, was sufficient humility to take advice, which he did on this occasion from his two ADCs, both experienced 'India men'. He determined on an immediate charge in the usual India fashion and, after carefully dressing his brigade, took off well to the fore of his squadrons. Though massively outnumbered and for a time almost overwhelmed, the Heavies broke the Russians who then galloped in disarray back whence they had come over the Causeway Heights.

Why the Light Brigade, sitting observing only five hundred yards away, did not support the attack or harry the fleeing Russians is as much a mystery as many another inexplicable nonsense in the Crimea. Cardigan maintained that his orders from Lucan constrained him from doing anything. Lucan maintained that they did precisely the opposite. Raglan watched the scene from his elevated vantage point on the Sapouné Heights with growing frustration and dismay at what he perceived to be both Lucan's and Cardigan's "wretched" mishandling of the cavalry.

Raglan was sixty-seven years old and not a 'field soldier'. At Waterloo he had lost his right arm, which gave rise to the fashionable Raglan-sleeve overcoat whose sleeves ran up to the collar rather than to the shoulder, but both there and in the Peninsula his service had been on Wellington's staff. Since 1815 he had been almost exclusively employed as a staff officer at Horse Guards, the Army Commander-in-Chief's headquarters, and shortly before the Crimean War he had been made Master-General of the Ordnance. He was polite to a fault and far from decisive. His orders were rarely expressed as such and invariably couched in imprecise terms. Lucan, no fool but dangerously irascible, invariably became exasperated with Raglan's unmilitary manner. Mistrustful too of Cardigan's competence, not without justification but aggravated also by family feuding (he and Cardigan were brothers-in-law), Lucan interfered too much with his subordinates, leaving them frequently unsure of the extent of their own discretion to act. The 'personal chemistry' could not have been worse, therefore, with the divisional commander at odds with both his commander-in-chief and the Light Brigade commander.

Before the first shots had been fired that morning, Raglan had sent messages to the Duke of Cambridge and Sir George Cathcart to bring up their infantry divisions. Their response had been astonishingly slow and, even by this stage in the battle, the Russian cavalry having retired beyond the Causeway Heights, the infantry were still not able to re-take the redoubts. In desperation the commander-in-chief decided to use his cavalry instead. As with his earlier orders, their purpose was obscured by the relative positions of the originator and recipient – Raglan on commanding ground with a panoramic view of the whole battlefield, Lucan 700 feet below with a very restricted one. If this were not bad enough, it took up to thirty minutes for an order to be carried by galloper from the commander-in-chief's position to his commanders below. Raglan's third order to the cavalry read

> "Cavalry to advance and take advantage of any opportunity to recover the Heights. They will be supported by the infantry which have been ordered. Advance on two fronts."

This message mystified Lucan. There was no sign of the infantry. He concluded he must wait for their support. It was not an unreasonable assumption.

What Raglan *meant* should happen was for the cavalry to attack there and then, panicking the Russians into abandoning the redoubts which would then be occupied by the infantry making their way slowly to the heights out of Lucan's sight. Had Raglan used the phrase "at once" after "advance" in the first sentence, and inserted the word "later" after "supported" in the second, Lucan would have been left in no doubt as to the requirement and could even have deduced the tactical purpose.

Lucan adjusted his dispositions slightly, placing the Light Brigade at the western end of the North Valley and the Heavy Brigade to their rear astride the Woronzoff Road. While Lucan waited thus for the infantry, Raglan watched these manoeuvres with growing agitation believing that with every minute that passed the opportunity to evict the enemy from the redoubts was receding. His exasperation finally got the better of him when he saw Russian gun teams with lasso equipment approaching the redoubts to carry away the abandoned Turkish guns. He turned to General Airey, acting as his chief of staff, and dictated his fourth and final order:

> "Lord Raglan wishes the cavalry to advance rapidly to the front – follow the enemy and try to prevent the enemy carrying away the guns. Troop Horse Artillery may accompany. French cavalry is on your left. Immediate."

If only Raglan had been more precise: "to the front" is relative, to say the least. If only he had not *assumed* that Lucan would automatically relate the order to the previous one. In fact, because it did not immediately appear to relate to the previous order, Lucan read it as a separate, unrelated one. If only Raglan had said entirely and precisely what he wanted: "Cavalry to advance immediately to the Causeway Heights to prevent enemy carrying away guns from redoubts. Infantry is moving towards Heights to support."

There was, however, one last chance that disaster could be averted. A galloper, what would nowadays be called an 'LO' (liaison officer), would deliver the order. He would be in the commander's mind and would be able to interpret the order to a subordinate in case of difficulty. This would be the 'failsafe' mechanism to avert confusion. Captain Louis Edward Nolan of the 15th Hussars thrust himself forward to take the piece of paper. He had left India in advance of his regiment and got himself attached to the staff for the war. Indeed he had already done invaluable work for the army by acquiring remounts in large numbers from all corners of Asia Minor. *No one* was better qualified to deliver this order than *he, Nolan.*

Captain Nolan thought not a lot of Raglan, but he was utterly contemptuous of Lucan and Cardigan, both of whose handling of the cavalry throughout the campaign he had continually and loudly criticized. Nor was this criticism merely an impudent young officer's contempt for authority: he had studied his profession deeply and written extensively on the subject. "He writes books," said Lord George Paget, commanding officer of the 4th Light Dragoons, with evident distaste. On this day Nolan had watched Lucan's faltering performance, to some extent real but largely apparent, with as much if not more anguish than Raglan. He believed passionately in the potential of light cavalry if handled boldly. As he turned away from Raglan and spurred his horse into a gallop, the commander-in-chief further fuelled his ADC's impatience by calling out to him, "Tell Lord Lucan the cavalry is to attack at once."

Nolan was also a superb horseman. Where other gallopers had picked their way down to the valley bottom, Nolan plunged headlong down the steepest, most direct route. The sight astonished A.W. Kinglake, the lawyer and later definitive historian of the war who had accompanied the army to the Crimea in a sight-seeing capacity: "the extremity of the possible" was how he described Nolan's 700 foot plunge, "straight, swift and intent – descending as it were on sure prey – he swooped angering down into the plain where Lord Lucan and his squadrons were posted."

Nolan galloped straight up to Lucan and handed him the written order. But it made no sense to him: the only guns he could see were those to *his* front, at the far end of the North Valley. Surely Raglan could not mean that the cavalry were to attack *these* guns, against every tactical principle? As Lucan re-read the order with growing puzzlement and consternation, Nolan let his impatience get the better of him and repeated with ill-concealed contempt Raglan's postscript that the cavalry should attack at once. Lucan's response was explosive: "Attack, sir? Attack what? What guns, sir? Where and what to do?" Nolan, now quite beside himself with contempt for this apparently wilfully stupid general, flung out an arm in frustrated anger and virtually shouted the words, "*There*, my lord, is your enemy, *there* are your guns." His arm appeared to Lucan to indicate the guns at the far end of the valley; they were indeed the only guns Lucan could see, or had seen that whole day.

When whole books have been written on the cause of the disastrous Charge of The Light Brigade, the most celebrated being Cecil Woodham-Smith's *The Reason Why*, it would be unreasonable to apportion blame in an analysis of a mere few pages. There is, however, an enormous irony which none of these histories highlights, and that is that Nolan, the very man who had written, and probably spoken, the most on the cavalryman's art should now make so grave an error. In the preface to his book *Cavalry; its History and Tactics*, he writes: "With the cavalry officer almost everything depends on the clearness of his *coup-d'oeil*, and the felicity with which he seizes the happy moment of action." Nolan had seen the battlefield from the commander-in-chief's viewpoint and was at this happy moment, uniquely, in a position to appreciate the disparity in perspective between the two commanders. His own *coup-d'oeil*, the 'comprehensive glance', should have told him instantly what and where the problem lay. It was the ultimate irony that this cavalry visionary's eye should fail him at the culminating point of his career.

Stunned by the implication of the commander-in-chief's wishes, seemingly as indicated by Nolan, Lucan passed the instructions to attack to Cardigan. Cardigan in turn pointed out to Lucan the danger and futility of such a course of action. Lucan acknowledged this objection but in turn insisted that it was Raglan's will. Even at this stage it would not have been impossible to devise a tactical plan, using the cavalry division, the troop of horse artillery and the small body of French cavalry on the left flank, to achieve Raglan's apparent purpose without monumental loss. Lucan's notion, however, and Cardigan's too, was for an unsupported frontal attack by the Light Brigade. So after some fussing over the dressing of the five regiments of the brigade, which numbered only 661 (the exact number varies, depending on sources, between 636 and 673) Cardigan gave the momentous order: "The brigade will advance. First squadron of the 17th Lancers [will] direct." Dressing and direction was therefore to be, as was usual, by the left, the 17th Lancers (now the Queen's Royal Lancers) being on the left of the first line, with the Thirteenth on the right. As a close-supporting second line were the 11th Hussars (now the King's Royal Hussars), with a third supporting line comprising the 4th Light Dragoons and the 8th Hussars (subsequently the Queen's Royal Irish Hussars).

The charge has been graphically recounted by many who took part. The brigade's progress along the valley bottom for the mile and a half to its objective, with artillery batteries and riflemen enfilading the regiments from either flank, and the batteries at the north end of the valley opening up with shrapnel and canister in the last half mile, has also been lyrically described by Alfred Lord Tennyson in his poem *The Charge of the Light Brigade*. Even without referring to these accounts it is not difficult to imagine the carnage.

Nolan, whom it is thought realized once the advance began that Cardigan was going for the wrong guns, rode out from the position he had taken with the 17th Lancers and frantically started to wave his sword at Cardigan. With the cruellest luck, virtually the first shell to explode killed him, thereby totally sealing the brigade's fate. General Bosquet, one of the French divisional commanders, with a clear view of the advance and with tears rolling down his cheeks, murmured the memorable protest against such futile courage: *"C'est magnifique, mais ce n'est pas la guerre"* – *It is magnificent, but it is not war.*

The Thirteenth had only been able to muster 128 officers and men that morning, slightly fewer than the 11th Hussars and 17th Lancers, slightly more than the 4th Light Dragoons and 8th Hussars. They were under the command of Captain J.A. Oldham because the commanding officer, Lieutenant-Colonel Charles Doherty, was sick. As they galloped through the hail of shot, shell and bullets, with gaps being torn in the ranks and the pace quickening with almost every stride, Mitchell remembers desperately praying, "Oh, Lord protect me, and watch over my poor mother", recalling that "oaths and imprecations might be heard between the report of the guns and the bursting of the shells, as the men crowded and jostled each other in their endeavours to close to the centre." No doubt they might be heard!

No one can swear quite like the proverbial trooper, and as

"Cannon to the right of them,
Cannon to the left of them,
Cannon in front of them
Volleyed and thundered"

these troopers could be excused the most violent of "oaths and imprecations".

In the final hundred yards or so of the charge the momentum was terrific. Lieutenant Anstruther Thomson recalled later that it was "a fine sight to see the fellows sit down and put their heads straight at the guns". An ADC recalls hearing one of the Thirteenth's troopers calling, "Come on; don't let those b . . . s [17th Lancers] get ahead of us!" All eight guns erupted simultaneously at this point and brought down many who up until then had done extremely well to remain mounted, let alone not be badly wounded. Cardigan galloped through the line of guns and was followed by the remnants of the first line, no more than fifty strong. A fight developed around the battery itself, some of the gunners diving for cover under the guns but many bravely trying to manhandle them away. Captain Oldham, whose horse had been brought down in the final few yards, was last seen crouching by one of the gun wheels, sword in hand, fending off several Russians.

Several groups of Cossacks made counter-attacks at the guns but with no great determination. The Light Brigade had clearly been spent, though, and there was little to be done other than to try to evade capture and to retire. There was only one way – the same way they had come, subject again to flanking artillery fire and now pursuit by the Russian cavalry. During this desperate race back Lance-Sergeant Joseph Malone won the newly-instituted Victoria Cross for rescuing a wounded officer of the 17th Lancers under fire, the first VC to be won by The Light Dragoons' forebears.

As the remnants of the brigade struggled back up the valley the French cavalry came to their support: two squadrons of the *4ème Chasseurs D'Afrique* charged the batteries on the Fedioukine Hills on the north side of the valley, silencing them before they could inflict more damage on the survivors. It was an action which led to the closest, and continuing, association of the two regiments, and every year an exchange of telegrams on 25 October marks the service the 4th Chausseurs rendered that day.

When the brigade re-formed it numbered only 195 mounted men, according to Cardigan's brigade major. Of the Thirteenth's casualties the best calculation is three officers and twenty-four other ranks killed, and fourteen men wounded sufficiently badly to be recorded – many wounds were considered insufficiently serious to record, especially if a few days' light duties were all that followed. Some had been taken prisoner; many were scattered about the valley having been unhorsed. At the rally the regiment could muster *mounted* only two officers and eight men. It was many months before the Thirteenth, and the other regiments of the brigade, were able to turn out in any effective strength.

* * *

The three actions that day at Balaklava undoubtedly shook the Russian cavalry's nerve: the offensive fizzled out and Balaklava port was saved. The Russians made one more attempt at a sortie in strength from Sevastopol before the hard winter set in. On 5 November, 1854, under cover of a thick fog, 42,000 Russians took the allies by surprise in their forward siege positions. The battle was a desperate affair, centred on Inkerman ridge: there was little tactical skill in the allied defence – it was more a business of pushing reinforcements into the fight as they arrived, and the day was carried by the bayonet and fighting spirit of the British infantry. Inkerman is indeed known as a 'soldier's battle'. The Thirteenth were mounted throughout the day but unable to take any active part, though they were awarded the battle honour.

When the Russians finally withdrew it signalled almost another year of siege operations. Sevastopol finally fell on 8 September, 1855, but the intervening winter brought terrible suffering to both troops and horses. The Thirteenth continued with both out-post and lines-of-communication duties throughout, on many occasions acting as no more than a baggage train for the siege trenches until proper transport was arranged. A young mid-shipman, Evelyn Wood, transferred into the regiment from the Royal Navy at this time. He had already distinguished himself in action ashore with the Naval Brigade and was to win the VC in India three years later, continuing to distinguish himself in colonial wars, of which more in the next chapter, and reaching field-marshal's rank.

The fall of Sevastopol effectively brought the war to an end but it was another six months before a formal peace was con-cluded. The winter which followed was this time made the more bearable by the massive help sent by the British public, including everything from warm clothing to food and even voluntary welfare workers, perhaps the most illustrious of whom was the Reform Club's head chef, the Frenchman Alexis Soyer, who patented a simple cooking stove and took it to the Crimea in person.

* * *

When Sergeant Mitchell climbed into his first bed in two years, in Cork Barracks, Dublin, he could have been forgiven for thinking that the powers-that-be were peculiarly insensitive to the conditions of service of the non-commissioned man in mid-Victorian England. Two days earlier, on 26 May, 1856, the Thirteenth had steamed into Plymouth harbour on board the *Assistance* and disembarked for Her Majesty's inspection (Queen Victoria had expressed her wish personally to greet any Crimea arrivals), keenly looking forward to marching thence to Exeter. After the Queen's inspection, and to everyone's dismay, they were ordered to re-embark for Ireland!

Although this was a time of sentimentality there was precious little time for sentiment: the demands of the Great British Empire were now making themselves felt, and Great Britain stood ready to meet the cost:

> "We don't want to fight
> But by jingo if we do,
> We've got the men, we've got the guns,
> We've got the money too."

The Army was about to be kept very busy indeed and more regiments would soon be needed, especially cavalry.

CHAPTER 8

Unavoidable Involvement in Colonial Wars

"For the first time since Waterloo British world power was
threatened by the rivalry of other great states. British commercial
supremacy was being eroded especially by united Germany.
In these new circumstances the British empire ceased to appear a costly encumbrance and began once more to seem a
source of power and opportunity. . . . Unavoidable involvement
in colonial wars gradually altered into more or less open imperial
expansion . . . the late Victorian army found a place in national
pride and affection never accorded to its predecessors. . . . The
nation cheered victories like Tel-el-Kebir."

CORRELLI BARNETT
Britain and Her Army

*19H and 18H re-raised; Home Service, Ireland and India; 15H
in Afghanistan 1878–80 and S. Africa; 19H in Egypt 1882–4;
1884–5: Tel-el-Kebir; Abu Klea; Nile.*

The Fifteenth returned to Britain from Bangalore in the middle
of 1854. Had they remained in India any longer they would have
been caught up in the great mutiny which broke out in the East
India Company's Bengal army in 1857. It was put down only
by the most strenuous efforts of the British and loyal native
regiments, and greatly shook the confidence of the Government
at home.

When the mutiny was over, the Company decided to raise
five regiments of British light dragoons to replace the Bengal

113

native cavalry which had proved unreliable. Accordingly, in 1857, recruiting began in Britain. There was, however, a dearth of recruits at this time, one of the reasons being famine in Ireland. This traditional source of recruits was drying up due to both death and emigration to America. Height restrictions were therefore lowered for the Company's recruits, 5ft becoming the minimum. Training was meant to be carried out in England, but the flood of 'bantam' recruits so took the Company by surprise that the idea was abandoned and the recruits were shipped straight to Calcutta.

It was not an auspicious start. Untrained, undersized men, without permanent officers were not going to become a disciplined fighting force quickly. When their horses arrived, for the most part wild unbroken bush horses from the Cape and Australia, and with them a few NCOs from other regiments who had been promoted too rapidly to be able to maintain respect and discipline, disaster appeared close at hand. One officer, writing forty years later, says, "No regiments were ever raised under such absurd conditions, and, if the object had been to prove them a failure, no course better calculated to achieve that end could have been pursued."

On 1 November, 1858, the Crown assumed the direct government of India, and the East India Company from that date effectively ceased to exist. So began the period, lasting to Independence in 1947, of the British *Raj*, the Hindi for 'reign' or 'rule'. The British Government's worries about entrusting India to a company of merchants had finally proved well-founded, and she was not going to risk another mutiny. Lord (Charles) Canning, the governor general during the mutiny, was the first Viceroy (exercising power on behalf of the sovereign), and he recognized the difficulties when he wrote: "I cannot forget that, in our Indian Empire, that greatest of all blessings depends on a greater variety of chances and a more precarious tenure than in any other quarter of the globe." Yet a mutiny of sorts is exactly what did occur again in 1859, but this time it was amongst the European troops formerly in the East India Company's employ – the so-called 'White Mutiny'.

26. *"Major Philip Chetwode, 19th Hussars, was President of the court . . . 'The farm had not been burnt. If it had been burnt it had not been burnt by the 18th Hussars!' "(p.148)*
Chetwode, later field marshal and Commander-in-Chief India, baled out
Major Percival Marling VC, 18th Hussars, from a potentially tricky situation.
Farm-burning and 'concentration camps' became unpleasant instruments of
Kitchener's determined policy to force the Boer guerrillas to give in.

27. *"Ceremonial played an important role"* (*p.163*), and it was still largely at individual expense to officers. A group of the Eighteenth's officers in 1906 at the Curragh, Marling commanding.

28. *"It was not all training."* (*p.161*) A remarkably relaxed group of (largely) 19th Hussars at Norwich, c. 1908. The contrast with the officer group is illuminating.

29. *"Advanced at the charge to within a few paces of where Her Majesty stood and with swords in the air gave her three resounding cheers."*(p.168) Queen Mary, Colonel-in-Chief of the 18th Hussars, visited them a few days prior to their sailing for France in August, 1914. Few could have guessed the nature of the coming conflict.

31. *"Generally in reserve."* The 13th Hussars near Ypres in March, 1915. The Cavalry were carefully husbanded throughout the war, but when committed, dismounted, they fought in some critical actions with great skill and courage. It was not until 1918 on the Western Front that mobile operations could be developed.

32. *"Late of the 19th Hussars, and lately CIGS."* Field-Marshal Sir John French, who had distinguished himself in South Africa, carried the burden of command of the British Expeditionary Force throughout the early months of mobile warfare, and the crippling Battle of Ypres.

All Company troops were arbitrarily transferred to the Crown's service in April, 1859. Many refused to comply on the grounds that they were not conscripts and had freely enlisted under strict terms of service which were being changed without their having the option of discharge. The 1st Bengal European Light Cavalry were one of the many regiments which refused to perform anything other than routine duties. Eventually, Canning backed down and granted the option of discharge. Ten thousand men elected to take their leave, of whom over a quarter re-enlisted on reaching England.

In 1861 it was finally decided to do away with European forces for service in India only. On 6 May the 1st European Light Cavalry was re-designated the 19th Light Dragoons, changing designation again on 17 August to the 19th Hussars. The same standards were then applied across the board and officers were permanently gazetted, many of exceptional quality.

It is possible that some of those discharged from the 1st Europeans found their way into the ranks of the 18th Hussars, for the Eighteenth were being re-raised at this time. By coincidence, too, it was the 15th Hussars who were charged with re-establishing the regiment. On 23 February, 1858, the Fifteenth's second-in-command, Major Richard Knox, was given lieutenant-colonel's rank and a warrant to raise the regiment at Leeds. So many men from the Fifteenth were transferred to the Eighteenth that the re-raised regiment was for some years referred to as 'the Young Fifteenth'. They wore green plumes and busby bags because, it is said, the Duke of Cambridge, who was the Commander-in-Chief, thought the colour appropriate to the regiment which had at one time been known as 'the 18th Royal Irish'. It was not until 1879 that the original red and white of the plume, and blue and white of the busby bag, were restored.

In 1864 the Eighteenth sailed for India where they spent the next eleven years, mainly in Bangalore, but seeing no active service. During this time, however, they lost ten officers and 158 other ranks to disease, mainly cholera. Cholera was still the Army's greatest enemy: its cause, contaminated water, was not finally established until 1886.

The Nineteenth 'returned' to England in 1870 to face disbandment for a second time. They had left India earlier than planned in order for the Indian Government to make economies, and the British Treasury was reluctant to take them on to the home establishment. It appears that the Franco-Prussian War, which broke out in July, settled the issue: the regiment was brought up to full strength and stationed on the south coast, moving to Ireland in 1876.

The Thirteenth, it will be remembered, had gone straight to Ireland from the Crimea. They returned to the mainland in 1859 and became hussars in 1862, there being by this time no effective difference between light dragoons and hussars save style. They went to Canada in 1866 when a Fenian invasion from the United States threatened: it did not materialize, however, so after three quite comfortable years in Toronto the regiment returned to England and relieved the Fifteenth at York. In 1873 they embarked for India, handing over their horses to the 21st Hussars. All, that is, except a twenty-five-year-old dark bay Irish mare called 'Butcher'. She had survived the Charge of the Light Brigade, though wounded by a musket ball in her upper leg, and had become a regimental favourite, being at this time the last equine survivor of the battle. She was presented to Queen Victoria who promised the regiment that "their old Crimean favourite would be kept in comfort for the rest of her days".

The Fifteenth had embarked for Dublin in 1859 and there they spent five years in support of the civil power until 1864 when they returned to England via twelve months in Glasgow. Five years later they were re-embarking for India, arriving at Mhow in Rajputana in early January, 1870. The whole journey had taken only six weeks, the railway from Alexandria to Suez allowing transhipping via the Mediterranean and Red Sea rather than the long Cape route. The Suez Canal, opening in 1869, was soon to make even the rail transfer unnecessary, and in 1870 a telegraph link direct from London to India was established, making the sub-continent less remote still.

At the beginning of the 1870s therefore, the Thirteenth,

Fifteenth and Eighteenth were serving under the same command, India, while the Nineteenth were thousands of miles away, in England, reversing the situation during the Napoleonic wars. The Army as a whole at this time was being shaken up by the Secretary for War in Gladstone's Liberal administration, Edward Cardwell, (another barrister and Liberal politician, Richard Haldane, was to shake things even more some thirty-five years later – of which more in Chapter Ten). Cardwell's reforms included the abolition of the purchase system, a further increase in the total strength of the Cavalry, and a re-equipment programme. The successes in colonial wars which were to follow in the next twenty years owe much to his foresight and energy.

General John Strawson, in his *Beggars in Red*, says that 1874 was a good year for Imperialism, with Disraeli re-elected prime minister, General Sir Garnet Wolseley's triumphs in the Gold Coast, and the birth of Winston Churchill! He might have added that Robert Baden-Powell joined the Army that year and, two years later, joined the 13th Hussars in India as a second lieutenant. General Strawson goes on to say: "The later 1870s and early 1880s were a good time for soldiers too, at least those soldiers who sought action and excitement. Ashantis, Zulus, Afghans, Burmese, Fuzzy-Wuzzies – there were plenty of natives awaiting the benefit of being subjected to disciplined fire from a square of British redcoats. . . And there was always the North-West Frontier of India." All four regiments, to a greater or lesser extent, were to become involved in campaigns against many of these tribesmen. And there was always the North-West Frontier – centre-stage for the 'Great Game'.

* * *

Captain Arthur Conolly of the Bengal cavalry is popularly supposed to have coined the term 'the Great Game' and he was killed playing it. It nicely captures the nature of what went on. As General Strawson notes, it had the character of a board game:

"The move and counter-move by the Russians and the British in the not quite no-man's-land between the Czar's domin- ions and British India, the chessboard formed by central Asia, Persia, the Punjab and Afghanistan."

It was undoubtedly 'Great' because the stakes were the highest, no less than the jewel in Queen Victoria's crown itself – India. It was a game which could prove costly after a wrong tactical move, as the disastrous losses in the First Afghan War of 1839-42 showed. But it was also a game which offered virtually continual sport for many, either in a team or as individuals: in *My Early Life*, Winston Churchill urges the young man who wants to enjoy himself, and wants to spend a few years agreeably in a military companionship, to join the British cavalry, but that if a young man wants "to make himself a professional soldier, an expert in war, a specialist in practical tactics, who desires a hard life and adventure and a true comradeship in arms, I would recommend the choice of some regiment on the frontier, like those fine ones I have seen, the Guides and the 10th Bengal Lancers." Fortunately, today, it is possible to do both. In fair- ness, too, it was possible to do so at that time in India, as will be seen. And if regimental life proved tedious to the officer in India, he could enter the Great Game as an individual, either as a political officer or a plain spy. To catch the atmosphere of life as a spy on the North-West Frontier there is nothing better than Kipling's novel *Kim* or John Masters' *The Lotus and the Wind*.

Both the Thirteenth and Fifteenth were to take part in one of the major rounds of the Game in 1878. The new Viceroy, Lord Lytton, had been attempting to persuade Sher Ali, the Amir of Afghanistan, to accept a British mission in Kabul and British agents at his frontier posts. In return, Britain would provide subsidies and military assistance if needed. Sher Ali refused: he was getting, to his mind, a better deal from the Russians, who established a mission in the capital in mid-1878. Lytton decided to force the issue by sending his own mission but it was turned back at the frontier. After an ultimatum, which was ignored, Lytton ordered an invasion.

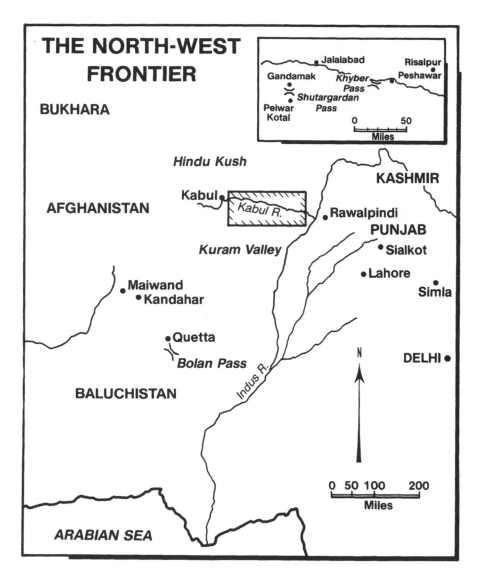

THE NORTH-WEST FRONTIER

BUKHARA

Hindu Kush

KASHMIR

Kabul•

Kabul R.

AFGHANISTAN

•Rawalpindi

PUNJAB

Kuram Valley

•Sialkot

•Maiwand
•Kandahar

•Lahore

Simla•

•Quetta

Bolan Pass

N

DELHI•

BALUCHISTAN

Indus R.

0 50 100   200
Miles

ARABIAN SEA

Jalalabad•   Risalpur•
Gandamak•   *Khyber*   Peshawar•
                Pass
            Shutargardan
        • *Pass*
Peiwar   *Pass*
Kotal
                0   50
                Miles

Three columns were formed for this. The first, more than 16,000-strong, was commanded by the legendary General Sir Sam Browne VC, who had raised the 2nd Punjab Cavalry (Sam Browne's Horse). He had designed the 'Sam Browne' belt after losing an arm. The column quickly overcame the frontier defences in the Khyber Pass and in mid-December occupied the town of Jalalabad, midway to Kabul. From here the column carried out operations against the Khugani tribesmen, who controlled the approaches along the valley of the Kabul River.

The second column, just over 5,000-strong, was commanded by another 'Mutiny VC' who would become even more of a legend than Sam Browne. Major-General Frederick Roberts, later Field-Marshal Lord Roberts of Kandahar, 'Bobs' to the soldiers and Kipling, was a diminutive figure possessing great energy and infinite good sense. This column, with great tactical flair, quickly captured the stronghold of Peiwar Kotal which totally dominated the Kuram Valley.

The third column, 7,500-strong, commanded by Lieutenant-General Sir Donald Stewart, included the 15th Hussars. It made equally good progress. They had plenty of skirmishing, but nothing on any large scale, and the column occupied Kandahar in early January, 1879. Sher Ali died while trying to escape to Turkestan and was succeeded by his son, Yakub Khan, who promptly signed the Treaty of Gandamak which agreed to the presence of a British resident in Kabul.

The columns then marched back to India. The Fifteenth calculated the distance they covered in this campaign to be 1,260 miles, much of it over roadless, mountainous country, intensely cold and often short of water and forage. It is interesting to note how their horses fared: of the three types with the regiment, Indian country-breds, Australian 'Walers', and Arabs, the Arabs proved much the hardiest, only 2 per cent of them having to be destroyed compared with 15 and 25 per cent respectively of the other types.

It was not long before Yakub Khan reneged on the treaty. In October the British resident and his escort were brutally murdered. The outrage was followed by re-invasion. Two armies were rapidly assembled, full use being made of the 9,000 miles of railway laid by British engineers in the previous twenty years. The 'North Afghanistan Field Force' was to be commanded by General Roberts and the 'South Afghanistan Field Force' by General Stewart, though neither of them included the Thirteenth or Fifteenth on this occasion.

Roberts's force reached Kabul on 13 October and Stewart's occupied Kandahar in November. Yakub Khan abdicated and a nephew, Abdur Rahman, replaced him. It was an already uneasy peace when in July, 1880, another claimant to the throne, Ayub Khan, another of Sher Ali's sons, marched on Kandahar with 11,000 men. Stewart, who had recently taken command in Kabul, had been replaced by Lieutenant-General James Primrose. Primrose lacked Stewart's vision and sent only a brigade to intercept this force. Though the brigade was probably strong enough its commander was inexperienced. The result was the Battle of Maiwand, one of *the* disasters of the late-Victorian age, where the brigade of 2,500 men was all but completely destroyed.

Kandahar was then besieged by Ayub Khan's army. When news reached Kabul, over 300 hundred miles' march away, a force of 10,000 was hastily assembled under Roberts for the relief of the fortress city. In the south, at Quetta near the frontier in what is now Pakistan, another relief force was being hastily assembled. Kandahar was half the distance from Quetta that it was from Kabul, and something of a race developed between the two relief forces, a 'Race for the Peerage' as one contemporary put it. The Fifteenth left Meerut to join the Quetta force in early August, and after five days in stifling heat by train, and a further five in temperatures of between 120°-130° marching the 100 miles from the railhead, they arrived at Quetta on 20 August, 1880. Several men and horses had died *en route* in the heat, and many more had had to be returned to Meerut.

The Fifteenth left Quetta with Major-General Phayre's relief force on 24 August and covered considerable distances over inhospitable country, always short of water, in very quick time. The regiment, together with elements of four regiments of Indian Cavalry, got to within twenty-five miles of Kandahar when it learned, on 3 September, that Roberts had won the 'Race for the Peerage' two days earlier, hence '1st Baron (later Earl) Roberts of Kandahar'. The Thirteenth arrived in the city as reinforcements in early December, having covered the 1,000 miles, as the crow flies, from their station at Lucknow in five days.

The new Viceroy, the Marquess of Ripon, had already decided, however, on a policy of disengagement. Abdul Rahman was confirmed as Amir of Afghanistan and, in exchange for a subsidy and promise of support against both Russian aggression and internal revolt, he agreed to British control of his foreign policy. The armies returned to India, the Thirteenth acting as rearguard on the arduous but uneventful march from Kandahar to the railhead south-east of Quetta. The Fifteenth, along with every regiment which had taken part in any of the operations of this Second Afghan War, were awarded the campaign honour *Afghanistan 1878-80*, but the Thirteenth, having arrived in the country after formal resistance had ceased, were not.

* * *

In December, 1880, soon after arriving back in Meerut, and in the middle of preparations to return to England, the Fifteenth received orders to proceed rapidly to South Africa. British involvement there had formally begun in 1814 when Cape Town and the hinterland was purchased for £6 million from the Dutch East India Company. Colonization had then taken place rapidly, Britons also settling in Natal and founding the port of Durban. In 1836 some 10,000 Dutch, wanting to escape British rule, set out north on the 'Great Trek' and founded the republics of Transvaal and the Orange Free State, also settling in northern Natal. Relations between the Boers, as the Dutch settlers became known (the word in Dutch simply means 'farmer'), and the British colonists were frequently strained, particularly after the discovery of diamonds at Kimberley in Cape Colony in 1867 which attracted prospectors with even fewer scruples than usual. In 1877 the Transvaal Republic surrendered its sovereignty in exchange for British help against the native Africans. The Transvaalers were not happy with this arrangement for very long, however, and in December, 1880, taking advantage of British losses in the recent Zulu War and continuing trouble with the Basutos, took up arms. The Fifteenth handed over their horses in Meerut, embarked at Bombay on 9 January, 1881, and arrived at Durban on the 25th.

The commander in Natal or, more correctly, High Commissioner, was Major-General Sir George Colley. He had distinguished himself in many a colonial skirmish but he was taken totally by surprise by the superb mounted infantry tactics of the Boers. Boer marksmanship was legendary, though sometimes exaggerated, and they were masters of fieldcraft. The British Army still fought in close order and wore red. Before the Fifteenth could be provided with remounts he had advanced to the Transvaal frontier with 1,500 men, but he suffered a sharp reverse at Laing's Nek where the Durban to Pretoria road crosses the border.

Colley withdrew to lick his wounds and to contemplate his next move. His second-in-command was Colonel Evelyn Wood VC, who had transferred from the Royal Navy to the 13th Light Dragoons in the Crimea. Colley's second campaign plan was, initially, to form two columns with which to invade the Transvaal, one to be commanded by himself, the other by Wood. While these columns were assembling, the Fifteenth did some valuable reconnaissance work with Wood on the frontier. The information gained could have been put to good use by Colley, but it seems that he had become obsessed with retaking Laing's Nek. He conceived the idea that taking Majuba Hill, a 6,000-foot feature on the flank of the Boer lines, would draw the enemy into the open and thence defeat. It was a thoroughly ill-judged concept, however, for possession of the hill would not have made the Boer lines untenable. Worse still, his tactical plan was even more ineptly executed. It started well enough when the hill was taken by stealth by 359 men, soldiers of three infantry battalions and some sailors commanded by Colley in person, during the night of 26 February, 1881. The Fifteenth were given lines-of-communication duties from the base at Prospect Camp a couple of miles to the south.

Once Colley's men had reached the small plateau on the summit, however, they made little attempt to fortify their position. No effective observation posts were set up and no artillery was brought up. Later that same morning the Boers, equally stealthily, made their way up the northern side of the

123

mountain, dismounting from their ponies short of the summit and creeping to the crest. When they opened a rapid rifle
fire at close range Colley's force was thrown into complete
panic. Three-quarters of them were killed, wounded or captured
within minutes. The remainder fled down the steep slopes as
fast as they could, Boer fire continuing after them. An intermediate supporting position of the 60th Rifles had to be withdrawn and this was covered by a troop of the Fifteenth which
had arrived earlier with water and rations. During the withdrawal the regiment rescued several wounded men, and sustained casualties themselves, including a troop sergeant major
killed.

Britain groaned at the disaster of Majuba Hill. Gladstone was
prime minister. He had opposed the annexation of the Transvaal
five years earlier, though he had not agreed to disannexation
on reaching office. Sir Robert Ensor, in his history *England
1870–1914*, asks: "What was Gladstone to do? Go on fighting
for annexation, in which he disbelieved, and risk a rebellion
of the Cape Dutch? Or make peace, conceding to force what
he had refused to reason, and leaving the Boers arrogant as
well as injured?" No British reverse that century had been left
unavenged but he decided to take the course of peace, recogniz-
ing Transvaal independence subject only to British control of
foreign policy. So in November, 1881, the Fifteenth sailed home
to England. But Ensor also poses the thought: "Perhaps, could
he [Gladstone] have foreseen 1899–1902, he might have chosen
otherwise." It is a sobering thought: 1899–1902, the Second
Boer War, was to account for 256 deaths in the Thirteenth,
Eighteenth and Nineteenth alone, as will be seen in the next
chapter.

* * *

The North-West Frontier and Southern Africa had kept the
Thirteenth and Fifteenth occupied in the first half of the decade
(the Thirteenth spent 1885 in Natal, having gone there from
India when trouble again looked possible) but it was Egypt,

.another colonial enterprise, which was to concern the Nineteenth and elements of the Eighteenth during the second half of the 1880s.

The significance of Egypt was, as in Napoleon's time, its position astride the route to India. After 1869 it became even more important with the opening of the Suez Canal. After 1878 Britain and France, the major shareholders in the Canal, effectively controlled the Egyptian economy. Earlier mismanagement by the Khedive (the Turkish Viceroy, Egypt at this time still being a province of the Ottoman Empire) had led to their intervention. The economies on which they insisted ultimately provoked the Egyptian army into a nationalist rebellion under Colonel Arabi Pasha. In 1882 fifty Europeans were killed, and as many injured, including the British consul, in riots in Alexandria. British and French financiers faced severe losses and the Canal itself seemed threatened. Gladstone reluctantly undertook to intervene militarily, though the French demurred, fearing that Germany might take advantage on her borders. Accordingly, General Sir Garnet Wolseley, recently appointed Adjutant General following his successes in Zululand, was placed in command of what has been described as the first purely imperialist British military expedition.

The expedition comprised 40,000 troops from Britain and India, and included the 19th Hussars. Attached to them, having answered the call for volunteers, was Lieutenant Bernard de Sales La Terrière of the Eighteenth. La Terrière had little time for anyone who had not been at Eton or who could not give him a good run in a point-to-point, which makes his autobiography *Days That Are Gone*, though racy, sometimes less than objective:

"Some notion of the curious discipline of the regiment can be gathered from my introduction by a junior subaltern (an Eton friend) to the major, in these words, 'Here you little Hindoo devil, here's a gentleman come to join!' The regiment was in an awful state of confusion. . . . The adjutant seemed to make a point of keeping out of the way, as did the colonel, and the most important man on such an occasion, the quartermaster, had 'gone sick' out of the way! . . . I never saw less enthusiasm among a regiment ordered on service."

Wolseley's concept of operations was characteristically simple. He intended deceiving Arabi Pasha into thinking the main offensive would be through Alexandria and thence to Cairo, whereas in reality there was to be a demonstration only against Alexandria, the main effort being directed first at the seizing of the Canal and then defeat of the Egyptian Army in the fifty miles of open desert between the Canal and Cairo.

The feint at Alexandria worked and the landings at Suez, Port Said and Ismailia on 20 August were unopposed. The Canal having been secured, Wolseley then switched his main effort towards defeating Arabi Pasha's army, numbering potentially over 60,000 with the reservists mobilized, in the desert. One troop of the Nineteenth was detailed to be Wolseley's escort and the remainder were divided into two columns to act as divisional cavalry for the 1st and 2nd Divisions. The last days in August and the first week of September were given over to consolidation along the Canal, patrols into the desert, and the establishing of an advanced base at Kassasin.

The patrols discovered that strong entrenched positions were being prepared at Tel-el-Kebir, covering the approaches to Cairo, and these became Wolseley's main objective. During the night of 12/13 August, 1882, he moved 17,000 men and 61 guns in what is always described as a brilliant approach march over the intervening thirteen miles of desert in order to be able to launch a surprise attack at dawn. Wolseley's reputation for organization and sound planning was such that the phrase *All Sir Garnet* had for some years been a synonym for things going like clockwork. Nevertheless, anyone who has taken part in a night march of any description will know that things rarely do go entirely so. La Terrière was with the Nineteenth's escort that night and his description of events would indicate that the brilliant approach march was not quite as *All Sir Garnet* as legend has it:

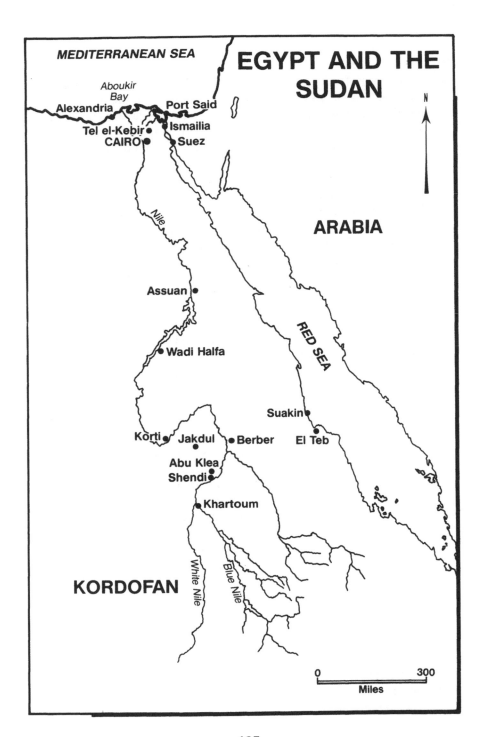

MEDITERRANEAN SEA

EGYPT AND THE SUDAN

N

Aboukir Bay

Alexandria

Port Said

Tel el-Kebir

Ismailia

CAIRO

Suez

Nile

ARABIA

Assuan

RED SEA

Wadi Halfa

Suakin

Korti

Jakdul

Berber

El Teb

Abu Klea

Shendi

Khartoum

KORDOFAN

White Nile

Blue Nile

0   300

Miles

127

"We were led by a naval officer (I forget his name, who was killed in the attack), and about six miles from the enemy's position, it being then about midnight, the whole army halted and lay down for a short rest. It was rather jumpy work moving along in the dark with all horses muffled and no talking or smoking allowed.

Shortly after we had halted, Wolseley did a thing which, if I hadn't heard and received the order myself, I should find it hard to believe. It *ought* to have upset the whole attack, and all his plans, and I can only conclude, either that he simply lost his head for the moment or didn't know what he was doing, or else a sudden recollection of the requirements of the drill-book (for which he was always a stickler) made him think that an army even advancing to the attack in strict secrecy in the dark, must have a screen of cavalry!

Anyhow, to my intense astonishment, which must have been shared by everyone who heard him, he said, 'We ought to have a few Hussars to the front,' and turning to Barclay of the 19th, who was with me and the escort, he told him to send out a line of scouts in front of the army. Some men were mounted in a hurry, making, as was natural, a considerable noise in the general silence, and proceeded to gallop off in all directions, just as if they'd been at an Aldershot field day. Wolseley didn't seem to think there was anything strange about it and we saw no more of them.

My servant Joe Hobbs, told me what happened afterwards, and how disaster was avoided. It was pitch dark, the men soon lost touch with each other, and their direction, and got lost in the desert. Hobbs himself, seems to have kept his direction, and probably drew the opening shot of the battle. About daylight he floundered almost into the enemy's lines, and as he described it, a gun went off and the shot carried away his haversack, and 'I've lost your razor that was in it,' he concluded! He and his horse – blown over but not hurt – lay still till our troops came up, when he joined them. I've often thought over this extraordinary incident and have been unable to account for Wolseley's incomprehensible action."

Nevertheless the attack was launched at 5.00 am, achieving complete surprise, and Wolseley's infantry were in possession of the defences after some hard fighting by 5.30. The Nineteenth exploited through a gap in the entrenchments, seizing Tel-el-Kebir station and bridge on the railway from Ismailia to Cairo, thereby cutting off the retreat of the Egyptian reserves. The pursuit continued for the rest of the day, Cairo falling on the following evening and Arabi Pasha surrendering. The war was over with little more than 400 British troops killed, the Nineteenth escaping even more lightly than most with only two wounded, both subalterns. The campaign's successes should not be overstated, however: most who had taken part agreed with La Terrière that Arabi's men were largely recruited by force: "Their officers were mostly cowardly and useless café loafers from Cairo, and a feebler enemy couldn't be imagined." The regiment was awarded the battle honour *Tel-el-Kebir* and the campaign honour *Egypt 1882* nonetheless.

The situation in lower Egypt having been restored, in November the Nineteenth received orders to prepare to re-embark for England. Scarcely had they begun preparations to do so when the news of revolt in upper Egypt and Sudan reached Cairo. A dervish chief had proclaimed himself *Mahdi* ('Messiah') and was raising an army to end Egyptian rule and to eject all foreigners. The regiment's embarkation was cancelled and they were placed on stand-by.

The dervish insurgents were an altogether more formidable enemy. A British-led Egyptian army was assembled and despatched to Khartoum (under Major-General William Hicks – 'Hicks Pasha'). It was not able to begin active operations against the Mahdi, however, until September, 1883. Two months later the force was utterly destroyed at Kashgil, 150 miles south of Khartoum, and Hicks himself was killed. This victory further fired the fanaticism of the Mahdi and his followers, and their revolt now looked like spreading from their strongholds in the south of the province to threaten Khartoum itself. The Egyptian government, encouraged by its newly appointed British adviser, therefore decided to evacuate the Sudan south of Wadi Halfa, the highest point to which the Nile is freely navigable.

Such an evacuation presented considerable difficulties of organization and control: there were many scattered Egyptian outposts, and the important garrison at Suakin on the coast, commanding the shortest route to Khartoum from the Red Sea, was already besieged by one of the Mahdi's lieutenants. To deal with this siege the government in Cairo again sent a force of Egyptian troops under a British commander, Major-General Valentine Baker – 'Baker Pasha'. In February, 1884, this force too was utterly defeated by the Mahdists at what became known as the first battle of El Teb, Baker himself only narrowly escaping death. It thus became clear to the Cairo authorities that without using *British* troops no success could be expected. A rapid reinforcement of Suakin was organized and by the end of February 4,000 British troops, including the Nineteenth, had been shipped from Cairo to the little port of Trinkitat, forty miles south of Suakin, under command of Major-General Sir Gerald Graham VC.

Graham lost no time in going onto the offensive. On 29 February, 1884, he advanced on the Mahdists' fortified camp at El Teb. The Mahdists numbered some 6,000, Graham's a little over half that number. His artillery soon silenced the enemy's and he was able to take their camp position with his infantry relatively easily. He then sent his cavalry, comprising the Nineteenth and the 10th Hussars, to pursue the enemy who were fleeing from the rear of the position. The two regiments quickly began to turn the defeat into a rout but were themselves counter-attacked vigorously by Mahdist horsemen who had been concealed in the scrub and broken ground.

Some desperate hand-to-hand fighting developed, many hussars being brought down by Mahdist swordsmen crouching in the scrub and hamstringing their horses. Of those brought down, not one survived except the second-in-command, Percy Barrow, who, with a spear still embedded in his side, was rescued by Quartermaster-Sergeant William Marshall. Marshall was unable to hoist him onto his own horse because of the spear, so he gripped his arm and literally pulled him to safety in the rear of a formed squadron. An indication of the ferocity of the fighting was the fate of Barrow's trumpeter, Fanning, who remained by him throughout and sustained *sixteen* severe wounds of which he later died. In all, the regiment's casualties were fourteen dead and twenty-two wounded. Barrow himself, against all expectations, recovered from his injuries, and Marshall was awarded the Victoria Cross, the first to be won by the regiment.

The second battle of El Teb was a clear victory but the local commander, Osman Digna, was not beaten. Another bitter action was fought a week later at Tamai, sixteen miles from Suakin. Here the Mahdists actually penetrated an infantry square, a remarkable achievement for men armed only with swords and spears. One hundred and nine British were killed and the same number wounded. The Mahdists lost over 2,000, though 10,000 managed to escape despite the efforts of the Nineteenth and the 10th Hussars.

These operations relieved the pressure on the Egyptian garrisons at Suakin, thus achieving the immediate object of the reinforcement, but overall they were inconclusive since the eastern Sudan still remained effectively in the insurgents' hands. Graham's force re-embarked on 1 April, 1884, landing at Cairo five days later. The regiments were awarded the campaign honour *Egypt 1884* for the battles at El Teb and Tamai.

As the Suakin operation was taking place, one of the great dramas of the late Victorian period was beginning to unfold. Against the advice of the government in Cairo, Gladstone had sent General Charles Gordon, the hero of the campaigns in China and against the slavers in Africa, to Khartoum. Gordon knew the Sudan well, having been the Khedive's governor general there until 1880. The Government thought that he might be able to persuade the Mahdi to permit the evacuation of the Khartoum garrison through Suakin, but his precise mission became confused. Arriving in Khartoum on 18 February, 1884, he managed to despatch 2,500 of the garrison down the Nile to safety in the first month but soon afterwards the Mahdi closed the ring around the city and communication with Cairo became extremely difficult. Gordon appears at this stage to have believed that his mission had, or should have been, changed to one of holding on to Khartoum while Wolseley's forces destroyed the Mahdi's army. There were so many factional interests that the *exact* purpose of Gordon's position in Khartoum was far from clear.

By April, Wolseley, who had returned to England, was seriously concerned for Gordon's safety. The Mahdists were consolidating their isolation of Khartoum, and he was in no doubt what prodigious effort would be needed to lift the siege: it would require "the biggest operation the English Army has *ever* undertaken" he wrote. At length, in the autumn of 1884, Gladstone agreed to a relief operation and Wolseley returned to Cairo to develop his plan to break through to Khartoum.

Wolseley had two options. Either he could take his force through the Suez Canal and, landing at Suakin, strike out through the desert to Berber and thence Khartoum, or he could choose to push his force up the Nile in boats as far as Khartoum itself. Despite the objections of many experienced soldiers on the spot, including Evelyn Wood, he chose the Nile option. In this he appears to have been strongly influenced by his success in the Red River expedition in Canada in 1870: he had organized and commanded the punitive operations against the *Metis* rebels in Manitoba and had covered the 600 miles from Lake Superior to Fort Garry in three months, all his force and its supplies having gone by boat.

This time he intended doing much the same despite the enormity of the logistical problems. His intention was to concentrate his army of some 95,000 men at Korti by mid-December. From here, if necessary, a dash could be made across the 200 miles of desert to Khartoum. Reinforcements began arriving from Britain, including a half-squadron of the Eighteenth which, together with detachments from other regiments, was to form a camel corps in the 'Nile Expeditionary Force'. On 25 October the Nineteenth, now under the command of an almost fully-recovered Barrow, set out by rail and steamer for Korti. They were to be the only horsemen with each force and were mounted on Arab ponies whose performance proved quite exceptional, as Chapter Ten will explain.

Delays of every kind put back Wolseley's programme by more than a month. "Had British soldiers and Egyptian camels been able to subsist on sand and occasional water, or had the desert produced beef and biscuit," speculated the *Official History* drily, "the army might, in spite of its late start, have reached Khartoum in November. But as things were, the rate of progress of the army was dependent on the rate of progress of its supplies." As a result, Wolseley modified his plans and decided to send the 'Desert Column' as soon as possible across the Bayuda Desert to Metammah and from there make a dash over the last hundred miles to Khartoum. Meanwhile the 'River Column' would move up to Shendi, opposite Metammah, and from here would be able to supply and reinforce the Desert Column. The plan required elements of the desert column to establish another forward base, at Jakdul, however, and this would add to the delay. The Nineteenth were to accompany the desert column, less one squadron with the river column.

The base at Jakdul, 90 miles from Korti, was relatively quickly established, the Nineteenth playing a key reconnaissance role. The whole desert column then set off from Korti for Abu Klea via the Jakdul base. Early on 16 January, 1885, the Nineteenth were ordered to push on to the Abu Klea wells, 53 miles from Jakdul. At the wells, unbeknown to the otherwise excellent intelligence staff, the Mahdi had concentrated 10,000 of his best troops. A patrol led by Major J.D.P. French (later Field-Marshal Lord French, CIGS in 1914 and subsequently commander of the British Expeditionary Force) managed nevertheless to pin the enemy until the main force could close up. Next day a savage battle developed: nine hours of the bloodiest fighting took place until the infantry eventually managed to break the Mahdi's defence, whereupon the Nineteenth advanced to seize the wells, though these could only be taken after heavy carbine fire. The Nineteenth shared the battle honour *Abu Klea* with the Royal Sussex Regiment whose use of the bayonet that day had been prodigious.

Late in the afternoon of the following day, 18 January, the column left Abu Klea to march the remaining 25 miles to the loop of the Nile where a junction with the river column could be expected. The Nineteenth led this march throughout the night and by daybreak were six miles from the river. Mahdist troops occupied the intervening ground, however, and another bloody fight ensued during which the column commander, Major-General Herbert Stewart, was killed. The Mahdists eventually broke, however, and the infantry pushed on to the Nile, which they reached just after dark. The Nineteenth, left guarding the defensive camp hastily constructed after sighting the enemy, and their horses beginning to suffer, followed up the next day. It was late in the afternoon of 20 January that half the horses had their first drink in seventy-two hours. Sir Charles Wilson, who had taken command after Stewart's death, wrote in his memoirs:

"The cavalry horses were quite done up. The way in which Barrow managed to bring the 19th Hussars across the desert is one of the best things in the expedition.... The scouting of the Hussars during the march was admirably done; they were ubiquitous.... They reached the Nile almost useless as cavalry, and could only be employed for scouting purposes, at short distances from the camp."

During the previous day's fighting the Nineteenth's Quarter-master, Lieutenant A.G. Lima, who had held the post for less than a year having previously been RSM, was killed. He was replaced by Quartermaster-Sergeant William Marshall VC, the hero of El Teb, who was still quartermaster when the regiment sailed for the South African War in 1900.

The river column was also making progress but slower than that of the desert column. Its squadron of the Nineteenth was involved in some brisk scouting actions on the west bank. The planned junction at Metammah was abandoned in early February, however, when it was learned that Khartoum had fallen and Gordon was dead. The regiment retraced their steps to Korti from where preparations were to be made for another expedition against Khartoum. Any attempts to relieve Khartoum in the short term were formally abandoned in April, however. Withdrawal to Cairo began in June and was completed on 14 August, 1885.

The regiment was awarded the campaign honour *Nile 1884–5,*

its fifth honour in three years. Even more honours were to be bestowed: in July, as they were returning to Cairo, the Nineteenth learned that Queen Victoria had conferred on them the designation 'Princess of Wales's Own' in recognition of "its distinguished services in Egypt and the Sudan". This was indeed a signal recognition by the Queen, who had taken an intense personal interest in Gordon's position in Khartoum and had repeatedly urged Gladstone to "*do* something". It is said that she never forgave him for Gordon's death.

The 19th Princess of Wales's Own Hussars returned to England in June, 1886, though not before, to the regiment's great sadness, Colonel Barrow died of the wounds he had received at El Teb two years earlier. He had joined the regiment in 1868 and was only 38 years old.

* * *

Queen Victoria realized full well the price of Empire: "If we are to *maintain* our position as a *first rate* Power," she wrote, with emphatic capitals and underlinings, "we must, with our Indian empire and large Colonies, be *Prepared* for *attacks* and *wars, somewhere* or *other*, CONTINUALLY." The 1880s had seen all The Light Dragoons' forebears mobilized to pay this price. The 1890s were no more peaceful, but the regiments themselves enjoyed a decade of relative peace. All less the Thirteenth returned to India at some stage to maintain the jewel in the crown.

Meanwhile, significant changes were taking place: khaki, smokeless powder, machine guns, magazine-fed rifles, barrel-recoiling artillery, telephones, type-writers and rapid printing methods, food in cans – these and others would have profound implications for tactics, command and logistics. To what extent these implications were promptly recognized and acted on can be seen in the biggest Imperial test Victoria's Army was to undergo – the Second, or Great, Boer War.

CHAPTER 9

No End of a Lesson

"The war was a most cruel one for the cavalry, who were handicapped throughout by the nature of the country and the tactics of the enemy. They were certainly the branch of the service which had the least opportunity for distinction. The work of scouting and patrolling is the most dangerous duty which a soldier can undertake, and yet from its very nature can find no chronicler."
Sir ARTHUR CONAN DOYLE

13H, 18H and 19H in South Africa 1899–1902.

As the 18th Hussars steamed from Bombay to Durban in the SS *Simla* in the middle of October, 1898, bets were exchanged with men of another regiment as to which would be the first cavalry into Pretoria, the northern Boer capital. The wager was eventually 'won' by the Eighteenth but in a fashion which they never would have imagined. Within nine days of the formal declaration of war, and on the first day's fighting in Natal, the whole of B Squadron, the maxim-gun section and regimental headquarters, including the commanding officer, were prisoners of war and on their way to Pretoria by train in open trucks. It was an inauspicious start, to say the least, to the war of which Kipling wrote:

"We have had no end of a lesson; it will do us no end of good;
Not on a single issue, or in one direction or twain,
But conclusively, comprehensively, and several times again."

The Eighteenth's wager was in any case jumping the gun somewhat, for war did not actually break out until a year after their arrival. They were simply taking over, on regular relief, from the 7th Hussars. The storm clouds were clear to see, however, and the regiment was immediately sent up to the Natal–Transvaal border, near Ladysmith, where they remained throughout the following twelve months' build-up to war.

Why was it that the Eighteenth, then the Thirteenth, Nineteenth and most of the rest of the regular and yeomanry cavalry, together with legions of infantry, found themselves in this corner of the Empire fighting these Dutch settlers? Why, to paraphrase Kipling, were these gentlemen in khaki *ordered south*? The reason was relatively straightforward, but dismaying. The peace terms at the end of the first Boer war in 1881, the short skirmish in which the Fifteenth had played an active role, had fudged the issue of British suzerainty over the Transvaal. When in 1886 gold was discovered there, multiplying annual revenue twenty times, and British settlers arrived, the issue began to take substance. The Boers began buying Mauser rifles and Krupp artillery from Germany in increasing quantities. The British Government and the colonial administration in Cape Colony mishandled the situation, being alternately too placatory and too arrogant. The astonishingly inept 'Jameson Raid' in 1895, largely conceived by Sir Cecil Rhodes, governor of the Cape, had already antagonized the whole of the Boer nation and won them support in many European countries, Germany in particular.

In 1899, with the storm clouds getting even blacker, the British Government decided to reinforce the 15,000-strong garrison in South Africa by 10,000 troops from India and the Mediterranean garrisons. These included the Nineteenth. President Kruger, with 50,000 mounted infantry (for that was what the Boer settlers were – skilled horsemen, excelling in fieldcraft, and superb shots) and some regular artillery, seemed determined on a show-down. In early October he issued an ultimatum demanding that all British troops on the Transvaal and Free State boundaries be withdrawn, and that the reinforcements which had arrived the previous month leave South Africa. On 11 October, no reply having been received, war was declared.

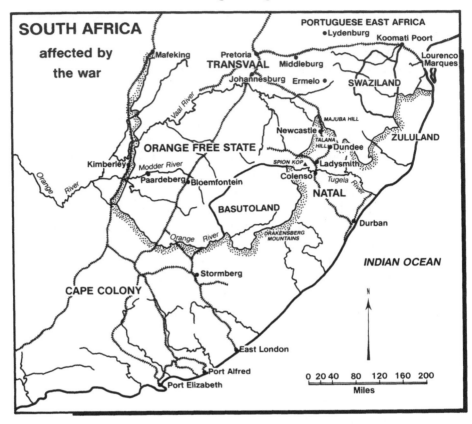

The area over which operations were to be conducted was as large as France and Germany combined.

The war divides into three distinct phases. The first phase, the Boer offensive and sieges of Mafeking, Kimberley and Ladysmith, lasted four months and saw some notable Boer successes: Stormberg, Magersfontein (just south of Kimberley), Colenso and Spion Kop showed the superiority of Boer field-craft, marksmanship, and tactics. But while these opening battles showed tactical ascendancy, the overall operational plan was faulty or, at best, faultily executed. The two-pronged offensive from the Free State and the Transvaal was intended to pin the British while the Boers seized Durban, Natal's only port, thereby confining the British operations to the long lines of communication from Cape Town, Port Elizabeth, Port Alfred and East London in Cape Colony. It was a sound enough plan, but instead of pinning the British at Kimberley, Mafeking and Ladysmith, these very sieges became the Boers' undoing: more and more of their troops had to be employed in the siege operations, fatally limiting their operational flexibility. Meanwhile, reinforcements from both Britain (including the Thirteenth) and India poured in through Durban, putting paid to all Boer hopes of knocking Natal out of the war.

During this first phase the Eighteenth both lost and regained their reputation. Their disaster on the first day's fighting, at Talana Hill near Dundee, seems to have been the result of a major miscalculation by the commanding officer, Lieutenant-Colonel B.D. Möller. He followed this initial mistake with a series of tactical misjudgments which ultimately placed him in a position whence he believed there was no escape. The German General Staff's official history of the war sums it up thus: "the British cavalry, which had been skilfully manoeuvred to the Boer rear, did not understand how to utilize their advantage and suffered heavy losses."

The regiment, about 500-strong, together with nearly 300 mounted infantrymen and a troop of Natal Carbineers, formed the mounted component of what was known as the Glencoe Division. This force of nearly 4,000 men and three batteries of 15-pounders was ordered to conduct a forward defence of Natal at Dundee some forty miles north-east of Ladysmith. It was not an easily held position, being overlooked on all sides by towering hills from which fire could be poured into the town. More graphically, a French observer compared the position with being in a chamber pot!

Before dawn on 20 October one of the three Boer columns which had invaded Natal nine days earlier occupied Talana Hill, two miles from the town. 4,000 Boers, four field guns and two Vickers Maxims under General Lucas Meyer, 'the lion of Vreiheid', had been able to take this dominating feature completely unbeknown to Major-General Sir William Penn Symons in Dundee itself. It was an extraordinary lapse in field security, and the defenders soon began to pay the price, for at 5.30am Boer shells began to fall in their camp. The Eighteenth were already saddled for the dawn stand-to and were ordered to move out of the camp to some cover in rocky ground. Symons then ordered them to make a wide flanking movement to the north of Talana Hill in order to cut off the Boer retreat which would surely follow his infantry's attack. This was of course to be a frontal attack preceded by the eighteen field guns' sharp bombardment of the hilltop. As Thomas Pakenham says in his history of the war, the plan showed all the originality and realism of an Aldershot field day.

The Eighteenth found themselves a good position immediately to the north of the hill, from where they were able to see over 500 of the Boer led-horses and ammunition details. One of the squadron leaders, Major P.S. Marling VC, who had transferred into the regiment from the 60th Rifles thirteen years earlier, asked the commanding officer for permission to open fire, but Möller would not hear of it. When he wanted Marling's advice he would ask for it, Möller replied! Worse still, Möller then took his force from this commanding position and moved south-east across the Boer line of advance for no apparent reason. They had a sharp encounter with twenty armed Boers, whom two troops of B Squadron charged, killing or capturing all of them, but still continued south-east.

At this stage the second-in-command, Major E.C. Knox, youngest son of Richard Knox who had re-raised the regiment, weighed in. Still Möller would not go back towards the enemy, but he did decide to let Knox take Marling's squadron and another while he himself led the third squadron, the mounted infantry and maxim guns in a retirement north-west.

By this time, however, the Boers were beginning to retire from Talana Hill. They had stood their ground during the initial assault, something they would rarely do again during the war, and Symons himself had been killed. After bitter fighting they streamed down the eastern slopes of the hill to their ponies. Knox wisely took evading action south-east, but Möller pressed north-west across the Boer line of retirement. The ground here offered neither Möller nor Knox the opportunity to enfilade the Boer retreat and their withdrawal went unmolested. Knox manoeuvred his two squadrons with considerable skill and managed to get back to Dundee during the late afternoon, but Möller walked into another Boer commando three miles north of Talana. This was under command of the able General S.P. Erasmus, whose marksmen opened an accurate long-range fire on Möller's group as they sheltered in a valley farm. Later in the afternoon Boer artillery opened up on them too, and at 4.30 Möller, believing further resistance futile, surrendered.

The capitulation had a profound effect on morale in South Africa and on public opinion both in Britain and abroad. A court of inquiry seven months later exonerated all concerned, but Lord Roberts, by then Commander-in-Chief South Africa, added a report which, though acknowledging no neglect or misconduct on Möller's part, nevertheless found that he had "shown himself but little capable of exercising command". Knox was promoted lieutenant-colonel to command, and when Möller was released the following year he was not permitted to resume command, instead retiring on half-pay.

Möller had risen unspectacularly to command of the Eighteenth. He was an entirely regimental soldier with no experience of active service. He was not untypical of a certain type of late-Victorian officer whose preferment followed a safe but unadventurous route, the promotion principle at that time being 'seniority tempered by rejection'. In contrast, the two officers from whom he refused to take advice were both experienced in active service in similar conditions. Knox had taken part in the Nile Expedition 1884-5, and Marling had fought in the 1881 Boer War, the 1882 Egypt campaign and in the Sudan in 1884 where he had won his Victoria Cross.

This was a humiliating setback for the Eighteenth, but it was only temporary. They were soon to regain their reputation during the prolonged defence of Ladysmith, and later in the war were described by one senior general as "the best mounted infantry in the country". They were joined at Ladysmith by the Nineteenth. Together with elements of the

5th Dragoon Guards (whom Baden-Powell had been commanding until recently), the 5th Lancers and Natal Carbineers, they formed Major-General John French's cavalry formation in the Natal Field Force. Major Douglas Haig, later Field-Marshal Earl Haig, was French's chief of staff.

Raising the sieges of Ladysmith, Mafeking and Kimberley became the British army's first priority: besides any military significance, public opinion in Britain expected no less after the appalling initial reverses. General Sir Redvers Buller VC was in overall command. He was an honest and brave soldier but he was totally overmatched by the ground and the enemy. In a series of faltering attempts to relieve the three towns he suffered setback after tactical setback. In the infamous 'Black Week' in December, General Gatacre was defeated at Stormberg, General Methuen at Magersfontein and Buller himself trying to relieve Ladysmith. In Buller's column were the Thirteenth, who had landed at Durban only a week or so earlier.

Something drastic had to be done, and it was. Field-Marshal Sir Frederick Roberts VC, who figured prominently in the preceding chapter, arrived at Cape Town on 10 January, 1900, to take command, with Major-General Lord Kitchener of Khartoum, of whom much more in Chapter Eleven, as his chief of staff. They immediately set to work reorganizing the army, in particular to make good the obvious deficiency in mounted infantry. Roberts also directed the main effort on one objective at a time, rather than on the three which Buller had done.

So began the second phase of the war. Within six weeks Roberts had manoeuvred a Boer army, under the redoubtable General Cronje, out of its powerful defences at Magersfontein, the key to the relief of Kimberley. He then cut off the Boers' retreat to Bloemfontein with a spectacular march by the cavalry division, recently arrived from England and under French's command (French had been recalled from the defence of Ladysmith and only succeeded in getting out of the town by lying on the floor of his railway carriage). Roberts took Cronje's surrender on 27 February after the Battle of Paardeberg.

At the beginning of March, after two more unsuccessful attempts, Buller's luck changed and he broke through at Ladysmith. Sadly, his tactical judgement had not changed and he expressly forbade any following-up of the retreating Boers. The cavalry, the Thirteenth as much as any, were mortified. Instead of a pursuit they found themselves spending a whole day cleaning up for the formal entry into the town. Even the war's official history, not usually a very critical document, says: "Both the Ladysmith Garrison and the Natal Force viewed the two days with a dull anger. Both knew what a chance was being cast to the wind."

Meanwhile, Roberts was pushing on to Bloemfontein, capital of the Orange Free State, which he captured on 13 March. He then had to order a halt, lasting seven weeks, in order both to resupply and to ride out an epidemic of enteric fever (typhoid) caused by infected water and poor sanitation. 8,000 British troops were to die of enteric in this war, slightly more than fell to Boer rifles and guns.

His army now reinforced to 75,000 men, Roberts resumed his advance towards Pretoria on 3 May. Over two hundred miles of *veldt* lay between him and his objective, yet in a fraction over a month he had taken it, and Johannesburg *en route*. Mafeking was relieved on 17 May by 'flying columns' from Rhodesia and the Cape. Its defence had been brilliantly conducted by Colonel Robert Baden-Powell. 'B-P' had joined the Thirteenth in India in 1876 and had been seconded to operations in Rhodesia and Matabeleland in 1896. In the following year he took command of the 5th Dragoon Guards in India, but while on home leave in the summer of 1899 he was summarily appointed to raise a force of mounted rifles, to be based on Mafeking, to patrol the north-west frontiers of Cape Colony. Thus, during the subsequent siege of his headquarters, he had no regular troops at all – only some 900 assorted local militiamen and volunteers, and a small group of regular officers, including the Prime Minister's son, Lord Edward Cecil. He built an intricate network of wire entanglements, trenches, forts and shelters and, crucial to any defence, conducted an aggressive policy of patrolling and sorties.

The garrison lost 200 killed, but the Boers lost five times that number. Infinitely more important, however, they had tied down a fifth of the entire mobilized Boer forces and a quarter of their artillery during the first six months of the war. The heroic defence also captured the public's admiration and did much to make up for the gloom which the several early defeats brought. B-P was certainly a self-publicist, but there is no doubt that the very 'hype' he created drew the Boers fatally into reinforcing a militarily useless operation. Queen Victoria was said to have been singularly unamused, however, when he issued siege postage stamps with his own head on them!

After the relief, Baden-Powell was promoted major-general, and Roberts commissioned him to raise the South African (Mounted) Constabulary. This he did with great success, and the force was to play a significant part in the third phase of the war. A year after the war ended he returned home to become Inspector General of Cavalry and was appointed Colonel of the 13th Hussars in 1911 and of the 13th/18th in 1922.

During Roberts's march through the Free State, the Natal Field Force had to withstand renewed pressure by the formidable commandant Louis Botha. The Eighteenth and Nineteenth were hastily reconstituted after the four months' deprivations of the siege. The horses, particularly, needed bringing back to condition, and many remounts were brought up. The Thirteenth meanwhile were sustaining steady losses on outpost duty around Newcastle, but generally the spring months – or, rather, autumn months in the southern hemisphere – were spent preparing for a general offensive astride the Newcastle–Johannesburg railway. The Eighteenth and Nineteenth were brigaded together in the Second Cavalry Brigade (together with the 5th Lancers) to form the spearhead of the advance.

Once Roberts's push towards the Transvaal gained momentum, Botha's position in the south-east became difficult, his lines of communication threatened and his commando susceptible to envelopment should part of Roberts's force turn south-east. General De la Rey, commanding the Transvaal commandos in the Free State, had cabled to him in the second week of

May that the advancing British were as "numerous as locusts" and "could not be shot back".

On 22 May, 1900, Buller's Natal Field Force went over to the offensive. The Eighteenth were the first to cross the Vaal River into the Republic, and during the next month the three regiments of the Second Cavalry Brigade saw sharp action. The Thirteenth, too, were kept busy securing the lines of communication. Roberts's advance was making such rapid progress, however, that Buller's force turned away from the railway to Johannesburg (the city surrendered without a fight to Roberts on 31 May) and advanced almost due north to Ermelo and Middleburg. At Ermelo the Eighteenth found Möller's charger, an event not unlike the rather more emotional one which occurred with the Thirteenth some seventeen years later at Baghdad – of which more in Chapter Twelve.

On 7 July Roberts's and Buller's forces made a junction at Vlakfontein, Pretoria having fallen on 5 June. Two weeks later Roberts began to advance eastwards along the railway to Koomati Poort and Portuguese East Africa, the Boers'. lifeline to the outside world. Buller's force renewed its advance towards Middleburg from the south, and the town was occupied on 27 July. Roberts's combined forces now numbered nearly 20,000, but opposing them in any further advance eastwards were 7,000 of Botha's burghers, all mounted, and twenty guns. Botha had disposed them along a twenty-mile front in mountainous country with virtually impregnable flanks, and there followed, on 27 August, the war's penultimate set-piece engagement. The ground was unsuitable for cavalry as a whole, but the Nineteenth's scouts, operating dismounted for much of the time, discovered a small gap in the defences. The offensive's main effort was switched to this weak spot in the Boer centre and, after some hard fighting, the position caved in.

After this battle, Bergendal, systematic Boer resistance ended and guerrilla warfare began. By 7 September the Second Cavalry Brigade had reached Lydenburg, a march of over three hundred miles from Ladysmith, and here they halted for a month.

The Orange Free State had been formally annexed, becoming the Orange River Colony on 24 May, and the annexation of the Transvaal had followed on 1 September. On 11 September President Kruger fled to Holland through Portuguese East Africa. No one in Britain thought that the capture of the Boer capitals, and sources of mineral wealth, could lead to anything less than a rapid surrender by the Boer commandos in the field. Roberts's brilliant achievements, in the space of less than six months, were being compared with his famous march on Kandahar twenty years earlier: all that was needed was a 'mopping-up' operation to deal with those Boers who had not given up their arms.

The 'mopping-up' operation was to take nearly two years' hard fighting, however: the principal Boer commandants, the Transvaalers Botha and De la Rey, and the Free Stater De Wet, would not concede defeat. They determined on a guerrilla war "to the bitter end" (thus "bitter-enders"). On the face of it, this was not a hopeless strategy: the British had conceded once before, in the war of 1881, when things went against them; international opinion was strongly supportive of the Boers – there was even hope of direct support from the French, Russians or Germans; the Unionist (Conservative) Government in Britain might fall to the generally anti-war Liberals; the Boer skill, and preference, for guerrilla raiding could exhaust British military resources, especially if the Afrikanders in the Cape Colony could be encouraged to join the fight.

None of these conditions for success materialized, however. It was Gladstone's Liberal Government which had conceded after Majuba Hill: the Unionists were returned to power in the September 1900 election on a wave of patriotic support following Roberts's victories, and British capitulation was not going to be won easily. Foreign opinion remained supportive of the Boers but it never turned to active support: the Kaiser even back-tracked considerably from his earlier outspoken support. The Cape Dutch failed to rise, and British military resources were not exhausted – though the war as a whole was eventually to see 400,000 British and Imperial troops committed, including 250,000 British regulars, and cost

33. *"High hopes of a major break-through which would finish the war."*(p. 196) The
18th Hussars massed in the Carnoy Valley, summer 1917, ready to exploit the gap
in the German defences which in the event was never made.

34. *"A gilded youth."*(p.200) The bronze memorial by Sir Alfred Munnings, and
stone plinth by Sir Edwin Lutyens, to Lieutenant Edward Horner, 18th Hussars,
killed during the battle of Cambrai, November, 1917. Mells Church, Somerset.

35. *"Despite its mauling, the regiment quickly recovered."(p.195)* After suffering heavy casualties in a mounted action at Lajj in March, 1917, the 13th Hussars were nevertheless the first mounted troops to enter Baghdad a few weeks later. In their two-year campaign in Mesopotamia the regiment won, inter alia, eight DSOs and fourteen DCMs.

36. *"She had a foal a few years later."(p.194)* Captain William Eve's favourite charger, Caprice, who survived the charge at Lajj outside Baghdad despite receiving seven bullet wounds in her neck and being 'lost' for over a year. Eve was killed at the head of his squadron of the Thirteenth, sword in hand. Silver commemorative statuette, copies of which were for some time the regimental officers' wedding present and one of which is now the trophy for the Duke of Gloucester Memorial Chase, run annually at Sandown.

37. *"There was some desperate fighting, and the Cavalry Corps . . . was used to fill gaps and generally act as 'fire brigade'."* (p. 204) Ludendorff's March, 1918, offensive was a desperate last fling but it nearly broke the allied defences. The photograph of men of C Squadron, 15th Hussars, taken after several days in continuous action, shows clearly their exhaustion.

38. *"Beyond the Rhine since December (1918)."(p.208)* The 15th Hussars mark the first anniversary of the Armistice in Cologne.

39. *"With a sorrow which no words can express I take farewell of my Regiment of Hussars."(p.212)* In the wake of peace came the reductions in the Army which brought about the 1922 cavalry amalgamations. Lieutenant-Colonel A W Parsons echoing the farewell of the 19th Hussars' Colonel-in-Chief, Queen Alexandra, to those remaining of the regiment in Tidworth, December, 1921.

the Exchequer nearly 225 million sterling. The final phase of the war began therefore in September 1900. It kept the Thirteenth, Eighteenth and Nineteenth fully occupied in uncomfortable, exhausting, tedious, dangerous and frequently distasteful operations for a further twenty months.

* * *

Roberts's first operational plan for this third phase used large troop concentrations to flush the *veldt* in order to drive the commandos on to columns placed astride stop-lines. This had been successful in the Free State in July when Prinsloo's commando, numbering 4,000 men, was captured in the Brandwater Basin, an area surrounded by mountains in which the passes were relatively easily blocked. Such countryside was not typical of the whole of the Free State and Transvaal, however, and the Boers, once bitten in this way, were twice shy thereafter. Their scouting system became highly developed and this, together with the exceptional visibility on the *veldt*, usually enabled them to keep several steps ahead of the 'sweeps'.

Roberts then ordered the burning of farms belonging to those Boers who had reneged on their oath of loyalty after surrender, and those close to where acts of sabotage had taken place. A real element of bitterness entered the campaign: the burghers were outraged and at first this hardened their resolve to resist. Those troops taking part in the burning, which included the destruction of crops and livestock, and on occasions the escorting away of the burgher's family, also felt the misery of such tactics. As the Thirteenth's history of the war records of one episode,

> "This was always an unpleasant duty, but on this occasion the women were particularly annoying and troublesome. One of them who insisted on being brought in going to the length of giving birth to a child on a wagon during the journey."

The farm searches were not without excitement occasionally. The Eighteenth had one incident which would be familiar to

147

later generations in Northern Ireland: two girls in their twenties were found

> "in a huge bed. The girls were given five minutes to dress whilst our party explored the rest of the building. On their return they found the girls nearly dressed and, on looking under the mattress, found two Mauser rifles and a lot of ammunition, and beneath the bed two Boer men."

There appeared to be no hard feelings on this occasion, however: "Good old Bojer!" records the diary!

Roberts became alarmed, though, by the way farm destroying was increasing, and at the end of November he ordered that it was only to be done on the specific orders of brigade commanders. His reasons were not entirely humanitarian: Boer commandants were saying openly that they welcomed the policy of farm destruction because the British, in looking after the refugees, removed the responsibility from their hard-pressed commandos. This regulation led to more reprimands and re-criminations, however, and there is little doubt that things got out of hand. Marling's journal recalls:

> "found an awful fat farm, which I burnt, and got eleven wagon loads of oat-hay for the horses, 2000 lbs mealies for the horses and mules and 3000 rounds of ammunition concealed in the roof. We also got fowls and eggs. There was trouble over this, as it was the farm that a certain general got his butter, eggs and fowls for his mess, and he was extremely annoyed and ordered me to assemble a court of enquiry, as he said that he had given the Boer a letter of protection. I then remembered that a Kaffir had come and given one of my subalterns a note, which was almost illegible. We duly held a court of enquiry, and found that nothing was known about the farm. The general then got furious, and ordered a Column Court of enquiry to be held, composed of officers not in the 18th Hussars. Major Philip Chetwode, 19th Hussars [of whom more in later chapters], was President of the court and played up well. He sent in the following finding:
> 1. The farm had not been burnt.

2. If it *had* been burnt it had not been burnt by the 18th Hussars."!

The affair appears to have fizzled out when the general concerned went home soon afterwards.

At this point in the war Roberts handed over to Kitchener and returned to England to an earldom and to the last appointment of Commander-in-Chief at the War Office. Kitchener had to make his own assessment as to how the guerrilla warfare could be ended. The big sweeps were not having any significant effect. Train wrecking, convoy capturing, patrol ambushing and general sabotage was increasing apace, and the small, marauding Boer commandos seemed also to be able to combine for larger operations with ease. Kitchener came to the conclusion that the answer lay in large measure with the burghers' families, notwithstanding what the commandants were saying about shifting the burden. The families and farms could offer far more support to the commandos, in material and intelligence, than the commandos could possibly give to the farms. The towns were firmly under British control, but the *veldt* could provide indefinite support to the commandos. To Kitchener it followed, therefore, that to remove this source of support was a prerequisite of success. Botha himself, still commander-in-chief and de facto president of the Transvaal too, in effect endorsed this estimate when he maintained that, under Transvaal law, he was empowered to force every man to join him and be provided with support from his family, on pain of confiscation of property.

Accordingly, in December, 1900, Kitchener issued orders for his land clearance policy:

"Memorandum:
The General Commander-in-Chief is desirous that all possible means shall be taken to stop the present guerrilla warfare. Of the various measures suggested for the accomplishment of this object, one which has been strongly recommended, and has lately been successfully tried on a small scale, is the removal of all men, women and children, and natives from the Districts

which the enemy's bands persistently occupy. This course has been pointed out by surrendered burghers, who are anxious to finish the war, as the most effective method of limiting the endurance of the guerrillas, as men and women left on farms, if disloyal, willingly supply burghers, if loyal, dare not refuse to do so. Moreover, seeing the unprotected state of women now living in the Districts, this course is desirable to assure their not being insulted or molested by natives.

... The women and children brought in should be camped near the railway for supply purposes... The Ordnance will supply the necessary tents and the District Commissioner will look after the food on the scale now in use.

It should be clearly explained to burghers in the field, that, if they voluntarily surrender, they will be allowed to live with their families in the camps until it is safe for them to return to their homes.

With regard to natives, it is not intended to clear Kaffir locations but only such Kaffirs and their stock as are on Boer farms. Every endeavour should be made to cause as little loss as possible to the natives removed and to give them protection when brought in. They will be available for any works undertaken, for which they will receive pay at native rates.

Pretoria, 21st December 1900"

The 13th/18th and 15th/19th Hussars were to be involved with a similar policy in Malaya fifty years on, as will be seen in Chapter Sixteen.

If the land clearance policy were successful in denying support to the commandos, it was still another thing to capture the most determined of them. Kitchener did not want to draw out operations any longer than necessary and was not prepared to wait for his policy to drive the commandos into surrendering. He therefore decided on two other innovations. The first was the scaling-down of the sweeps. They had not proved cost-effective. Instead he subdivided the *veldt* into smaller, brigade-sized tactical areas of responsibility. In these areas the allocated brigades were expected to become thoroughly acquainted with the country and its population and to keep up a continuous pattern of patrolling and ambushing, especially at night during the cold weather when the commandos tended to lay up in farms and move only their supply wagons. The Eighteenth and Nineteenth, usually brigaded together, spent much of 1901 operating in this way and took part in a number of sharp night actions. They saw some sharp daytime actions too. In July two troopers of the Eighteenth were scouting forward of A Squadron at Springbok Laagte on the *veldt* west of Ermelo when the Boers opened fire at a range of 100 yards. Private Harry Crandon rode back under heavy fire to where Private Berry, who had been hit twice, had fallen from his disabled horse. He put Berry over his own horse's saddle and ran back 1,100 yards (bringing Berry's rifle with him too) to where the rest of the squadron had dismounted. The action won him the VC. Had he been killed it would not have, for at this time the VC was not awarded posthumously. A similar rescue in the Thirteenth the previous year, depicted in a clever watercolour sketch by Baden-Powell, could gain no recognition.

There were some poor tactical judgements from time to time, however. On 16 August at Vrieskraal in the eastern Transvaal two squadrons of the Nineteenth were ambushed by the Johannesburg Commando. They had been advancing without proper scouts through thick bush country and, on seeing cattle placed as bait by the Boers, had broken ranks to round them up. Fortunately, the Eighteenth were not far behind, being the other regiment in a column commanded by Kitchener's brother. Although casualties in both regiments were not heavy, the Boers made off with thirty-five horses, thirty rifles and 2,000 rounds of ammunition. Such successes helped significantly to sustain Boer operations when most other sources of supply were being closed off.

Even this incident was not without a certain lightness which characterized the war right to the end. Fighting for the Boers were a number of Irish-American volunteers. Neither the Irish nor the Americans were enamoured of the British at their colonial best, and the Irish Americans combined both emotion and principle in their opposition. At Vrieskraal the Commando took, and released the same day, twenty-four of the Nineteenth, one of the Boers recording that he:

"found a few of our Irish Americans swapping clothing with the captured soldiers. Some of the Tommies who were relieved of their boots had rolled their puttees around their feet as protection against the thorns. . . I met Joe Wade, neatly dressed in the uniform of one of the 19th talking amiably to a soldier who was wearing in exchange Joe's tattered trousers patched and torn to ribbons. . . A little distance away stood a young Hussar, wearing the limp and greasy hat of his captor. . . One man was allowed to retain his trousers, because, it was thought, he had received too great a fright"!

The second of Kitchener's innovations was the extension of the 'blockhouse' system. After Pretoria had fallen, Roberts ordered the construction of blockhouses at one-and-a-half-mile intervals along the length of the Pretoria–Newcastle railway. Each contained a section of six men and they were successful in limiting attacks on the line. Kitchener decided to extend the system to other lines and into the *veldt* itself. Long cross-country lines were constructed during the latter half of 1901 and their effect was very marked: they provided the features, in the absence of natural ones, on which the ambushing, patrolling and sweeping could pivot. By the end of the war there were 8,000 blockhouses, some at intervals of a mile or less, strongly fortified, linked by telegraph or flare signalling, often with barbed wire between and many with machine guns on fixed lines. The manpower bill for all this was not small: 50,000 soldiers or constabulary at any one time were deployed on these lines.

The Cavalry, however, were spared the tedium of blockhouse duty. Instead, their mobile operations between the lines were stepped up, unfortunately just as the wet season was beginning (September). The three regiments caught a great many Boers, their cattle and wagons, in both day and night operations, though at a small but steadily mounting cost in men and at a much greater one in horses. The Eighteenth's history describes a typical operation:

"Sighting them [a large commando under Botha] after a long march, we gave chase as far as Kaffirstad, and succeeded in capturing thirty-six of them, with a number of wagons and cattle. Forty miles having now been covered, we halted for the night, the Regiment as rearguard, with the enemy close on us, and by the time we got back we had lost thirty-seven horses through fatigue and exhaustion, all of which had to be shot."

There were occasional problems with 'friendly fire': on 30 March, 1902, two troopers of the Nineteenth were injured when several blockhouses opened up on their column.

Kitchener's operational concept worked, however, because he was given the resources to pursue it and he personally possessed the ruthlessness to see it through. The destruction of the farms was a particularly savage variation of the old-fashioned 'scorched-earth policy' and required a ruthless resolve. In the so-called 'concentration camps', not in any way to be likened to those bearing the same name in the Second World War, there was terrible loss through disease and faulty nutrition: probably not less than 20,000 Boer women and children died in them. This was no conscious part of policy, but it had its effect on the burghers. Kitchener's resistance to changing this policy in the face of growing public disquiet took a remarkably steady nerve. In May 1902 the Boers, split by internal dissension over continuing the resistance, agreed to an effectively unconditional surrender.

The Thirteenth and Eighteenth left for Aldershot by the end of the year and the Nineteenth left the following April for the Curragh. Their losses and honours had been remarkably similar. The Thirteenth lost eighty men in all, seventeen killed in action, the remainder dying of various causes including forty-six from enteric. The regiment were awarded a CB, four DSOs and five DCMs. The Eighteenth lost ninety-three men and won a VC, CB, eight DSOs and ten DCMs (and fifty-seven Mentions in Despatches). The Nineteenth lost eighty-three men and gained a CB, three DSOs and eight DCMs. The campaign honour *South Africa 1899–1902* is shared by all three regiments, as is the battle honour *Ladysmith* – the Eighteenth and Nineteenth for the *Defence of* and the Thirteenth for the *Relief of*.

The regiments' performance, the Cavalry's as a whole, had been uneven. Conan Doyle's belief that the Cavalry's opportunity for distinction had been limited seems correct, but at an individual level the honours and awards testify to resourcefulness and courage. The casualty figures, though not high by the usual standards, showed nevertheless the truth of his other assertion that "The work of scouting and patrolling is the most dangerous duty which a soldier can undertake."

CHAPTER 10

Charging Ahead

"Short service cavalry are necessarily at a disadvantage in that the recruit has to learn to ride as well as to learn all the other requirements of a cavalry soldier in a limited period of time, and in this respect the British and Indian armies have a considerable advantage over the cavalries of the Continental Powers, which should, to a certain extent, make up for deficiency in numbers."

Lieutenant-Colonel F.M. EDWARDS, 1910

Legacy of the Boer War; 18H and 19H in England and Ireland; 13H and 15H in India; 15H in South Africa; 15H returns to England. The coming of War in Europe.

In 1910 Colonel Edwards, a noted military commentator and later commander of the Meerut Cavalry Brigade, could point with some confidence to the British cavalry's qualitative edge over their potential continental adversaries and allies. In 1914 there was little doubt whatever about it, and after a few months' fighting, as will be seen in the next chapter, the edge had been demonstrably established. A decade earlier, however, it was certainly not the case.

At the end of the Boer War the Government wanted to know why it had taken almost three years of hard fighting by nearly half a million British and Imperial troops, 250,000 of which were British regulars, to subdue, at most, 50,000 armed Dutch settlers. A royal commission and several committees were set up to find the reasons. A very public debate took place in parallel. The official findings did not fudge the issues: the conclusions were that, save in one respect alone, courage, the Army had faltered in every way, and from top to bottom. Only the relatively recently formed Army Service Corps received praise for its professional performance.

The Cavalry in particular drew heavy criticism. The standard of training among their officers was said by the Akers-Douglas committee to be the worst in the Service. The German General Staff's report on the war concluded that the Cavalry "was trained first of all for attack, but only insufficiently in the use of the carbine, and, as was the case with the infantry, it had not sufficient facilities for training. The want of these rendered it all the more difficult for the cavalry to understand the tactics of the other arms."

Most alarmingly, however, the Cavalry seemed unable to keep their horses fit for service during arduous field conditions. The Army as a whole employed more than half a million horses during the war, and destroyed 350,000 of them in the process. The 6th Dragoon Guards destroyed 3,750 horses in two and a half years, one horse for every three and a half miles the regiment covered, five horses per man during the war. There is nothing to show that this regiment's horse management was notably worse than any other's. The British cavalry's horsemanship had often been criticized. In the Peninsular War it was remarked that their horses were often worn to rags whereas those of the King's German Legion always seemed to keep their condition. General Sir John Burgoyne, who had raised the 16th Light Dragoons, had pointed to this contrast during the American Revolutionary War, saying that the Hanoverians were always able to put 100 horses in the ranks to the British ten. Captain Cavalié Mercer, of the Horse Artillery, wrote after Waterloo that the German dragoon would sell everything he had to feed his horse whereas his British counterpart looked upon the animal "as a curse and perpetual source of drudgery to himself" and would "sell his horse itself for spirits". The state of things in the Cavalry Division in the Crimea forty years later was notorious, as was seen in Chapter Seven.

There were exceptions to this. It all depended on the knowledge and diligence of the officers. Sir Charles Oman, writing of the Peninsula, says, "the trooper of 1810 was, when not well looked after by his officer, a bad horsemaster, careless as to feeding his mount, and more so as to saddle-galls, and such like." Presumably, when the officers did *their* job the trooper did *his*. There was a notable feat of exemplary horsemastership in 1885 during the Nile campaign. The 19th Hussars substituted their big English and Irish troop horses with Syrian Arabs, and covered over 1,500 miles during the seven months' operations. Water and forage were in continual short supply, but of the 350 ponies which began the campaign, only forty-eight died of anything but enemy fire. "The horses were saved on every possible occasion, and by every possible device," the commanding officer's report says. "The men never sat on their horses' backs for a moment longer than necessary. Marches in column were avoided, extended line being used, so that each horse had pure air to breath; when picketed, horses always had plenty of room and their heads to the breeze; when possible, they were washed two or three times a week, which tended much towards their healthy condition."

As a 19th Hussar, Lieutenant-General Sir John French, who had been knighted in the war honours, knew the standards attainable. He told the Royal Commission that training, especially in the regiments from England, had been too narrow:

> "They understood stable management better than the care of horses in the field. . . . For example, at the commencement of the campaign, partly owing to strict orders re looting, many opportunities for foraging were neglected. . . . Few officers or men understood how to feed horses on maize, barley or wheat, which were often to be found on the farms; they either over-fed them, thereby impairing their digestion and giving them Laminitis, or refused to risk this evil, neglecting available supplies."

If all this had changed by 1914, what had happened to bring these changes about?

The regiments themselves knew that something had to be

done, and this was probably the most important factor. But they were aided by changes in organization, equipment and training methods, and by the direction they received from the War Office. The Thirteenth and Fifteenth, in India throughout most of the period, trained under the energetic direction of the young Major-General Douglas Haig, who had been rapidly promoted after the war and was Inspector General of Cavalry there. Haig had seen much in South Africa, where he had served at regimental duty and with the staff, and was a 'thinker'. In England and Ireland the Eighteenth and Nineteenth came under the supervision of the young Major-General Robert Baden-Powell, who had also been rapidly promoted and was Inspector-General of Cavalry Great Britain and Ireland. B-P was a thinker too, but in a very down-to-earth, practical way. Between B-P and Haig almost every cavalry issue, from the highest level to the simplest issue of horsemastership, was thought through. At the tactical level they took the Cavalry way ahead of all but that of the United States.

Horsemastership in the field was improved by a combination of more field training and by troopers being taught in a more practical way rather than by the formality of 'riding school'.

"Our training now," wrote Baden-Powell in 1906, "has to be effected by *instruction* rather than mere drill . . . the useless N.C.O. who was formerly considered efficient if he was able to throw up his chin and to spout, parrotwise, a string of aids to a squad of men, no longer passes muster where 'instruction' to each recruit is required in his own words and by his own demonstration."

The post of riding master was in fact officially abolished, and responsibility for training passed from the adjutant, RM and RSM to the squadron leader and his officers. In short, by 1914 each trooper knew how to keep his horse in condition in the field because he had received appropriate individual training by the men with whom he would actually be fighting.

There were important equipment innovations too. The short-magazine Lee-Enfield rifle, the 'SMLE', with which the whole of the British Expeditionary Force went to war in August 1914, was issued to all the cavalry. It was short enough for cavalry work, and infinitely superior to the carbines with which the French and German cavalry were equipped. Once they had the same rifle as the infantry there was no longer any reason for cavalry fire tactics to be neglected: in 1909 the Thirteenth's annual musketry returns show 271 marksmen, 250 first-class shots, 27 second-class and no third-classes. The Fifteenth carried off many shooting trophies at this time too, and in 1909 Sergeant Hanks won the 'Gold Jewel' for best marksman in India, the first time it had been won by a cavalryman. The BEF's commander-in-chief was to have good cause to be grateful for cavalry marksmanship when the Eighteenth and Nineteenth, dismounted, held vital sectors of the line at the first and second battles of Ypres.

The thorough overhaul of cavalry tactics resulted in new training manuals with less emphasis on the squadron charge in line and more on such things as scouting. B-P's subsequent founding of the Boy Scout movement is not always associated with his development of cavalry scouting principles. There was, too, a good deal of heated argument as to whether there was any future for the '*arme blanche*', the sword and lance; many believed that cavalry combat would in the future be a matter of the rifle only. While the arguments raged, and whole books were written on the subject in Britain and abroad, most regiments simply got on with balanced training in both. In the event, they seem to have achieved the correct balance, as will be seen in the next chapter.

Large-scale manoeuvres took place in southern England with increasing regularity, following the continental pattern. In 1910, for instance, work-up training at brigade and divisional level took place throughout south-west England preparatory to the 'Army Manoeuvres' themselves in September. The Eighteenth, who had moved to Ireland in 1907, together with the rest of the 3rd Cavalry Brigade from The Curragh, acted as enemy for these manoeuvres. "Billeting on large farms was practised," records the regiment's diary, "and we made many friends among the large dairy farmers in the West of England."

The establishment of permanent brigades, with dedicated commanders and staff, was a relatively new departure. Hitherto, they had been largely ad hoc affairs thrown together for a particular operation, as were divisions. In 1906, however, the Secretary of State for War in the new Liberal government, Richard Haldane, had begun the process which put this chaotic system to rights. He was not a soldier: he was a lawyer, and he had the lawyer's sharp and uncluttered mind. He asked the fundamental question, "What is the Army *for?*" and would not proceed until everyone was clear about the answer. What emerged as the answer was that the Army's purpose was to fight beside the French in case of German aggression. From this followed a re-shaping of the higher organization of defence and the Field Army.

The brigades were the focus for tactical debate and training. Almost all their commanders had distinguished themselves in South Africa and were clear about the vital relationship between fire and manoeuvre. Lord Carnock's *History of the 15th The King's Hussars 1914-1922* sums it up admirably: "The British Army, of all those engaged on the Western Front, had at this period the greatest experience of the power of modern weapons. . . . It might therefore be suggested that the training of the British Army was in many respects far in advance of that of the other Powers." Correlli Barnett puts it even more enthusiastically: "Not since the days of the Commonwealth had the British Army been so generally gripped with a sense of professional purpose in peacetime."

But while the British cavalry's lead over the continentals was widening through the positive efforts of its commanders it was also being widened because of the astonishing conservatism in the German and French armies. The 1902 *Review of Reviews* describes the Kaiser's autumn manoeuvres:

"Lord Roberts, Mr Brodrick [war minister], General Kelly-Kenny and General French attended the scene of mimic war. These soldiers, fresh from the realities of war in South Africa must have smiled in their sleeves at the puerility of the imposing display which took place when the Kaiser, placing himself at the head of his cavalry brigades, led several thousand men for four miles in what was meant to be a dashing charge upon the enemy's flank. In real war every saddle would have been empty long before the foremost files had got within eight hundred yards of the enemy's position."

This might have been forgiven so soon after the Boer War had finished, and before the German General Staff's thorough examination of the war's lessons had been drawn, but the faults persisted. Observers were reporting the same scenes at the annual manoeuvres ten years later.

It was not all training of course for the British: there was plenty of sport and games. Polo emerged as *the* game for the officers. It had been popular for decades in India but only began to take root in England in the last quarter of the Nineteenth Century. The accolade of 'father of English polo' belongs by tradition to a Thirteenth officer, Captain John Watson, who helped devise the rules of the modern game and who, in 1886, captained the first British international team. Cricket and football were enjoyed by all ranks. The 'Cavalry Cup', which originated in 1896, was by this time a keenly contested football competition and one in which The Light Dragoons' forebears established an early reputation. Hunting was actively encouraged; indeed it was considered to be indispensable training in developing an officer's eye for ground. There can be no doubt that it was. Nor could there be any doubt that steeplechasing tested his courage. England and Ireland were perfect for cavalry training at this time: there was little wire in the countryside and the railway network was so extensive, and trains so frequent, that returning to camp after covering miles in the hunting field simply meant going to a nearby station and arranging for the horsebox in the siding to be attached to the next train.

From time to time the Cavalry was still called on to assist the civil powers. 1910 and 1911 were particularly troublesome years in the coalfields and docks. In August 1911 a squadron of the Eighteenth was attacked while escorting prisoners to jail in Liverpool. Two rioters were killed and two wounded in the follow-up. The dress for these duties is interesting: khaki, introduced in the 1890s, and by 1904 universal for field dress, was worn with the busby minus plume instead of the khaki forage cap. The reason for this is not entirely clear, but it was probably for regimental 'show' and for some measure of protection to the head, steel helmets not coming into general service until 1916.

Life for the Thirteenth and Fifteenth in India mirrored that of the Eighteenth and Nineteenth at home. The British Army in India, and the Indian Army, were not there simply to hold the country against its native population. Kitchener, who had taken over as Commander-in-Chief India shortly after returning from the Boer War, had made it clear that their chief role was to defend the North-West Frontier from a Russian invasion through Afghanistan. From this followed much the same equipment and training requirements as for Haldane's army at home.

Sport was encouraged as much as it was in England and Ireland. If hunting were not so smart as it was in Gloucestershire it was a no less useful form of training, for the jackal was every bit as cunning as the fox. Pig-sticking and big-game shooting were additional tests of skill and courage. Only the 8th Hussars won the Kadir Cup, the 'blue riband of hog hunting', more times than the Fifteenth during the seventy-three years the competition ran. In 1883 the Cup was won by Lieutenant Baden-Powell who then, characteristically, wrote a handbook on the sport. Rough shooting was available to all ranks. Unfortunately, history does not relate what happened to the two troopers of the Thirteenth who brought down a brace of peacocks in the hills near Meerut: peacocks were sacred birds to the Hindus and were protected by the severest penalties. Football, cricket and athletics were promoted vigorously and hockey, still a relatively new game, was popular. Show jumping, though not yet called that, was also beginning to gain popularity among the NCOs and troopers, and tent-pegging, a by-product of pig-sticking, was universally popular.

Inter-regimental sport was also seen as a powerful aid to building *esprit*, both regimental and brigade. Strong bonds were established between regiments at this time. In India, where longer periods stationed together presented greater opportunities for regiments to become thoroughly acquainted, some particularly strong links between British and Indian regiments were forged. None have been quite so enduring, however, as those between the Thirteenth and Skinner's Horse. It began in Meerut in 1914: a subaltern's letter home records, "Skinner's Horse are in Meerut with us now. They are an extraordinarily good and very sporting lot." How this chance stationing together led to today's affiliation will be seen in subsequent chapters.

Ceremonial played an important rôle in the duties of a regiment in India. It was part of the panoply of the Raj's power, an intangible but real factor in the acquiescence of the Indian princes. The Thirteenth and Fifteenth took part in the two great *durbars* of the decade, the grand assemblies of princes and other potentates to honour the Crown. The first was in 1903 to mark the accession of King Edward VII, where the Fifteenth found escorts for the representative royal parties. The second was in 1912 to mark the accession of King George V, who attended in person with Queen Mary, where the Thirteenth furnished the escort for the Queen's visit to Agra. On each occasion the regiments fielded a representative trumpeter to join with others for the great fanfares. The trumpets and banners used on these occasions, together with the one used by the Fifteenth to herald the proclamation of Queen Victoria as Empress of India, are preserved in the Light Dragoons' officers' mess.

The Fifteenth left India for South Africa in 1909 to begin three years' garrison duties at Durban. They were entirely peaceful years. The South Africa Act had received royal assent in September 1909, creating the Union of South Africa, a dominion under the British crown with equal status for people of British or Dutch descent. In the following year Louis Botha's moderate Boer nationalist party won the election. So the man who only a few years before had led the Boer commandos with such tenacity now became the Union's first prime minister.

These three years gave the Fifteenth even more opportunity for worthwhile field training and on their return to England in January, 1913, after an absence overseas of thirteen years, they were as proficient as any regiment at home thanks to the systematic approach to doctrine and training which had been applied by Baden-Powell, Haig and their successors.

* * *

It was a strange turn of events which saw, by 1914, Britain's traditional allies, the Germans, and her traditional enemy, the French, with their roles reversed. Anglo-German relations had been deteriorating for two decades due to naval rivalry and, to an extent, trade competition. Conversely, Anglo-French friction had been all but eliminated in 1904 by the signing of an agreement which settled a number of minor, though provocative, colonial disputes. This, the '*Entente Cordiale*', though neither an alliance nor anti-German in intention, strengthened Anglo-French military collaboration in the face of the growing German threat. In 1907 Britain added an 'understanding' to the *Entente* with France's ally Russia. Europe began increasingly to cleave along the lines of the 'Triple Alliance' (Germany, Austria, Italy) and the 'Triple *Entente*' (France, Russia, Great Britain). The general staffs began to elaborate their war plans in the event of diplomacy failing.

On 28 June, 1914, a chance occurrence set in motion the whole complicated machinery of mobilization plans throughout Europe. The Austrian Archduke Franz Ferdinand and his wife were assassinated by a Serbian nationalist in Sarajevo, capital of the Austrian province of Bosnia. The occurrence itself was hardly cataclysmic but Austria could not ignore it without appearing weak and thereby encouraging further Russian influence with the Slavs. It also gave Austria the pretext, however, to deal with Serbia, for, as she saw it, the Serbs never lost an opportunity to stir up sedition in her neighbouring Slav provinces. Serbia was given an impossible ultimatum, and Austria declared war when the reply predictably failed to satisfy her.

But Serbia enjoyed the 'protection' of Russia. Russian plans did not, however, allow for partial mobilization against Austria, but only for full mobilization against both Austria *and* Germany. As soon as Russia announced general mobilization, therefore, Germany had little alternative but to mobilize. This was because the German war strategy, acknowledging the dangers of fighting on two fronts simultaneously, required the rapid defeat of France so that forces could then be switched to the east over the superior German railway system to deal with Russia. 'Rapid' meant only six weeks and, according to the 'Schlieffen Plan', of which more in the next chapter, this meant an attack through neutral Belgium as soon as mobilization was completed.

Britain was not bound by treaty to come to France's aid, though the strategic interest and moral obligation to do so was widely acknowledged: at the very least, inaction would have been a betrayal of the trust implicit in the previous eight years' staff talks (none of which, incidentally, had ever been submitted to Cabinet approval). But Belgian neutrality was another matter. In his magisterial work *Dreadnought – Britain, Germany and the Coming of the Great War*, Robert Massie sets the issue in its broader historical context:

"Since the sixteenth century, England had been unwilling to see the Low Countries in the hands of a Great Power. To keep the Channel coast out of threatening hands, England had fought Philip II of Spain, Louis XIV, and the Emperor Napoleon. The nation of Belgium had arisen from the ruins of Bonaparte's empire, and in 1839 its perpetual neutrality had been guaranteed by France, Britain, Prussia and Austria. When war broke out between Prussia and France in 1870 [the war which probably saved the Nineteenth from disbandment again], Gladstone made certain that Bismarck understood Britain's commitment to Belgian neutrality. The Prussian Chancellor gave assurances and the army of the elder Moltke advanced into France without trespassing on Belgium. The language of the 1839 treaty was unusual on one point: it gave the signatories the right, but not the duty, of intervention in case of violation."

Germany declared war on France on 3 August, 1914, and invaded Belgium the same day. Britain declared war and began mobilizing the following day. Over-rigid military planning had precipitated hostilities. As the historian A.J.P. Taylor has described it, this was war by railway timetable.

CHAPTER 11

Still a Use for Cavalry

"The latter course of the war made cavalry unusable, and many sarcastic things have been written about it. . . . But August 1914 had not yet seen that transformation take place; there was still a use for cavalry, if properly trained and handled. Ironically, it was only the British cavalry, under some of the generals who came in for so much scorn later, that was so trained".

JOHN TERRAINE, *Mons*

15H, 18H, 19H with the BEF to France; 13H from India to France; 1914-1916 battles.

Sometime during the evening of 7 August, 1914, the commanding officer of the 18th Hussars (Queen Mary's Own) received a telephone call to inform him that Her Majesty the Queen intended to come to Tidworth the next day to bid farewell to her regiment before its departure for France. Although the Eighteenth had become the 'Princess of Wales's Own' in 1903 to mark their services in the Boer War, and 'Queen Mary's Own' in 1910 on the accession of George V, the Queen herself had not been appointed Colonel-in-Chief until June, 1914. Lieutenant-Colonel C.K. Burnett, who had assumed command only six months earlier, having previously been the senior major, must have had mixed feelings: the regiment was in the middle of its mobilization, including the return of reservists to the colours and the collection of the additional horses needed to bring it up to war establishment, and now the Queen of England was going to visit. There is no record of the ensuing instructions, but Burnett met Queen Mary at Bulford station (long since demolished and the line lifted) the following morning and conveyed her to Aliwal Barracks, where the regiment was drawn up on parade by the cricket ground ready for inspection. The district and brigade commanders were also present for good measure!

The Eighteenth's history records that "in a short time the Regiment marched past complete for war in every detail, together with its first line transport, and forming up again advanced at the charge to within a few paces of where Her Majesty stood and with swords in the air gave her three resounding cheers." No doubt not *every* detail was complete for war, but it is certainly true that mobilization of the entire army went with astonishing, and unprecedented, smoothness. The Fifteenth, at their barracks in Aldershot, noted that reservists arrived punctually, "equipped and accoutred to the last button". They were also pleased that "splendid horses joined – many from famous hunt stables". The regiment had been dismayed on returning to England eighteen months earlier to find that their remounts were cobs from the mounted infantry, the concept of 'MI' having been abandoned. The cobs soon found favour, however, and won high praise subsequently as troop horses in France.

In India the Thirteenth fretted. It was not at all clear whether they were going to be needed. On 9 August Lieutenant G.R Watson-Smyth wrote home: "I have just gone to the Club, and a wire has come in saying that the Brigade is not for it. Rotten luck." Again, a fortnight later, he wrote: "We are carrying on in the same way as if there were no war in the world. . . . It really is a bit too thick that here are we, the most efficient Cavalry in the world, stuck in this horrid country. . . . Not a hope of our going to war." Twelve months later Watson-Smyth was carried wounded from a trench in France. The war was meant to have been over by Christmas.

The plans agreed by Haldane in the preceding decade, and subsequently worked at in great detail by the general staff, were for a British expeditionary force (BEF) to comprise two corps and a cavalry division of five brigades. The Eighteenth had since 1910 been part of the 2nd Cavalry Brigade at Tidworth, together with the 9th Lancers and 4th Dragoon Guards, under the command of the immensely able Brigadier-General H. de B. de Lisle, an infantryman who had commanded his mounted infantry column in South Africa with conspicuous success. De Lisle had no doubt about the nature of what was facing them: at an officers' study period during the build-up he told his brigade, "Make no mistake, gentlemen, we are in for a long and bitter war." One of the other cavalry brigades, the fifth, was under the command of Brigadier-General Sir Philip Chetwode who had joined the Nineteenth in 1890 and won a DSO with them in South Africa.

The Fifteenth and Nineteenth were (infantry) divisional cavalry. This was a relatively new concept and one which both regiments had done much to develop. It was not as glamorous as working in Major-General E.H. Allenby's Cavalry Division; it was, however, often infinitely more arduous because the squadrons were frequently integrated with the infantry brigades. At mobilization, A Squadron 15th Hussars were under command 1st Division and B Squadron were with 2nd Division. In the 2nd Corps, C Squadron were with 3rd Division, A Squadron 19th Hussars were under command 5th Division, and B Squadron were with 4th Division. Regimental headquarters of both regiments did not initially deploy to France. The BEF itself was commanded by Field-Marshal Sir John French, late of the 19th Hussars and lately CIGS.

On 5 August, the first day of full mobilization, commanding officers received files of documents, all *Top Secret*, detailing precisely their regiments' movements to their un-named ports of embarkation. They were not over-wordy:

"Train No 287Y will arrive at siding D at 1235 am August 15th.
You will complete loading by 3.40 am.
This train will leave siding E at 9.45 am, August 15th.
You will march onto the platform at 9.30 am and complete your entraining by 9.40 am."

Many officers thought it all rather un-British, but it worked with clockwork precision. Not that at this stage anyone in the regiments knew their ultimate destination, or even port of disembarkation. Nor did the captains of the transports: the three regiments, along with most of the BEF, sailed from Southampton, but it was only once the ships had put out to sea that their masters were allowed to open their sealed orders to discover their destination.

The Eighteenth discovered theirs was Boulogne, the port from which most of the cavalry had returned to England after the Peninsular Campaign exactly one hundred years and one month earlier. Officers were puzzled, therefore, that the men began singing "Here we are, here we are, here we are again"! For the Nineteenth it was the first time they had set foot or hoof on continental Europe.

By train, the regiments moved to the BEF's concentration area around Maubeuge on the Belgian border. Here it was intended that the British force was to extend the French left flank to meet the German swing through Belgium. Within days, all three regiments would be in contact with the enemy, contact which, though occasionally broken and rest snatched, would continue until the middle of November, after which the long stalemate of the trenches would begin. The next three months dashed German hopes of rapid victory. To understand the significance of these three months, and of the part which the Fifteenth, Eighteenth and Nineteenth played in the dashing of these hopes, and why their subsequent four years were spent in and out of the trenches in this corner of Flanders and north-west France, it is necessary to understand the German operational plan – the *Schlieffen Plan*.

Field-Marshal Count von Schlieffen was Chief of the German Great General Staff from 1891 to 1905. His plan, adopted in 1905, made bold use of Germany's excellent railway system. Calculating on Russia's much slower mobilization, her railway system being quite the opposite of Germany's in efficiency, his plan allowed for only ten divisions to hold a Russian offensive against East Prussia. The whole weight of the rapidly mobilized

German army would be thrown against the French and, after victory in six weeks, the army would then be transferred by the super-efficient German railways to confront the Russian masses in the east.

The difficulty in achieving a six-week victory lay in the powerful fortress system which France had constructed on their common border after the Franco-Prussian war of 1870. It would be necessary to outflank these defences, but this could only be done by violating Belgian (and Luxembourg) neutrality. No delay through Belgium could be afforded: the Belgian fortresses would have to be quickly reduced and her army would have to be swept aside by overwhelming numbers. The great wheeling movement through Belgium would have to be so deep and strong that it would outflank any extension of the French line towards the Channel. Schlieffen therefore planned the movement to be like a ball on the end of a chain, the chain itself anchored in Alsace-Lorraine with eight divisions. The chain and ball, some fifty-four divisions, would swing through the Ardennes, Brabant, Flanders and Picardy, past the left of the French line, curving round the west of Paris, masking the capital and pinning the French armies *from behind* against their own fortress system.

There was only one way to defeat such an operational plan and that was to destroy the momentum of the ball itself: the rest of the chain was of secondary importance. The allied main effort should therefore have been from the outset in the west, in Artois and Picardy. It wasn't. The French, with their belief in the absolute superiority of the offensive, attacked straightaway along the German border. The danger in this was that it was playing into the hands of the Schlieffen Plan itself. Basil Liddell Hart, the great post-war military analyst, likened it to a revolving door: "If a man pressed heavily on one side, the other would swing round and hit him in the back." By not strengthening the left, and pressing heavily on one side, the French were only hastening the swing of the door and the blow on the back. Two things prevented the revolving door effect, however. First, the Germans did not give the door a strong enough initial push, and secondly, a small but irritating obstruction, a thin end of a wedge, arrested the swing. This small obstruction was the BEF, what the Kaiser referred to as "Sir John French's contemptible little army", and forever afterwards 'The Old Contemptibles'.

The weakened push was the result of Schlieffen's successor, von Moltke, having a fainter heart. He had strengthened both the defences in East Prussia and at the pivot (Alsace-Lorraine) at the expense of the right wing. The concept of main effort was crucial to the whole plan: von Schlieffen's dying words in 1913 are reported to have been, "It must come to a fight. Only make the right wing strong." But in 1914 Moltke feared the immediate implications of making the right wing strong. Much has been written to challenge the notion that the Schlieffen Plan was a beautifully-crafted and infallible plan which failed only because Moltke departed from its prescription. It is not that simple, and *no* plan can approach infallibility, but it is certain that without an immensely strong right the plan's chances of success were low. The German right *had* to outflank, and envelop, the French left, and this would mean a wheeling movement so wide that, again in Schlieffen's own words, the Germans would be "brushing the channel ports with their sleeves". In the event, they were not strong enough to wheel within arms' length of the coast.

The Belgian army's resistance was greater than had been expected, and the German advance was therefore slower than predicted. This gave the allies the opportunity for offensive action rather than preparing for a passive defence along the Belgian border.

The British were hesitant at first but the French pushed ahead. On 21 August the BEF finally crossed the border and began moving up to Mons, on the exposed left flank of the French 5th Corps. They were expecting to take part in a counter-move against the German 1st Army. The Cavalry Division covered this move and contact was made with the German cavalry early the following day. The 4th Dragoon Guards, in the 2nd Cavalry Brigade with the Eighteenth, fired the first shots in the BEF's war and captured several prisoners. During this action Allenby's cavalry formed the impression that the Germans were

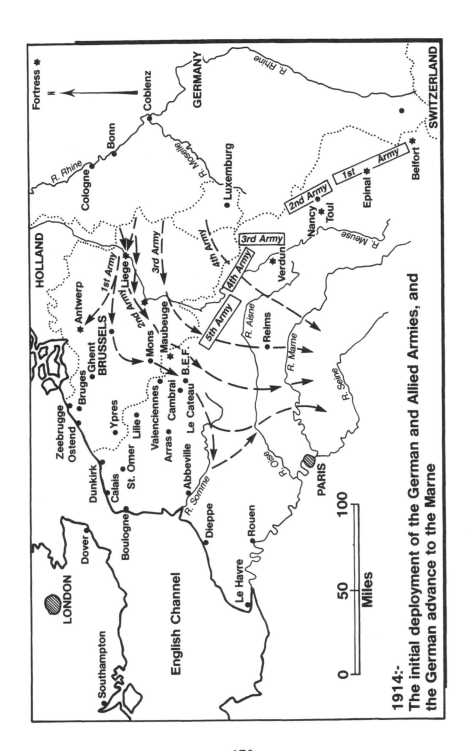

1914:-
The initial deployment of the German and Allied Armies, and the German advance to the Marne

173

following up in strength, and this was confirmed by the Royal Flying Corps' reconnaissance. It was, too, the commander of the French 5th Army's impression: General Lanrezac began to worry about *both* his flanks being enveloped – he was in something of a salient and appeared to have two armies bearing down on him, for the Germans had 'hooked in' short.

Lanrezac asked the BEF to hold at Mons for twenty-four hours while he extricated himself from the potential noose. It was not ideal ground for a defensive battle. It had not been selected as such – it just happened to be the place where the BEF had halted in the advance that never came off. The British divisions hastily occupied defensive positions among the slag heaps and colliery buildings of this coal-mining district (The Light Dragoons, Yorkshiremen and Geordies, will recognize the sort of scene). As was remarked earlier, the Cavalry Division may have been the more glamorous with its long-range scouting and opportunities for dashing action, but the divisional cavalry, like sheepdogs, really had their work cut out to get their infantry brigades into position.

The next day, 23 August, the Battle of Mons was fought in earnest. Some of the first fighting fell to A Squadron 15th Hussars, reconnoitring east of Mons for 3rd Division, soon after first light. Two troops sustained several casualties, many of which could not be recovered. The squadron second-in-command fell close to the main road but was rescued by a passing civilian car, despite rifle fire and shelling, and carried to a dressing station. The two troops only managed to extricate themselves with great difficulty, for a machine gun was enfilading a wire fence which blocked their line of escape: Corporal Charles Garforth, under intense fire, dismounted and ran forward to cut it in several places, and through these gaps the troops were able to gallop to relative safety.

The day's fighting was to be a triumph for the Infantry's disciplined and deadly-accurate sixteen-rounds-per-minute rapid fire. The German strength was growing, however, and towards the end of the day the general line had been pushed back in a number of places. The enemy had succeeded earlier in crossing the Condé Canal, which ran east-west across the defensive front and gave the position its only semblance of strength, in some numbers. These bridgeheads were rapidly reinforced during the day and proved too strong to counter-attack.

Withdrawal was ordered that night in order to conform with 5th (French) Army's retirement on the right. The following day, 24 August, was intensely busy for all three regiments as they covered the general withdrawal. The Eighteenth were badly mauled, losing a large number of horses. Cohesion in the 2nd Cavalry Brigade was lost for some time after a mounted charge by the 9th Lancers and 4th Dragoon Guards ran into trouble. The Fifteenth and Nineteenth had as hot a time, though less confused. Nonetheless, the best part of a squadron of the Fifteenth was cut down by machine-gun fire in the streets of one village after following up retreating German cavalry. B Squadron of the Nineteenth, 4th Division's cavalry, were delayed in the move up to Mons and only detrained at St Quentin on the afternoon of the 25th. They bivouacked that night at the village of Bohain having got lost trying to make contact with the division. At 2.00am, according to the diary kept throughout the war by Sergeant D. Brunton, there was:

"A sudden alarm. All around us was chaos and confusion. Details of various cavalry and infantry regiments, remnants of their units, and badly broken up, came hurrying past our little bivouac. We now hear that our little Army had been overwhelmed by the Germans and that we were in full retreat. . . . We now moved off to stop the rush of the enemy, and came into action at Monteoinet, under a heavy Artillery fire."

The divisional cavalry system on the whole worked well, however, during the withdrawal from Mons. The techniques evolved in training stood the test of action. The squadrons deployed a thin screen between the enemy and the infantry rearguard. The squadron leader kept a small fighting reserve centrally under his control, and a troop was detached to divisional headquarters for liaison and protection of the commander, with orderlies attached to the signal company. Lord Carnock's history best sums up the nature of this work:

> "It was said of the Rifles during the Peninsular War that the first shot and the last shot of every engagement were fired by a rifleman, and the same might apply to the 15th Hussars during the retreat from Mons."

By 27 August 1st and 2nd Cavalry Brigades had had to be combined, so great were the losses: of their six regiments, there were none with more than two squadrons, some with only one. On 29 August there was a general halt in 1st (British) Corps, and it was much needed. The horses had hardly been unsaddled since the 23rd and many badly needed shoeing. No doubt everyone needed sleep, but instead they worked. In the Fifteenth "every article of equipment was cleaned and repaired as quickly as the time allowed." The pause was covered by the Cavalry Division and the infantry brigade outpost lines. The heat continued to be stifling.

The pause was interrupted abruptly in the afternoon by orders to move patrols forward, and some sharp exchanges with the German cavalry developed, but they never seemed keen to press home their attacks or to follow up local successes vigorously: at this stage there were many gaps in the outpost lines which could have been penetrated. The retreat resumed at 4.30 the following morning, the sixth consecutive day of withdrawal. Other than the stand at Le Cateau, at which a squadron of both the Fifteenth and Nineteenth were present but did not play a major part, there had been nothing but withdrawal, and this was beginning to take its toll on morale across the whole of the force. But things could have been a lot worse: during the whole of this withdrawal south towards Paris there was nothing of substance on the British left, just bewildered French territorials and some of Sordet's cavalry.

While the BEF had been withdrawing, however, Joffre had begun assembling a new army, the Sixth, between Amiens and Paris. This comprised mainly troops brought by rail from the eastern fortresses and had initially been meant for the defence of the capital. By 30 August it, too, was being obliged to fall back in order to conform to the BEF's and the 5th (French) Army's retirement. The existence of this new army, makeshift though it was at this stage, posed a potential threat, however, to the German right flank which it overlapped. Orders were therefore given to the German 1st Army on 3 September to echelon itself slightly behind the 2nd Army, in order to be able to guard the flank, but to continue the pressure south on the BEF and 5th (French) Army.

The German 1st Army commander, General von Kluck, saw immediately that to do as ordered would inevitably mean a slackening of pressure on the allied left (his leading corps was fourteen miles ahead of 2nd Army and he would therefore have to pause for at least twenty-four hours to echelon as instructed). The German high command's intention of enveloping the French by swinging *west* of Paris had already had to be abandoned through insufficient strength and the tiring delays at the hands of the Belgian army (which had by this stage retired into the defensive perimeter of Antwerp). It was therefore essential to push the BEF and the 5th Army *south-east*, taking them away from Paris lest they should be able to make an effective junction with the 6th Army and the Paris garrison. If *this* occurred, then the only way the Germans could effect a turning movement would be to revert to the Schlieffen Plan's concept of encircling Paris – and 1st German Army no longer had the strength to do it. Initially, therefore, Von Kluck ignored the order to echelon and kept pushing the BEF.

The next day, 4 September, von Kluck began feeling distinctly uneasy about his right flank and signalled Moltke at Supreme Headquarters in Luxembourg for more information on Maunoury's 6th Army. The growing peril to the right flank was now plain to Moltke, and that evening orders were sent by wireless for both 1st and 2nd Armies to change direction and face south-west to guard against the anticipated attack by Maunoury. Wireless orders took a long time: besides the laborious manual encoding and decoding, the French were enjoying considerable success with jamming from the top of the Eiffel Tower. Moltke therefore sent a staff officer to explain the order so that the headstrong von Kluck could not wilfully misinterpret it.

The liaison officer arrived at 1st Army HQ during the evening of 5 September. The wireless message, sent at 7.45 the previous evening, had reached von Kluck at only 6.00 that morning. Since his army had resumed its advance at 4.00 am he had ignored the order, maintaining instead one corps to guard his open flank. By the time Moltke's emissary arrived, however, this corps had had a sharp brush with some of Maunoury's troops and von Kluck was distinctly less headstrong. He agreed to comply. He turned his army westward to counter the growing threat from Maunoury, and in so doing opened a gap between himself and 2nd Army.

The Eighteenth had felt the pressure slackening as early as 3 September, and the whole of the Cavalry Division had had two nights of relative rest. They were now in the eastern environs of Paris, "passing the outer fortifications and watching the morning trains take their quota of businessmen into the city". Fighting seemed unreal in these surroundings, and all were getting concerned because they had outrun their maps and the right ones were not forthcoming except from guide books and the like. The Fifteenth had felt the pressure slacken too, although they had a few sharp exchanges with cavalry patrols while screening the preparation of bridge demolitions over the Marne. Corporal Garforth, under intense fire, returned and rescued his troop sergeant who was pinned under his own horse, having come down at a ditch which his patrol had had to cross at a gallop to escape from two enemy squadrons which had caught them by surprise. For this, and his brave conduct at Mons, he was awarded the Victoria Cross.

On the morning of 6 September Maunoury struck. Reinforced by 6,000 of the Paris garrison hastily conveyed from the city in Renault taxicabs, the brilliant improvisation of the veteran city commandant General Gallieni, it achieved complete tactical surprise. It was but one part of Joffre's grand counter-offensive, however, which included the 5th Army, under a new commander, its previous one having been sacked for timidity, and the

40. *"Even allowing for the absence of female company it was an officer's life verging on the ideal."* (p.216) Young officers of the 15th/19th Hussars and their personal servants at Risalpur, 1930.

41. *"A thinker, but in a down-to-earth, practical way."* Lieutenant-General The Lord Baden-Powell, Colonel of the 13th/18th Hussars, addresses the regiment at Shorncliffe, 1928.

42. *"Determined to modernize the Army as much as was politically and economically possible - and as rapidly as its conservative elements would permit."(p.218)* It was 1936 before the 15th/19th Hussar began to feel the effects of the policy of mechanization, however. Part of the Signal Troop on exercise in Dorset that year.

43. *"Did not actually receive its Vickers light tanks until the middle of 1939."(p.220)* A few training prototypes arriving within the 15th/19th Hussars at York the previous year.

44. *"When 13th/18th's motorbikes arrived there were still no instructors. The bandsmen were simply given the handbook, told to teach themselves driving and maintenance, and generally to 'get on with it!'"*(p.221)

45. *"They managed somehow."*(p.222) By the summer of 1939, when Queen Mary again visited her regiment on the eve of war, in Shorncliffe, both 13th/18th and 15th/19th had been officially mechanized. There were grave deficiencies in equipment, however.

46. and 47. "'Sitzkrieg' at least allowed for some desperately needed training."(p.225) 13th/18th Hussars in France, 1939.

9th Army on its right. Between Maunoury's 6th Army and d'Esperey's 5th Army the BEF also went on to the offensive, hesitantly at first, but then with zeal and boldness, plunging deep into the gap between the German 1st and 2nd Armies, a gap which was eventually to widen to some thirty miles.

The boost to morale was instantaneous. The squadrons of the Fifteenth and Nineteenth moved off at dawn to take up positions with the advance guards of their divisions. The Cavalry Division led the whole movement, keeping in touch with the French cavalry on the right. Each of the next twelve days saw fierce fighting with the German screen in the gap and with the flank guards of the 1st German Army.

On the 6th Sergeant Brunton's horse came down in a charge: "Had to shoot her as she had an open joint at knee." But he was back in action the following day "and had a splendid charge at some motor cyclists and infantry. Thoroughly routed them and took about 40 prisoners." The remarkable Corporal Garforth distinguished himself again too, his steady rifle fire pinning down two lorry-mounted machine guns which had cut up the patrol he was in, so that the casualties could be extricated.

Although by 8 September Maunoury's counter-attack had been beaten off, the German 1st and 2nd Armies were retreating. 6th and 5th French armies on the left and right, and the BEF in the middle followed up. They withdrew, or were pushed, to the River Aisne, elements of the Cavalry Division, including the Eighteenth, penetrating up to forty miles to the rear of von Kluck's army. Even allowing for exaggeration in descriptions of the outrages committed by "fiendish hordes of Germans" there is no doubting the unpleasantness of some of the scenes the regiments found during this counter-move. Sergeant Brunton, with the British regular's innate sense of chivalry, describes riding through La Pountains: "Germans have destroyed and burnt the town and committed acts on the female population too awful to write about", remarks reminiscent of the Eighteenth's diarist after Waterloo – and in almost the same place – one hundred years earlier.

By the middle of September the Germans had recovered themselves sufficiently to make a strong stand along the Aisne, including some fierce counter-attacks by both artillery and infantry. Entrenching began and the cavalry were withdrawn from the firing lines though they remained at short notice to turn out to deal with any threatened penetration.

It was widely reported, though never verified, that on 10 September, 1914, von Moltke informed the Kaiser, "Majesty, we have lost the war". What is certain is that rapid victory, victory by *manoeuvre*, was no longer possible. The BEF's part in the defeat of the Germans' high hopes is clear, and the part played by the Fifteenth, Eighteenth and Nineteenth in the BEF's operations was continuous and significant. The Cavalry had gone to France confident but nonetheless slightly apprehensive of the Kaiser's cavalry, which had been impressing foreign observers so much at the annual manoeuvres in the previous decade. At the end of the retreat from Mons, when spirits might have been at their lowest, the GSO2 of the Cavalry Division wrote in his diary: "our men do not fear the German cavalry in the slightest and in every action, however small, have done well". The BEF's cavalry had matched them in horsemanship, excelled them in dash and with the sword and lance, and outshot them with the Lee-Enfield. Rarely can training have felt so worthwhile.

* * *

The Eighteenth were looking forward to the change: "We had had enough for a time of this semi-siege warfare and of long tramps from our horses, though we did not realize at the moment that this was only child's play to what was in store for us at no very distant date." In the closing days of September, 1914, Sir John French suggested to Joffre that the BEF be moved north-west into Flanders to shorten its lines of communication through the channel ports. This was agreed, and in little more than a fortnight the BEF was in its new position. This complex redeployment went without a hitch and without the Germans discovering the movement. The Cavalry Division marched the hundred and fifty miles or so from the Aisne to their new area between Armentières and Ypres; the rest of the army, including the two divisional cavalry regiments, were transferred by train.

Joffre intended going on to the offensive again on the Germans' right flank. This time he intended doing so in Flanders where the German right lay in the air and where the small Belgian army, besieged in Antwerp, could assist. He therefore moved more French troops from his right. The Germans, now under the overall command of Field-Marshal von Falkenhayn, who had replaced Moltke, began doing likewise when fighting on the Aisne became deadlocked. There were a hundred miles of open flank between the Aisne battlefield and the coast. The month's fighting which followed is sometimes referred to as 'the race to the sea'. It was, in fact, a race to outflank which was ended when both sides reached the sea at roughly the same time and then began entrenching.

Fighting around Ypres was at first very fluid, and the cavalry, the Fifteenth and Nineteenth with their divisions, could still be employed in the classic manner. Indeed, the number of cavalry brigades was increased to nine with the arrival of four more from Britain with the Third Cavalry Division. The Second Cavalry Division was also formed and a corps headquarters under Allenby was established. They were all needed. Seizing important ground, screening, guarding flanks, manning defensive lines dismounted, and particularly communication work, these were the constant demands on Allenby's regiments and those of the divisions. On 14 October Sergeant Brunton's squadron "charged the town of Bailleul at point of sword. Germans hastily retired towards Armentières and Dieppe." His day was somewhat marred, however, by the loss of his tobacco pouch and jack knife.

Above all, though, patrolling was required, day and night, to relieve the infantry of the requirement so that they could strengthen defensive positions or prepare for attacks. Dismounted work *and* attending to the troop horses meant that the squadrons rarely got as much rest as they needed, and certainly not as much as they appeared to the staff to be

ARTOIS AND FLANDERS
SHOWING MAIN RAILWAYS IN 1914

getting. There could be no skimping with grooming, watering and feeding if they were to be ready, at a moment's notice, for exploitation or reaction to a German break-through – and each looked as likely much of the time. C Squadron 15th Hussars were not allowed to unsaddle for *twenty-one days*, but there was not a single case of sore-back.

In the middle of November the German 6th Army made one more attempt to break through at Ypres. It was their last chance. To their right the twenty miles of the Ypres–Nieuport Canal and the River Yser were held by an ad hoc French army and the remainder of the Belgian army under King Albert which had withdrawn down the coast from Antwerp. The King ordered the locks on the canalized river at Nieuport to be opened, and the sea water inundated the low-lying fenland in the enemy's path. The whole weight of the German right wing's attacks fell therefore on the British in the Ypres Salient and on the junction with the French. This was only defeated by the most stubborn fighting and determined counter-attacks. Most of the BEF's cavalry were in the trenches at some time during the last German push. The machine-gun sections were particularly busy and suffered badly. The weather was atrocious – the Eighteenth's war diary complains that:

> "Sleep was impossible for those who in turn were allowed to try and enjoy an hour or so of it, and the long night through we waxed colder, until the first streak of dawn stopped further pretence of courting repose, and enabled us to stamp our feet in the sloshy mud and try to regain some feeling in our frozen extremities. It snowed all night of the 18th and lay quite deep next morning."

With the failure of this last German offensive the battle which was to become known as 'First Ypres' ended. Falkenhayn wrote after the war: "That which had to be attained under any circumstances, if the war was to be carried on with any hopeful prospects, was attained." He meant the stabilization of the Western Front from the Alps to the North Sea. But that was not what his aim had been: his aim had been to break through to Calais and envelop the allied left.

Envelopment had also been the allies' hope, but while it was desirable for them to break through it was not essential. It was essential for the Germans, for time was not on their side. The cost of that month of fighting to both sides was enormous. Numerically, the Germans suffered far greater but the BEF's infantry, the core of the regular army, had been all but destroyed. The cavalry had not been decimated because, though exhausted by their exertions as 'fire brigades', they had never become decisively engaged by complete squadrons or more. The regiments needed many men, and remounts, to bring them up to strength (the Eighteenth had lost 37 per cent of their war establishment in casualties) but their command structure was mercifully intact.

* * *

At 4.00 am on Balaklava Day (25 October) the Thirteenth at last received the orders they had long awaited – to mobilize. On 13 November they left Meerut by train and embarked at Bombay three days later, twenty officers, 499 other ranks and 560 horses. The heat was intense. It got much worse in the Red Sea and Suez. Below decks it was, in one officer's words, "absolute hell". Several horses fell dead from heat exhaustion alone.

By rail from Marseilles, they arrived at Orleans a little after midnight on 17 December: "It was bitterly cold, with a white frost and icy wind, and we had to turn out, detrain, and load up all our kit, saddles and arms on to motor lorries, and then march, leading our horses six miles out to our camp here in pitch darkness." It was a rude shock, but the regiment was given a fortnight to acclimatize itself before proceeding to the front. The main feature of this for the soldiers was exchanging their tropical khaki for something more appropriate. The horses could only grow their own thick coats, however.

Meanwhile, the other three regiments were settling to the routine of trench warfare. Occasionally they took a turn in the firing line, but in the main the divisional squadrons were involved in rear-area security and communication work, whilst the Eighteenth, with the Cavalry Corps, were generally in reserve, rotating through various states of notice-to-move with the other regiments and brigades.

All the regiments tried to make themselves, and especially the horses, as comfortable as possible in the farm billets behind the lines. Trickle leave home began and training was started. Games flourished, football especially, the odd divisional competition being held. Shooting for the pot, pheasants and hares, was popular. In the 2nd Cavalry Brigade the 9th Lancers organized a steeplechase meeting and the 4th Dragoon Guards had a pack of beagles sent over. Sometimes things could be really quite convivial.

The Duke of Wellington's headquarters in Portugal had had a pack of foxhounds, but it was perhaps not surprising that a ban on hunting and shooting was eventually imposed by GHQ in France. The shooting was a cause of friction with French farmers and landowners, and in any case gave rise to alarms, and the hunting gave the allies the impression that the British were not taking the war entirely seriously. This was a pity, for the Eighteenth's "wind and condition generally were getting into fine order . . . ; so for the future we had to content ourselves with football and cross-country runs."

The King visited; food and clothing parcels arrived by the lorry-load from an admiring British public, and on Christmas Day every man in the BEF received a Christmas card and a commemorative tin box with pipe and tobacco or writing materials from the King and Queen Mary. Winter passed, on the whole, relatively comfortably. Spring brought renewed activity as both sides tested the strength of each other's defences and hoped for a breakthrough. In April the organization of the cavalry was changed and the Fifteenth and Nineteenth ceased being divisional cavalry and were instead brought together as regiments in the newly-formed 9th Cavalry Brigade in the 1st Cavalry Division.

In late April the Germans began using gas in the Ypres Salient. The cavalry, dismounted, had to be used several times to restore the situation and on one occasion, in late May, the Eighteenth's commanding officer was caught in one such attack, resulting in his permanent invaliding home. The Fifteenth missed the same gas by minutes.

During these weeks, as fighting became more desperate in the Salient, the regiments frequently found themselves in the firing-line trenches. Occasionally they needed to fix bayonets, a weapon not seen by them in peace, the sword being the cavalry's 'cold steel'. For the cavalry were reliable: for the most part they were still regulars and under command of their own officers. The newly-raised and Territorial units could hardly be expected to be as steady. Little wonder dismounted cavalry became an expedient. Between 10 and 24 May the Fifteenth lost in killed and wounded nine officers and 138 other ranks. They had not given one inch of ground unless ordered. In the Nineteenth it had been the same: on 13 May alone the regiment had over a hundred casualties including seven officers, one of which was the commanding officer, Lieutenant-Colonel G.A. Egerton, who died of wounds. After this Second Battle of Ypres, as it became known, Sir John French visited the 9th Cavalry Brigade and praised their "splendid conduct and personal gallantry and . . . wonderful performance in the trenches".

Captain William Eve, 'D' Squadron Leader 13th Hussars, writing home, was possibly a little exaggerated in his judgement, but not much: "You say you are watching for news of the Cavalry. Well, you have it now in the Casualties List. That is the British Cavalry. It is, I think, wicked, for they are men we can't replace, but the fact is they can't trust any but the very best up there at Ypres, and that's why they sent for the Cavalry."

The rest of 1915, and the following winter, was sheer hard work interspersed with danger and disappointment. Trench-digging parties, dismounted duties in the trenches, training, standing-by for the break-through – the regiments saw it all. They also saw the arrival of the 'new armies'. In August, 1914, the Secretary for War was Field-Marshal Lord Kitchener. The Liberal government had appointed him in the aftermath of the enforced resignation of his predecessor over the mishandling of the Army's involvement in Ulster in the event of the Irish Home Rule Bill's being enacted – the 'Curragh Incident'. Kitchener, in one of his characteristically instinctive decisions, set about the raising of a vast citizens' army in addition to the Territorials. His accusing stare and pointing finger on the famous "Your Country Needs *You*" poster brought in volunteers by the hundred thousand. But recruits were one thing; experienced officers for these new battalions, brigades and divisions quite another. The regular army was trawled for NCOs of quality and experience to be officers in the 'New Army'. Throughout 1915 the Fifteenth, Eighteenth and Nineteenth sent some of their very best NCOs back to England for officer training, the Fifteenth no less than thirty-eight during the course of the war. Sergeant Brunton, recovering from wounds and now with the ribbon of the DCM on his chest (the medal having been presented to him in the field by the King) was offered a commission in the Infantry: "Refused, as I prefer the Cavalry."

One of the Eighteenth's nominations was a trooper, Sidney Carlin. His story is one of quite astonishing courage and determination, the equal of Douglas Bader and *Reach for the Sky*. Carlin had won the DCM 'For Conspicuous Gallantry' in a demolished trench on 13 May, 1915, after all his seniors had been killed. After recovering from severe wounds he was commissioned into the Royal Engineers and won the MC in October the following year during a German attack. He was again severely wounded and had a leg amputated. Appealing against a medical discharge he applied for transfer to the Royal Flying Corps but was turned down. Undaunted, he took his discharge, learned to fly at his own expense and was then accepted into the RFC. He won the DFC in 1918, "A gallant and determined pilot who sets a fine example to his Squadron", having shot down four balloons and two fighters. He was shot down himself and spent the closing weeks of the war as a prisoner. The story does not end there. In 1939 he returned to England from his new home in Africa to join the RAF and was posted to a squadron equipped with Defiants, the two-seater gun-turreted night fighter. He fought throughout the Battle of Britain and was at RAF Wittering on 8 May, 1941, when the airfield was 'jumped' by *Junkers* 88s. Instead of sheltering, as everyone else did, Flying Officer Sidney Carlin MC DFC DCM, aged 52, climbed into a grounded Defiant's gun turret and fought back. He died there in the turret, the only casualty of the raid. What *quality* there had been in the ranks of Britain's regular army in 1914.

* * *

In March, 1916, the Cavalry Corps was disbanded, and one of its divisions was attached to each of the four British armies now in France, the fifth division being kept as a GHQ reserve. The 1st Cavalry Division, with the 2nd and 9th Cavalry Brigades, was placed under the 1st Army. Expectations of a break-through in the coming months were high: the Cavalry were confident that their turn would soon come. The great 1916 allied offensive on the Western Front was being planned to coincide with Russia's in the east and Italy's, who had entered the war in May, 1915, against the Austrians. This coordinated strategic offensive held high hopes of actually ending the war. The British attacks were to be on the River Somme in the southern part of the British sector.

The Somme offensive opened on 1 July. By nightfall 60,000 British troops were dead, wounded or taken prisoner. The offensive continued, however, at varying degrees of intensity, until November. Tanks made their first appearance in small numbers on 15 September. They had remarkable tactical success, but there were far too few of them, only thirty-one crossing the German lines. The Cavalry Corps was hastily re-formed, but only waited: in the four months of fighting not a single opportunity for exploitation was created. The Corps' chief of staff, Brigadier-General Archibald Home, whose comments as a major on the regiments' ascendancy over the German cavalry closed the first section of this chapter, recorded in his diary at the end of October: "The mud up there is awful – horses are simply over their hocks in it. . . I am sorry to say that I came to the conclusion that the Cavalry as a mass cannot be employed before next spring. I don't believe the horses would get through the mud and, if they did, they would be stone cold after a very short time." Many infantrymen would have been grateful for a similar high-level analysis of their own predicament as they struggled in the same mud.

On 7 November, 1916, all further attacks in the Somme sector were abandoned, and the cavalry marched into winter quarters. The Battle of the Somme was the costliest miscalculation in the Army's history. The preceding paragraph can hardly do justice to a battle which, for no territorial gains worth speaking of, had cost 600,000 allied casualties. The Germans had lost over two-thirds this number. In attritional terms it had had some success therefore: German manpower became critical, forcing them to introduce universal adult conscription for the Army or for war work.

1st Cavalry Division now wintered near Boulogne. It was their third and severest winter to date. Hard training continued, but it took all the regiments' efforts to keep their horses in condition during these bitterly cold, wet months. Everyone told them they would be needed *en masse* for the 1917 offensives which, this time, would be sure to lead to a break-through.

CHAPTER 12

Going the Distance

"The years 1917 and 1918 were marked by continental strife and suspicion between Haig and Robertson (the C.I.G.S) on the one hand and Lloyd George, the War Premier, on the other ... Haig and Robertson continued to believe that the war could only be decided by defeating the main body of the German army, which lay in France. Lloyd George flinched at the cost of going fifteen rounds with such a heavyweight. He favoured action anywhere but on the Western Front."

CORRELLI BARNETT – *Britain and Her Army*

13H in Mesopotamia; 15H, 18H and 19H in France and Belgium, 1917–18: the 1917 Offensives; Cambrai; Hindenburg's 1918 Offensive; the 1918 Counter-Offensive; Armistice.

A colourful Christmas card from the Russian Front reached the Thirteenth in 1917. The greeting ran:

"The Hussars of the Thirteenth Narva Regiment of Russia send most fraternal greetings to their valiant and noble comrades of the Thirteenth Regiment of Hussars, proud and happy in being united with them in cordial cooperation against a common enemy."

The Narva Hussars had sent it to the Western Front where they believed the regiment to be enduring another winter fighting the Germans. The card was forwarded instead to Mesopotamia, where they had been fighting the Turks for several months.

The Mesopotamia campaign began in November, 1914, when three British-Indian brigades seized Basra in order to protect the Persian Gulf oil refinery at Abadan from Turkish attack. The force beat off subsequent Turkish counter-attacks and began to move up the River Tigris towards Baghdad, the Poona Division advancing to within twenty miles of the capital before being checked by greatly superior numbers. The division had to withdraw to Kut-el-Amara where its soldiers withstood a five-month siege before the commander, Major-General Sir Charles Townshend, was forced to capitulate. Kut was a blow to national pride reminiscent of some of the earlier set-backs in the South African war. Besides the strategic significance of operations in Mesopotamia, there was clearly going to be some imperative to avenge the Kut disaster.

The Thirteenth had had a frustrating time in France. They had taken turns in the trenches, in quiet sectors, and had done a good deal of trench-digging fatigues. Training had continued, and morale was good: a marked camaraderie had formed within the Meerut Brigade, and relations with the 18th King George's Own Lancers, predominantly Mohammedans, and with Skinner's Horse could not have been better. Nevertheless everyone craved for real action. Captain Eve wrote home,

> "We sit back here well within the sound of the guns, and go on with more or less peace-training and try to be patient. Whenever there is a big show on, off we go up behind the line, and every time we think our time has really come; but every time we come back again in a few days – a sort of mobile reserve, that's all. We are known out here as the 'Iron Ration', only to be used in the last emergency!"

In the early summer of 1916 the Indian Cavalry Corps was thinned out and the Meerut Brigade returned to India under orders for Mesopotamia. The 18th Lancers remained in France, however, because it was considered prudent not to put a predominantly Mohammedan regiment against the Turks. Even

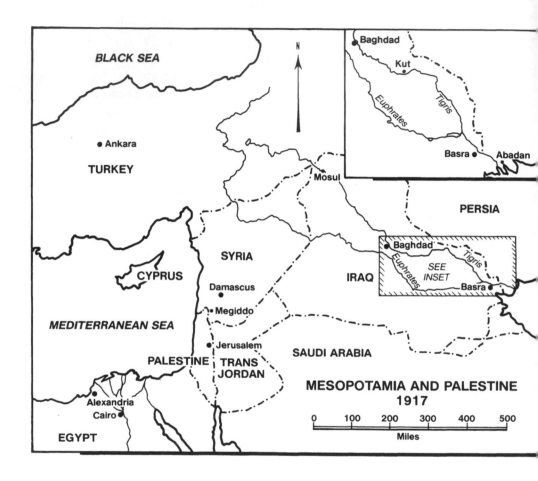

more disappointing, Skinner's Horse learned on arrival back in India that they were not to proceed to Mesopotamia either, and it was to be a dozen or so years before the two regiments renewed their friendship. Two Indian lancer regiments, the 13th and 14th, replaced the 18th KGO and Skinner's in what was now designated '7th Cavalry Brigade (Mesopotamian Field Force)'.

Fresh troop horses having been acquired in Bombay, the Thirteenth, with the rest of the brigade, sailed for Basra in the middle of July. There they began a remarkable chapter in their history, without doubt the most spectacularly successful, and at a time when virtually all but they and the 14th Hussars (in the 6th Cavalry Brigade) of the British regular cavalry were locked in static warfare on the Western Front. The campaign lasted a little over two years, and although the Force commander, Lieutenant-General F.S. Maude, lacked the flair of Townshend, who had done so well up to the fall of Kut, the Turks were systematically defeated. In essence, Maude's campaign was a methodical advance up the Tigris, capturing Baghdad and exploiting almost to the Turkish border. If he showed none of the instinctive skill and *élan* in the handling of his cavalry which Allenby was to display in Palestine, there were nevertheless many occasions on which mounted action proved not only possible but essential, and these were eagerly seized by the Thirteenth.

Though there had been a fair amount of cavalry skirmishing during the winter advance to Baghdad, it was initially a rather plodding business. Just outside the capital, at Lajj on 5 March, 1917, however, the Thirteenth were really tested. They were wrong-footed because of faulty information provided by spotter aircraft and armoured cars. Advancing to attack a Turkish convoy, they were caught in the open by entrenched infantry who had not been discovered. There was no option but to force the position with a charge, which was carried out by three squadrons in echelon. Losses were almost 50 per cent and included the commanding officer wounded; fifty horses were killed and thirty-six wounded. The position was taken after some fierce dismounted fighting.

Captain Eve, who had so often chafed at the Cavalry's inactivity in both France and the early part of the Mesopotamian campaign, was killed at the head of his squadron, sword in hand. He had written home disconsolately only three months earlier: "Personally I see no show ever for us. . . I shall never get a gallop with my squadron."

His favourite charger Caprice, who had been with him for years and had seen him through the best part of two winters in France, had an extraordinary escape. She was seen galloping off with several bullet wounds in her neck and was presumed to have died. She was found by Eve's former batman over a year later, however, in the ranks of an Indian cavalry regiment in Baghdad, where she was reclaimed and returned to England after the war to Eve's widow, no less than *seven* scars from bullets in her neck. She had a foal a few years later, and the two were modelled in silver as a memento. For many years, copies were given as the regimental officers' wedding present. The atmosphere of the charge is perfectly caught in the following extracts from a letter from Second-Lieutenant Guy Pedder, one of Eve's troop leaders in D Squadron. It was written only seven days after the action, in the field hospital at Kut:

"My Dearest Mother.

No doubt you will have heard by now how we ran into it on the 5th but in case you haven't I will try and give you a rough idea what happened . . . .at 1030 we moved off again, and almost immediately a sandstorm started, the strong wind taking all our dust out in front of us, we went about 5 miles when one of our armoured cars brought in a Turkish officer and the news that there were a few of the enemy scattered about who were probably only waiting for us to collect them as prisoners. . . Eve told us this and quickly changed on to his favourite mare. Three squadrons moved out to the right, the 4th right out to the flank, A B and D then advanced in line of troop column extended and almost immediately came under heavy rifle fire, we walked about ½ mile and then trotted, the dust was awful and you cldn't see more than 100–200 yds in front, all of a sudden thro' the dust I cld see a lot of Turks in the open and in a nullah Eve gave the order 'draw swords – form line – gallop' and before we knew where we were we were into them, some stood up and surrendered others lay flat on their backs and shot us at 2 and 3 yds range, . . . the noise was tremendous bullets from revolvers, rifles and machine guns cracking all round. . . I lost sight of Eve who was just in front of me at the first nullah but his orderly who was shot (wounded) close by him tells me he was shot from 2 yds range as he was bending down to charge a group of Turks. At any rate he must have been killed instantaneously. There were a great many empty saddles and dead horses by now so I tried to rally all the men who were near me. It was extremely difficult as we were under v. heavy fire at v. short range, there was deafening noise and a loud wind blowing and if you collected men in bunches the bunches wd v. soon have a machine gun on them, so what men I got under hand I kept extended and galloped a fair way back and handed over the horses and went up dismounted, the Turks guns had now got our range and were v. annoying, but their skills were bad or I shldn't be writing to you now . . . we all went on by short rushes together until we met the colonel who told us roughly where to go and we got into the nullah we had first charged and then we held on till dark when we collected the wounded who were lying out in front. I was hit clean through the shoulder about 2 P.M. having got thro' the charge and dismounted attack and when I was sitting in the nullah talking to the colonel who got hit in the arm v. shortly after me."

Despite its mauling, the regiment quickly recovered and in the following eighteen months carried out four more mounted actions, all successful and at relatively small cost. Three of these actions were against machine-gun positions and succeeded due to clever use of ground and dismounted supporting fire. On the last occasion, at Hadraniya near the Turkish border on 29 October, 1918, they carried out a truly brilliant 'mounted infantry' action, winning universal praise. The Turks were occupying some commanding cliffs, or 'bluffs', outside the town, and the clearing of this position had become a matter of some urgency: the 11th Brigade had worked its way to the rear of Hadraniya but were then sandwiched between its defenders and reinforcements coming from the opposite direction. With artillery and machine-gun fire supporting, the Thirteenth in two squadron waves galloped across 1,400 yards of exposed valley and dismounted at the foot of the bluff, in the lee of its craggy face, and then scaled the steep cliffs to carry the positions on the top with the bayonet. The Turks surrendered or fled. The action thereafter became known as 'Richardson's Bluff', after the commanding officer, and is commemorated in a vivid painting in the officers' mess.

In their two-year campaign the Thirteenth had eight officers killed and sixteen wounded, of whom two were taken prisoner, and ninety other ranks killed and 176 wounded. They won eight DSOs, sixteen MCs, fourteen DCMs, fourteen MMs and *seventy-eight* mentions in despatches.

* * *

While the Thirteenth were 'knocking away the props', as the eastern strategy was described, the Fifteenth, Eighteenth and Nineteenth faced the prospect of 1917 at the coal-face once again. But there were high hopes of a major break-through which would finish the war. In March the Germans began a systematic retirement to the 'Hindenburg Line' (sometimes called the 'Siegfried Line'). This was a formidable defensive line on commanding ground. The retirement also had the merit of pinching out the bulge in their line between Arras and Rheims, releasing more men to the reserve. The Germans laid waste to everything between the old line and the new, even cutting down fruit trees and poisoning the water, as well as mining and booby-trapping.

This retirement brought into doubt whether the cavalry could be used, for the abandoned ground was appalling going, but planning went ahead. The Cavalry Corps of five divisions, including two Indian divisions, remained concentrated, the 15th and 19th Hussars still together in the 9th Brigade, and the 18th Hussars in the 2nd Brigade. There were some early successes. The Canadians took Vimy Ridge in April and Allenby's 3rd Army made gains at Arras, but there was no break-through. General Sir Herbert Plumer's 2nd Army, in a fine, methodically planned operation, took Messines Ridge in June, but again there was no break-through. It was going to have to be another attempt in the Ypres Salient. An attack on a four-corps front was therefore planned, centred on the remains of the village of Passchendaele. When the War Cabinet discussed the plans, Lloyd George nearly forbade the attack. Haig's confidence, buoyed by the earlier successes and what proved to be exaggerated reports of the poor state of the German defenders, carried the day, however. More was the pity.

The attack began just before dawn on 31 July, 1917, after a protracted bombardment. The artillery had been devastating – they had totally destroyed the Flanders drainage system. What was not flooded fenland was liquid mud. The Germans, prudently, had largely abandoned trench defences here and had instead constructed concrete pillboxes housing machine guns. Three months and 250,000 casualties later, the offensive was abandoned. Passchendaele Ridge was taken finally by the Canadians, but there was still no break-through. How the cavalry could have crossed the sea of mud is in any case beyond imagination. One more attempt to force a decision would be made before the winter closed down offensive operations – at Cambrai.

Cambrai was conceived initially as a massed tank raid, that is to say the force would withdraw after striking its objective. There was no thought of a break-through. The new commander of 3rd Army, General Sir Julian Byng (Allenby had been elevated to command in the Middle East), had grander ideas, however. He believed that the tanks *could* make a break-through. The immediate result of this would be the capture of the bridges over the River Sensée which would threaten the German lines of communication and thus force their withdrawal. This in turn would expose the German flank and leave them open to being 'rolled-up' from the south. Byng's plan allowed for no effective tank or infantry reserve, however: resources were scarce. In effect, the Cavalry Corps, awaiting the break-through, were Byng's reserve – an unpromising bit of 'double-hatting'.

Things went extremely well to start with. The tanks, 374 of them, were moved up to their concentration area then dispersed in woods and ruined buildings in complete secrecy. There was to be no protracted preliminary artillery bombardment, only a rolling barrage 200 yards in front of the tanks. Two hundred and seventy-five British aircraft, Sopwith Camels, Scouts, Bristol Fighters and DE '4s and '5s, would sweep ahead strafing the German defences and keeping the Germans from flying. This way, the Germans would get no advanced warning and would not be able to move reserves in time, and the ground would remain unbroken.

Three divisions of the Cavalry Corps moved up to their concentration area on the night of 19/20 November, 1917, ten miles in pitch darkness without a hitch. The other two divisions were echeloned in support. The plan was for the cavalry to be ready to move forward at $H+150$ (minutes) – 8.50am, by which time it was hoped that the infantry divisions would have occupied the ground up to a line from Flesquières, through Marcoing, to Masnières. Then the 2nd and 5th Cavalry Divisions were to advance south of Cambrai, and the 1st, with 15th, 18th and 19th Hussars in their usual brigades, was to isolate Cambrai from the strong defensive position at Bourlon. From then on they would develop an advance north, securing the Sensée bridges, breaking up railways, overrunning batteries and headquarters, and pressing north-east towards Valenciennes in preparation for a general rolling-up of the front.

The tanks achieved rapid success through total surprise. The forward defensive lines were quickly overrun and progress initially was excellent. The attack achieved a large measure of dislocation in the sector, but in some places there was stubborn resistance, sometimes *after* the assaulting troops had pressed on. Mopping-up was not always thorough. There would have been no need for it to have been too thorough if the tanks themselves had been following through, but instead it was the cavalry who found themselves held up by machine-gun fire in several places. The Eighteenth, in 2nd Cavalry Brigade, had only been able to get to Nine Wood by mid-afternoon and were still immobilized by fire, as was the rest of the brigade, from several points west of the St Quentin Canal. Meanwhile the Fifteenth and Nineteenth, in the 9th Cavalry Brigade (the 1st Cavalry Division's reserve brigade) were moving up to Havrincourt Wood to await progress by the 2nd, but were well out of contact.

The depth of the Hindenburg Line's defences, the rallying of the defenders after the initial shock and, more than anything, the lack of infantry and tank reserves to deal with local checks, now led to a fatal loss of momentum. 2nd Brigade were instructed to hold between Nine Wood and the canal. The 9th Brigade bivouacked in Havrincourt Wood. It poured with icy rain all

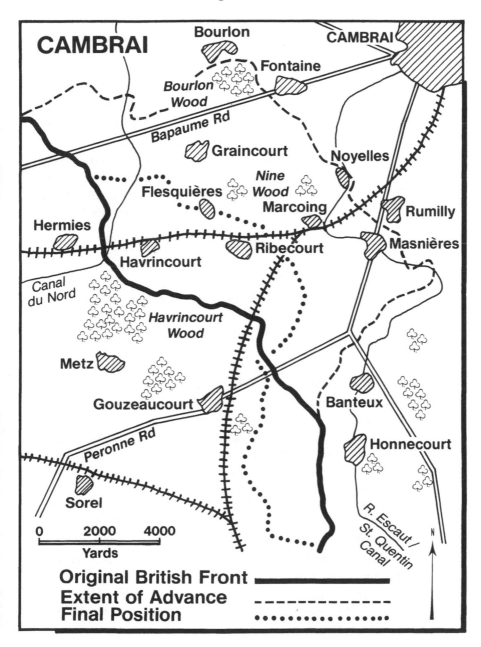

night. At about 6.00 am on 21 November the Germans counter-attacked the Eighteenth at Noyelles, but were beaten back. They attacked again at 8.00, but were again brought to a halt, although they gained a lodgement in the village and kept up sniping for much of the day. Three officers in A Squadron, including the squadron leader, were hit. One of these was Lieutenant Edward Horner who died later that day. Horner was a gilded youth, the son of Sir John and Lady Horner of Mells in Somerset. His mother afterwards commissioned a bronze memorial equestrian statue of her son in uniform. The commission was undertaken by Alfred Munnings, the pre-eminent equestrian artist of the age. The magnificent statue, with the inscription "An Officer of Hussars", stands in Mells Church.

No forward progress could be made by 2nd Cavalry Brigade in this sector and their casualties were beginning to mount steadily. The 9th Brigade were moved up to support them and both the Fifteenth and Nineteenth helped to clear several pockets of Germans. 2nd Brigade were withdrawn that night to Ribécourt and the 9th Brigade were told to go firm in 2nd Brigade's positions of the previous night because the infantry had still not been able to break through in the key area of Fontaine. No crossings over the St Quentin Canal had been found intact, so the advance was stalled until Fontaine, and to an extent Bourlon to its west, were cleared.

The following morning, 22 November, 9th Cavalry Brigade were ordered to concentrate with the rest of 1st Cavalry Division back at Metz, a return march of about nine miles which they completed in the middle of the afternoon after handing over to an infantry brigade. The division spent the night in Metz, and 9th Brigade received orders to move forward the following morning in the hope of slipping between Bourlon and Fontaine, the intention being that the villages would be cleared by two infantry divisions at first light.

The brigade marched at 8.30am, the Nineteenth leading. The roads were congested so the move was made cross-country. This proved difficult going due to the old trenches and wire, and Flesquières was only reached at 11.00. It mattered little, however, for the attacks on Bourlon and Fontaine had not been successful. A second attack on Fontaine in late afternoon might have been successful if tanks had been available but, after two and a half days of fighting, the crews were exhausted and tanks could not be moved across to Fontaine before last light. 9th Brigade were therefore told to off-saddle where they stood.

Late in the afternoon the Germans vigorously counter-attacked 40th Division at Bourlon Wood and at 6.30 pm the 9th Brigade were put under the division's command. Each regiment hurriedly mustered three dismounted squadrons and moved up to the wood, the remainder and the led horses returning to Metz. The dismounted squadrons managed to receive orders and get into some sandpits south of the wood, in reserve, by about 3.00 am, but they were in action soon after daylight when the Germans began a series of determined counter-attacks which were to last for nearly thirty-six hours. During this time both the Fifteenth and Nineteenth were continually in action, alternately pouring steady, accurate fire into the German rushes, then counter-attacking with fixed bayonets. Throughout the night of 24/25 November the German attacks continued, and increased in strength after daylight. The Fifteenth ran out of ammunition at one stage that morning.

At 2.00 pm a relatively fresh battalion was brought up, the 2nd Scots Guards, and these succeeded in finally clearing the wood. The dismounted elements of the 9th Brigade were withdrawn to Flesquières that evening and the following morning they returned to Metz. The brigade left behind a considerable number of dead, the Fifteenth alone losing two officers and twenty-eight other ranks killed.

The divisional commander wrote to the Cavalry Corps commander shortly afterwards and said, "I wish particularly to bring to your notice the gallant conduct of the 15th Hussars, who on several occasions charged the enemy, and when our right flank was thrown back, assisted in repulsing the enemy and restoring the situation." The Commander-in-Chief, too, especially mentioned the regiment in his own despatches. It seems that the gratitude was genuinely felt, for when the 40th

Division disbanded at the end of the war, a salver and cup were presented to the regiment in recognition of these desperate thirty-six hours' fighting.

The 1st Cavalry Division as a whole now went into reserve. There was little rest, however, for the virtually incessant rain and sleet which had fallen on the horses and wagons during the battle meant that a thorough overhaul of saddlery and harness was necessary. It took almost forty-eight hours to strip everything down, clean it, repair or strengthen where necessary and re-assemble. Cavalry soldiering was not as 'cushy' as many an infantryman thought.

By early December the Cambrai offensive had fizzled out. There was bitter disappointment in many quarters that the cavalry had not been able to break out into the Germans' rear. The disappointment turned to criticism of the handling of the cavalry itself. The Corps Commander, Kavanagh, came in for sharp criticism of his command and control arrangements. J.F.C. Fuller, the military theorist and post-war proponent of '*Blitzkrieg*', sums this up as follows:

> "in spite of the obvious necessity for a free hand, the Cavalry Corps commander, strange to say, tied his command down in such a way that in any conceivable set of circumstances, it would have been impossible for it to develop its mobility. . . . What was wrong was not the dispositions but the leadership. In place of moving as close up to the front as possible, the Cavalry Corps headquarters remained at Fins, six miles in rear of the nearest point of the front line and some twelve miles from Masnières [the crossing point of the canal], and as no action was to be taken except by order of these headquarters, this meant that opportunity would be lost as all information would have to go back to headquarters and from there be transmitted to cavalry divisions and by them to brigades and thence. . . "

Fuller then asserts, "The truth is that, possibly for the last time in the history of war, the cavalry were offered a chance of operating as a mounted arm."

Were the cavalry offered a chance which they missed? Fuller was not entirely impartial – the tanks' rôle at Cambrai had been planned in large part by him. No gap was made through which a division, let alone the whole Cavalry Corps, could pour into the rear area. It was the tanks' and infantry's job to secure a corridor through the front and support lines so that the cavalry could be launched against un-entrenched enemy – gun positions, headquarters, reserves on the move. The corridor was never made because the force ratio was wrong – Byng simply did not have enough tanks and infantry to be sure of success. Instead he *hoped* for it.

But the cavalry should have done better – and could have done, because at the tactical level there was no lack of offensive spirit. If the cavalry had been expected from the outset to *fight* to get a break-out then they might well have done so effectively. There were virtually twelve hours of darkness each night, and it ought to have been possible, if they had anticipated the need to bridge the St Quentin Canal, to make use of that darkness to outflank or infiltrate. Horse artillery could have been used aggressively in intimate support, and there was also scope for using armoured cars as heavy machine-gun carriers (a whole tank battalion had been put at the Corps' disposal to help get the cavalry forward, but no tanks had been used). All this would have needed de-centralized control: it was needed anyway. It is difficult to comprehend how the nature of the coming battle should have been so misunderstood by both Byng (a cavalryman himself) and Kavanagh as to contrive such a passive and cumbersome command and control system. There *were* some local successes, but they came to nothing through lack of support. A squadron of Fort Garry Horse from the Canadian Cavalry Brigade in 5th Cavalry Division got across the canal by a footbridge on the afternoon of the first day but were later cut up by machine-gun fire and, without support, had to withdraw.

Why the divisions were kept so far back is difficult to understand save in one respect: if the big hole were going to be punched at some place in the line it would best be exploited by the cavalry *en masse*, and concentration was easier to achieve by keeping some distance back and using the road system which favoured movement north-west, north and north-east but did not help lateral movement. Once the first day's fighting had developed as it did, however, it is difficult to see why the divisions were pulled back. When Bourlon Wood was cleared in the middle of the afternoon of 24 November the Corps was ordered to push as much cavalry through as possible, but the nearest division was twelve miles away – a two-hour fast trot, if the route were clear, which would have left the horses, with their twenty-stone loads, all but blown. What had happened to battle procedure in 3rd Army and the Corps – 'anticipation of future tasks'? Was the attack on Bourlon Wood not expected to be successful? If not, why was it launched? If it *were* expected to be successful why was there no means of exploiting the success?

On the morning of 21 November, after news of the impressive advances on the 20th had reached London, the church bells rang out for the first time since the start of the Great War. Hidden in these joyful peals was a death knell for the horsed cavalry.

* * *

And so the regiments began their fourth winter in Flanders. The same routine of training and keeping horses in condition was interspersed with more turns in the trenches. The Germans launched a massive, last-fling, offensive towards the end of March, 1918, astride the junction of the British and French armies at Amiens. They made impressive advances, breaking through the fixed defences and getting into open country. There was some desperate fighting, and the Cavalry Corps, reduced by two divisions during the winter (the Indian divisions were sent to Egypt and many of the Yeomanry regiments were re-assigned to dismounted duties), was used to plug gaps and generally act as 'fire brigade'. The regiments again acquitted themselves well, fighting both mounted and dismounted.

After two weeks' fighting, the German offensive petered out. Their commander-in-chief, Ludendorff, had failed to drive a wedge between the two armies. His intention had been to drive the wedge in so deep that the British would begin to fall back on their lines of communication with the channel ports, opening a wide gap and unmasking Paris. Ludendorff's offensive, though its initial gains were impressive, had neither the infantry and tank strength to maintain the pressure, nor, ironically, the cavalry with which to exploit the break-throughs he *did* make.

Once the offensive had been halted, the Germans were in a critical situation. They had lost heavily during the fighting, but they had also abandoned their well-constructed defences and were extremely vulnerable to a counter-offensive. The Americans had entered the war by this stage and their divisions were becoming battleworthy. The Royal Air Force (formed from the RFC and elements of the Royal Naval Air Service earlier in the year) had 22,000 aircraft of all types, and the Tank Corps had assembled nearly 500 tanks by the summer of 1918.

Throughout June and July pressure was kept on the German line while preparations to counter-attack were made. The Cavalry Corps carried out intensive training with the infantry and new command arrangements were made to permit rapid exploitation of opportunities. In early August all three regiments were in action at Amiens in support of the Canadian divisions' attacks. The Fifteenth, *en masse*, made a 2,000-yard gallop on 8 August to seize their objectives. Though they were shelled and machine-gunned, the sheer momentum of the advance, on horses in the peak of condition, carried them the distance with remarkably light casualties.

The same feat was attempted two months later by the Nineteenth near Le Cateau, the allies' advance having remorselessly continued since August. On this occasion, however, the German rearguard's determined use of machine guns nearly destroyed the regiment: frustrated by the hold-ups which interlocking machine guns and field batteries were causing, and the country being unbroken, the commanding officer, Lieutenant-Colonel G.D. Franks, decided to try to break through the rearguard at the gallop. In two successive attempts, all the Nineteenth's officers were either killed or wounded, Franks himself falling dead riding fifty yards ahead of the regiment. Brunton, having recovered from a second set of wounds, with a bar to his DCM and now C Squadron sergeant major, records the scene:

> "Our objective was two batteries of field guns and a nest of machine guns about 1000X away on high ground. The charge was sounded, squadrons rapidly formed into line, and away we went hell for leather; it was a mad ride through shell fire. We rode clean through the guns, killing many gunners by the sword. Those that were spared bombed us as we passed through."

So close to the end of the war, this was a particular tragedy. It does, however, show how determined the cavalry were to appear not to be shirking at this late stage. They had had things easy in comparison with the 'PBI', the 'Poor Bloody Infantry', and now with the return of mobile warfare, the type of warfare for which they were most suited and in which expectation they had been husbanded by the high command, they were going to see it through. There was no bravado, beyond the understandable exhilaration of a gallop. Franks had been commanding since the middle of 1915 and knew his business. The regiment was the corps advance guard that day and they had a job to do: it was done with the sword as the infantry would have done with the bayonet.

* * *

Just before eleven o'clock on the morning of 11 November, 1918, the Fifteenth were ordered to halt and off-saddle in a field near the village of Maffle, beyond Ath on the Lille-Brussels road. They were twenty miles from Waterloo, and fourteen from Mons where they had fired their first shots four years before. The regiment had spent the previous day pursuing the German rearguards and had had a sharp time towards evening driving them out of Ath. Billets that night were in a convent, and the advance was resumed after first light on the 11th. At 11.00 news was received that hostilities had ceased. The Fifteenth's trumpeters sounded the regimental call followed by the 'Cease

Fire'. The regiment cheered. It would have been understandable if a huge party had followed. Instead, however, the commanding officer ordered the trumpeters to sound 'Stables' and everyone calmly got on with grooming and watering the horses.

In his final despatch, Field-Marshal Haig addressed the value of cavalry in modern war:

> "From time to time, as the war of position dragged on, and the enemy's trench systems remained unbroken, while questions of man-power and the shortage of shipping became acute, the wisdom or necessity of maintaining any large force of mounted men was freely discussed. In the light of the full experience of the War, the decision to preserve the Cavalry Corps has been fully justified. It has been proved that Cavalry, whether used for shock effect under suitable conditions, or as mobile Infantry, have still an indispensable part to play in modern war. Moreover, it cannot be safely assumed that in all future wars, the flanks of the opposing forces will rest on neutral states or impassable obstacles. Whenever such a condition does not obtain, opportunities for the use of Cavalry must arise frequently. . . . There is no doubt that, had the advance of the Cavalry been allowed to continue, the enemy's disorganised retreat would have been turned into a rout."

The debate about the Cavalry's future had not even been resolved by four years of high-intensity warfare. So far as 13th/18th and 15th/19th were concerned, it was not resolved for another twenty years – not until the very eve of the Second World War itself.

CHAPTER 13

Amalgamation and Mechanization

"In 1919 Lloyd George told the service chiefs that they need not anticipate a major war within the next ten years. In 1925 the service chiefs asked again and were given the same answer. . . This answer was repeated in 1926 and 1927. Finally, in 1928, the service chiefs were told, on Churchill's prompting, that they need ask no more: the ten years' freedom from major war began automatically each morning."

A.J.P. TAYLOR, *English History 1914–1945*

"I feel sure that as time goes on you will find just as much use for the horse – the well-bred horse – as you have done in the past."

Field-Marshal Lord HAIG, 1925

Aftermath of the Great War; the 1922 Amalgamations; 13th/18th and 15th/19th on Home Service, in the Middle East, and India; the 'Gathering Storm'; Mechanization; War.

The regiments started to come home in 1919 once order had been assured in Germany. They had been beyond the Rhine since December, the Eighteenth being the first British troops to cross this symbolic frontier of Germany's heartland. There had at first been some concern that civil unrest would detain them, but the Germans' desire to get back to normal was on the whole stronger than the communist revolutionary forces at work. Revolution came later, of course, although fascist not communist.

The 15th Hussars left Germany with mixed feelings. They were just beginning to enjoy themselves. They were sent to Ireland after a relaxed summer of occupation duties, and immediately found the atmosphere ironically tense. There was no welcome – no salute to the home-coming victors after five years' active service. Instead the regiment marched to the barracks in Kilkenny with loaded rifles. Once inside, the gates were shut and armed sentries took post on the walls. They were once again in hostile country.

The Eighteenth and Nineteenth did not have much of a stay in England. They were needed in India. They left for the east, however, with 'Royal' added to their titles, the personal interest of their royal Colonels-in-Chief, Queen Alexandra and Queen Mary, in obvious evidence. The Thirteenth, who left Baghdad for Aldershot early in 1919, were the only regiment who seemed set for a decent stretch of service in England.

These were the regular regiments, of course. A year after the Armistice, the great military machine assembled by Kitchener and the other war leaders had been almost entirely dismantled, its new regiments and battalions disappearing from sight if not from memory. The brief experience of the 'Citizens' Army' was over; the sharp divisions between civilians and soldiers returned. Correlli Barnett, in *Britain and her Army*, maintains that the 'Ten Year Rule', explained in the heading to this chapter, removed the spur even to theoretical studies: "The Army was thus put back to the 1890s, a colonial gendarmerie with no major role to play or plan for."

The Great War had, after all, been 'the war to end all wars'. "The nation lost all concern with its defence from 1918 until late in 1938," continues Barnett. "The very existence of even a comatose army seemed indecent to public opinion in the 1920s and early 1930s, in the prevailing pacifistic climate of belief in disarmament and the League of Nations."

The country was also broke – or very nearly. There was an immediate post-war boom based on the war's increased production, but this was over by 1922. Chapter Two described how the Younger Pitt's policy of strict financial economy all but ruined the Army. History was about to repeat itself as "men grasped at the old remedy of public economy" in Professor Taylor's words.

Enter a man called Geddes, Sir Eric Geddes. He was a remarkable man in his way, possibly unique in that at one moment he was a major-general in the BEF and at the next he was a vice-admiral in the Royal Navy. Equally spectacularly, he reached the rank of major-general in one bound from being a civilian. A Scot, he had been the general-manager designate of the North Eastern Railway before the war and had been seconded to Haig's staff in France to direct the BEF's rail transport. He had done so with outstanding success, and from France he went to the Admiralty to organize naval supply. After the war he had been made Minister of Transport and had produced some far-reaching schemes to modernize the railways. These had been an early victim of economy, however. An embittered Geddes was then asked to chair a committee on government expenditure. It reported in February, 1922, and the so-called 'Geddes Axe' began to swing. It swung widely in all directions: public health, education and the civil service were major targets. So too were the Army and Navy.

Unlike the immediate years following Waterloo, the Cavalry did not escape the reductions in the Army. The prospect of another continental war, and its requirement for large numbers of cavalry, seemed utterly remote. The Indian Army's cavalry was steady, loyal and professional, so only a few British regiments would be needed there too. Ireland would need some, but the calls from the civil powers both there and on the mainland were much reduced: there were now efficient police forces throughout the Kingdom and better communications allowed infantry to be moved more quickly and cheaply than the cavalry.

Fourteen regiments were amalgamated to form seven, but the process was at first unusual. The four most junior regiments, including the 18th and 19th Hussars, were to be *disbanded*. The process had actually begun when it was then decided that amalgamation should take place instead. In most cases the pairings seemed haphazard: regiments were amalgamated 'like with like'

48. *"After months of waiting, most of the BEF heard the news of the German invasion of Belgium on 10 May, 1940, from the BBC. The order for the move to the forward line on the Dyle arrived soon afterwards".(p.227)* A Mk VI of A Squadron 15th/19th Hussars crossing the Franco-Belgian border.

49. *"Orders were received for a general withdrawal to the River Escaut."(p.229)* 15th/19th carriers withdrawing through the bombed and shelled streets of Louvain, 14 May, 1940.

50. *"The wretched Covenanter 'cruiser' tank, mechanically unreliable, under-armoured and under-armed."(p.240)* 15th/19th Hussars on a recruiting drive 'somewhere in England', 1942.

51. *"A training programme which had taken them all over the country."(p.240)* Which meant at some stage, of course, Salisbury Plain where, in 1943, the Prime Minister, Winston Churchill, reviewed the 13th/18th Hussars.

52. *"It really had only one disadvantage - its late arrival."* (p.244) The Sherman was a dramatic improvement on anything the British had seen so far in the war. 13th/18th Hussars converted in 1943 but did not receive the DD version until just before D-Day itself.

53. *"The brainchild of the Hungarian-born engineer, Nicholas Straussler."* (p.241) All flotation training was carried out by both regiments in DD Valentines.

54. *"All his forces were embarked in appallingly cramped conditions."(p.246)* Loading began on 4 June, 1944, for the 13th/18th Hussars but D-Day was postponed for 24 hours because of the weather.

55. *"The Lesson of Greatest Importance . . . is the need for overwhelming fire support, including close support, during the initial stages of the attack."(p.240)* The lessons of the Dieppe raid were well taken: 13th/18th DDs on the beach ahead of the Infantry.

(hussars with hussars, and so on), but following no set formula. In some cases the pairings were felicitous – the 15th and 19th had fought side by side in the Great War for instance. On the other hand, the last time that the 13th and 18th had paraded together was on the field at Waterloo (though the 13th had 'rescued' the 18th at Ladysmith). Were the pairings really arrived at by the Colonels drawing the numbers from a bag in a smoke-filled room at the Cavalry Club, as tradition has it?

In any case, were they at this time true amalgamations? Army Order Number 133 reads:

> "His Majesty the King is graciously pleased to approve of the reconstruction of four Cavalry Regiments recently disbanded and for regiments to be amalgamated as under:
>
> 15th Hussars, 2 Squadrons)
> 19th Hussars, 1 Squadron) to form 15th/19th Hussars
>
> Composite Regiment to be treated as a complete regiment, but each squadron to retain name of its original regiment in order to preserve its identity."

Similar orders applied to the other junior pairs. In these orders there was more than a hint, to many, that the 'reconstruction' might be temporary. Had there not been many such temporary expedients with battalions of the same regiments of infantry in the recent war?

When in 1941 the Royal Armoured Corps was being rapidly expanded, in addition to the many extra Royal Tank Regiments six new 'cavalry' regiments were raised – the 23rd Hussars, 24th Lancers etc. Rather, they were *re*-raised because they had all enjoyed a brief existence during the Napoleonic wars. It was all a bit of a conceit, perhaps, but a successful one. Nevertheless, Churchill was not convinced. In December, 1941, he minuted the CIGS:

> "Surely it was a very odd thing to create these outlandish numbered regiments of Dragoons, Hussars, and Lancers, none

of which has carbines, swords or lances, when there exist already telescoped up the 18th, 20th and 19th Hussars, 5th and 21st Lancers. Surely all these should have been revived before creating these unreal and artificial titles. I wish you would explain to me what was moving in the minds of the War Office when they did this."

It is a classic Churchill memorandum. Fortunately, it had no effect on plans: re-amalgamation would inevitably have occurred as soon as the war ended and it would have been 'back to square one' again. The Prime Minister was so informed.

For the 18th and 19th Hussars it must have seemed more like a 'takeover' because of the disparity in strength. Queen Alexandra sent her regiment the following deeply personal message shortly before disbandment:

"With a sorrow which no words can express I take farewell of my Regiment of Hussars. I had always hoped that long after I was gone the regiment might have still been in existence to maintain its reputation and to carry on the glorious traditions handed down from Seringapatam, Assaye, Egypt, The Soudan, South Africa, to the Great War, . . . and I had been proud to think that my name was borne by the regiment who had thus fought its way over the world and I hoped that perhaps my memory might be associated with its tradition in the name the regiment bore. . . I have made every effort that was possible to save the regiment and to retain it in the army but without avail and to the requirement of military necessities I have to see my regiment swept away. To me the blow is bad enough but to you it is terrible. . . I ask you to do what is hardest of all, to face this decision of disbandment both as a body and individually with the same courage and discipline that has won the regiment its good name throughout its history and I ask you to remember in whatever other units you may be called on to serve that with the recollection of your old regiment you carry with you the discipline learnt in the 19th Royal Hussars . . . wherever you may be. To my Dear Regiment with unspeakable sadness I now bid farewell and for the last time I sign myself

Muttra 23/9/21.   Alexandra: Colonel in Chief.

Queen Mary sent a similar message to her own regiment, though by this time it was known that they were amalgamating not disbanding and, with nice touch, the new Colonel of the 13th/18th Hussars, Baden-Powell, wrote to them:

> "I want in the name of the 13th Hussars to condole with you in the reduction of your Regiment under the new scheme of organization, and at the same time to tell you how glad we are to find a silver lining to the dark cloud in that we are in the future to be associated with the 18th.
>
> May I say how greatly we welcome this particular alliance under the circumstances. Speaking for myself, you may be sure that I shall do all in my power to uphold the prestige of the 18th, and I shall be glad to receive any views or suggestions which, from time to time, Officers, past or present, may wish to put forward."

From the start the 13th/18th Hussars seemed to have an amicable arranged marriage. Based on mutual respect, there was no reason why it should have been otherwise. But the terms of the War Office orders were not as precise as they should have been. Associations and aid funds were not combined for some time because of the thought of dis-amalgamation. Queen Mary continued to return loyal greetings to the officers of the "18th (Queen Mary's Own) Royal Hussars" at their annual dinner, though she was Colonel-in-Chief of the amalgamated regiment. Uniform, which by definition is meant to unite, in fact perpetuated the differences. Seemingly in the spirit, if not the letter, of the War Office orders, the squadrons wore the uniform of their former regiments. Only in full dress was there agreement to standardize on the senior regiment's pattern, though full dress for the whole regiment was by this time a thing of the past. It was not for another ten years that a unified regimental badge was produced and worn.

While the 13th/18th Hussars, their title shorn of all embellishments, enjoyed a relatively straightforward honeymoon, the 15th/19th Hussars, likewise shorn of embellishments, needed marriage guidance from the outset. The officers refused to sit at the same table for the wedding breakfast and for some time afterwards. Queen Alexandra had become Colonel-in-Chief of the new regiment but there was a dual colonelcy with General Sir William Peyton (late 15th) and Field-Marshal Lord French (late 19th). This worked as well as might be expected but after French died in 1925 his place was taken, unofficially, by Field-Marshal Lord Chetwode, also late 19th and a powerful serving officer. By the end of the decade all the regiments had begun to realize that the amalgamations were permanent and that what the 1922 orders had laid down was not really practicable. It was generally decided that thorough fusions should be made.

The question of names therefore arose. No longer did they have to reflect two separate regiments in one. In 1935 13th/18th were redesignated 'Royal' and 'Queen Mary's Own'. Three years earlier 15th/19th had become '15th The King's Royal Hussars'. This was a mistake: it completely submerged the 19th's identity and for no real purpose. What had happened, apparently, was that Chetwode had advised the King that this was the wish of the regiment. It appears that it was certainly *not* the wish of the '19th Hussars' officers. The field-marshal would regret his ill-researched advice: it is said that the great man, Commander-in-Chief India, could not go into the Cavalry Club without former 19th Hussar officers throwing things at him – no unruly Roman forum could match the Cavalry Club in that mood!

A petition was sent to the King and a question asked in the House of Commons. The lobbying bore fruit the next year when the regiment was redesignated '15th/19th The King's Royal Hussars'. And so, for nearly sixty years, the titles of the two regiments remained unchanged. In 1941, a little before Churchill's memorandum, there appears to have been an attempt by 15th/19th to call on the War Office to honour the promise implicit in the 1922 orders, that is to say, to *dis*-amalgamate. The reply was that which the Prime Minister later received.

✳ ✳ ✳

After amalgamation the 13th/18th Hussars, at Aldershot, and the 15th/19th Hussars at Tidworth, began to follow each other around the world. 15th/19th moved to Egypt in 1924. There was still a large garrison there, its purpose twofold – to guard the Suez Canal against external attack, and to provide for internal security. Egypt, it will be remembered from Chapter Eight, had been occupied by Britain in 1882 after the Ottoman Turks had mis-managed the country's economy (Cyprus had been occupied four years earlier in much the same circumstances). In 1914, however, Turkey no longer an ally, Egypt had been made a protectorate by Britain, and this remained effectively her status until after the Second World War.

In the aftermath of the Great War there were frequent anti-British demonstrations and Egypt would not have been a total 'sunshine posting'. Nevertheless there was excellent scope for training in ideal cavalry country and plenty of opportunities for games and sport. Polo had been revived in the regiment in Tidworth and was now flourishing. No doubt, too, after the sullenness of Ireland and the austerity of post-war Britain, those not playing polo found Cairo a fascinating diversion. It only lasted four years, however, an unusually short posting, but Egypt was being used as a transit garrison for India. In 1928 the 15th/19th Hussars sailed for the familiar sub-continent, to be stationed this time at Risalpur on the North-West Frontier.

Meanwhile, the 13th/18th Hussars had left Aldershot and had moved to Edinburgh. For four years they had, it seems, returned to the pre-war routine of hunting, horse shows, and lots of games. There was nothing like the large-scale exercises over the countryside which the decade before the Great War had seen: the Country would not stand for it. So the regiments did their best at home to maintain enthusiasm and standards, but it was an uphill struggle.

The 1926 General Strike might have afforded some excitement, especially since C Squadron was sent to Glasgow, but even that proved a damp squib. Another move, in 1927 after two years in Scotland, hardly enlivened things. Miller's history of the regiment records forlornly:

"Shorncliffe had little different in the way of soldiering to offer. Training areas were very restricted, and it was difficult to exercise the horses except on hard and slippery main roads. Recruit and individual training, musketry, education, courses and minor tactical exercises were the normal order of the day."

The one change of pace seems to have been the mechanization of the regiment's two machine-gun troops, which were provided with Morris six-wheel trucks, and of the first-line transport. It was 1929 and, according to the 'Ten Year Rule', defence spending was still limited because no major war in Europe was contemplated within ten years. This partial mechanization was a beginning, at least, and elsewhere in the Army there were far-sighted experiments, but always under impossibly restrictive conditions.

In September, 1929, the 13th/18th Hussars sailed for Egypt to take up the life which 15th/19th had left the previous year, but after only two years they followed them again to India. They were stationed initially at Sialkot and then moved to Risalpur three years later.

Life for both regiments in India followed the same pattern. There was occasionally civil unrest, especially in the frontier provinces and Bengal, for which they sometimes deployed. The deployment invariably achieved its deterrent effect, the situation quietened and the regiments returned to their cantonments. But besides these occasional excitements the pattern was of training, games and sport. Even allowing for the absence of female company it was an officer's life verging on the ideal: everything was affordable, polo was played almost every day, there was plenty of shooting and wonderful camaraderie. Variations of English field sports, such as hunting jackal with 'bobbery packs', kept officers in touch with life at home.

For the soldier it was not quite the same, but India was popular nonetheless. First and foremost it was no longer a place where they died in large numbers because of disease. Nor was it a posting of interminable length: ten years, maximum, overseas was the rule, often with two or three changes of station, and good stretches of home leave. Some marrieds could be accompanied, the majority in fact, though marriage in the junior ranks was not nearly so common then. But how did the soldier manage without female company? The answer is that he didn't always. Marriage with Indian girls was strenuously discouraged but it happened occasionally. And there was always the red light district. Each cantonment's *lal* (red) *bazaar* had by this stage become less conspicuous as a result of reforming zeal at the turn of the century: nevertheless brothels were almost an official part of the scene. The curious thing was that, like mess subscriptions, charges were *pro rata* – two rupees for a sergeant, one for a corporal, twelve annas for a lance corporal and eight for a trooper.

And the officers? There is no record of 'rates' having been advertised. Officers had hill stations. A vivid picture of social life in these can be seen in Paul Scott's novel *The Jewel in the Crown*, a generation or two after Kipling's stories about Mrs Hauksbee and her cronies.

The real purpose of the hill station was to escape the heat and dust of the plains in the summer. Most regiments were allocated a permanent site and spent much effort improving them – accommodation, sports grounds and general amenities. Families went up for the whole of the summer and all ranks had trickle leave there.

Although these were the twilight days of the Raj, mutual respect between British and Indian officers, in spite of conventions which today would seem outrageous, was probably at its greatest. The 'Indianization' of the Indian Army was moving apace and some of the Indian officers were being trained at Sandhurst. There was genuine affection and fellow-feeling between British and Indian regiments. The 13th/18th Hussars found themselves in Risalpur alongside Skinner's Horse again, and they immediately resumed the rapport which had developed in Meerut before the Great War. It was to lead eventually to a formal alliance.

The 15th/19th Hussars returned to England in 1934, remaining for a year in both Shorncliffe and Tidworth before moving to

York in 1936. In the wake of limited re-armament, mechaniz-ation was gaining pace. There had still been a place for the horse in a colonial police role, which was in effect the regiments' role in India, but Haig's assertion that there would *always* be a role for the horse, "the well-bred horse", was hopelessly wrong.

It was not in the end the machine gun which concluded cavalry warfare: until the time when reconnaissance, battlefield mobility and shock action could be reliably provided by an armoured vehicle there was often no alternative to using horsed cavalry – whatever the cost. It was the development of the tank as a reliable alternative which sealed the fate of horsed cavalry – or, the alternative viewpoint, released legions of future horses from privation and horrific injury.

* * *

It had not been widely recognized in Britain after the Great War that full mechanization was only a matter of time. The prevailing view was that tanks would be an adjunct to the cavalry and infantry rather than a revolutionary piece of technology. Even Churchill, who had done so much to encourage the tank's earlier development, later confessed that the implications of massed armour had escaped him despite the growing evidence. In the immediate post-war years the Royal Tank Corps had only just managed to keep the flame alive against a chill wind of apathy. In 1926, however, a Gunner, General Sir George Milne, took over as CIGS. He had no experience whatever of armour, having served throughout the war in the Middle East and Salonika. As is often the case, this very lack of experience made for impartiality. Milne had indeed thought out the position from first principles, and by the time he arrived in Whitehall he had distilled his thoughts. He was determined to modernize the army as much as was politically and economically possible – and as rapidly as its conservative elements would permit.

In 1924 the War Office had formed a Directorate of Mech-anization, and Milne, with Fuller as his military assistant, now insisted on the formation of "a mechanized division capable of covering at least 100 miles per day across country", at the same time demanding "as rapidly as possible the modernization of the existing formations". It was 1929 before 13th/18th saw anything of 'mechanicalization', as indicated earlier, but the seeds were sewn. The Indian Army itself showed little sign of interest, in spite of a highly successful demonstration in 1925 of two 'whippet' tanks over long distances and different terrain. Throughout both 13th/18th's and 15th/19th's time in Egypt and India, however, there was a growing realization in the regiments as to where the future lay – as will be seen.

An experimental mechanized force (EMF) was set up in 1927 and in the same year the Army Council decided to convert two cavalry regiments to armoured cars. The 11th Hussars and the 12th Lancers were chosen as the two most junior of the regiments not amalgamated in 1922. To the great surprise of many not a single officer resigned.

It was only three years later that the 'National Socialist German Workers' Party', soon derisively nicknamed '*Nazi*', became the second largest party in Germany. Their democratic success was the result of a number of factors – a general disillusionment with the other parties, rising unemployment, the provision of a scapegoat in the notion of the 'treacherous Jew', superior propaganda and the backing of leading industrialists who saw communism as the greater threat. After the successive failures of three Chancellors in as many years, President Hindenburg appointed Hitler to that office in January, 1930. During the next few years, by a skilful combination of intrigue, blackmail, street thuggery, murder, and more, Hitler eliminated the democratic opposition. On Hindenburg's death in August, 1934, he proclaimed himself '*Führer*' of the German *Reich*'.

The following year in Germany saw the formation of three *Panzer* divisions, the introduction of conscription and the announcement of an air force. All these were in direct contravention of the Versailles Treaty which had sought to emasculate German military power after the Great War. In this same year the League of Nations failed to prevent fascist Italy from conquering Abyssinia. Collective security had failed, as Hitler expected, but

Britain and France had failed unilaterally too, and this was even more significant. It signalled to him that their resolve to resist his own expansionism would probably be weak.

In March, 1936, the German army re-occupied the Rhineland violating its demilitarized status under the Versailles and Locarno treaties. The British and French governments contented themselves with protests. There were some politicians who did not – in England, Winston Churchill for one. He had been out of office since 1929 and had been advocating re-armament with increasing vigour.

In 1937 Japan, which six years earlier had been the first to expose the feebleness of collective security by refusing to comply with the League of Nations' demand to withdraw from Manchuria, began a large-scale conquest of China. Gradually Neville Chamberlain's Conservative government began to see that armed defiance might in the end be the only way of stopping ruthless aggression. That year, therefore, an extensive programme of re-armament began. The Army Council decided in October to mechanize the remainder of the Cavalry less two regiments, though not the Household Cavalry and not all the Yeomanry. Again there were fears of high numbers of resignations and again they proved groundless. The Greys and the Royals were the two regiments selected to remain horsed being "oldest by date of raising". It is interesting to note how mechanization, as in 1927, was still not regarded as the *privilege* and that seniority carried the 'privilege' of remaining horsed.

15th/19th's mechanization came in 1938, the year of the German annexation of Austria (the *Anschluss*) and of the Sudetenland in Czechoslovakia. More correctly, the regiment lost its horses in 1938 (April) but did not actually receive its Vickers light tanks until the middle of 1939. Rearmament for the Nation was a case of 'too little too late', but for the Army and industry it was mainly a case of 'too much too quickly'.

But what happened to the horses? In fact they did not all disappear. The troop horses were sent to the remount depots or to contractors who supplied the Yeomanry, but the officers' chargers remained, on a reduced scale of one per officer. To

what purpose? Astonishing as it may seem, the Army Council
was still obsessed with the notion that officers might resign in
large numbers and so it decided to keep half the chargers to
maintain morale. The principle applied for some years even
after the war had ended. Even courses at Bovington were 'sweet-
ened' by allowing the charger to accompany the officer. The
Quartermaster-General pointed out forcefully that this was not
even-handed, so the Tank Corps were allocated five horses there
too!

While 15th/19th were struggling to re-train on the few obsolete
tracked carriers which arrived in York in the summer of 1938,
13th/18th were preparing to return to England to begin their
mechanization. They were able to do some familiarization training with the Tank Corps in Peshawar but they were fully expecting, as no doubt 15th/19th had been, a comprehensive conversion
programme to be in place on their reaching England. They arrived
in Shorncliffe at the beginning of November full of eager anticipation but were immediately disappointed at what they found.

What they found, in fact, was *nothing*. Everything would have
to be done from scratch. The War Office made a training grant
to equip a driving and maintenance school – £10! This was to
enable engines and parts to be bought for instructional purposes.
It was an impossibly small amount, even by the standards of the
time: as Miller's history of 13th/18th recalls, "It was only by the
generosity and patriotism of the Rootes Group, Lucas Ltd., and
the local garages, who gave freely almost everything necessary,
that it was possible to set up a school at all." Others were less
impressed by British industry: Gardner's Horse officers, whom
the regiment had said farewell to in India, were apprehensive
about being able to master the techniques of mechanization, but
on the initial training "were grateful to Lord Nuffield for the
slowness and poor acceleration of his products", relates Major
Narindar Saroop in *A Squire of Hindoostan*.

The bands of both regiments were equipped as motor cycle
troops. When 13th/18th's motorbikes arrived there were still
no instructors. The bandsmen were simply given the hand-
books, told to teach themselves riding and maintenance, and

generally to 'get on with it'. They managed somehow, and were able to give a passable motor-cycle display for Queen Mary when she visited in July.

A limited number of Vickers Mark VIs arrived at about the same time as 15th/19th received theirs, but most were well-worn. The majority of them failed to make it to the barracks from the railway sidings. It can have done little to inspire confidence amongst the onlookers in Shorncliffe but for 13th/18th it was thoroughly disheartening, for by this time the further carve-up of Czechoslovakia had taken place and it was clear that Chamberlain's policy of appeasement was failing. Guarantees to Poland were given by Britain and France in the event of further German aggression and there were few people who did not expect war soon. A limited mobilization was in fact taking place with the call-up of the Militia, Reserve and Special Reserve. More equipment began to arrive with both regiments but it was still woefully inadequate.

History usually has it that, while the much-vaunted German *Blitzkrieg* army relied heavily on horses for both transport and artillery, the BEF of 1939 was a mechanized force with *no* horses. The War Office branch responsible for the equipment programme, 'SD7', could report in the summer that the Mark VI was "the main fighting vehicle of the four Divisional Cavalry Regiments". But the reality was nothing like so cut and dried. Out of 13th/18th's twenty-eight Mark VIs, for instance, only twelve had gun shoulder pieces and were thus in a condition to fight. Many drivers had not driven off the training field and the gunners had had only three days on the ranges: more would in any case have been pointless with only two belts of ammunition per gun. It was only on the day before leaving Shorncliffe for France that the regiment received its full complement of transport. This arrived in the afternoon – bakers' vans and grocers' lorries in every colour. The last evening was spent painting them khaki.

While the BEF of 1914 has been described as "the best equipped, organized and prepared army that Britain had ever sent abroad at the beginning of a war", conversely John Strawson has written of the BEF of 1939: "The fact was that the British army was totally inadequate in size, in equipment, in doctrine and in training". Hitler's invasion of Poland on 1 September, 1939, had set Europe on a final course to war. When the Franco-British ultimatum expired on 3 September Britain's war officially began. 13th/18th landed in France on 19 September; 15th/19th landed on 4 October having only received their last tanks and echelon transport (of the same description as 13th/18th's) on 28 September. They and the BEF as a whole were lucky that, unlike 1914, the enemy were not already on the march. It was not *Blitzkrieg* they faced but 'Sitzkrieg'.

CHAPTER 14

The Road to Dunkirk

"I remember little of the crossing except a very welcome whisky and soda before dropping to sleep in a luxurious double cabin with Captain Harrap (Adjutant) in the other bed. We were called by a steward in the morning with a cup of tea, who said: *'We are just approaching Dover Harbour, Sir'*."

Lieutenant-Colonel D.A. STIRLING,
Commanding 13th/18th Hussars, June, 1940.

13th/18th and 15th/19th with BEF to France; the 'Phoney War'; Advance to the Dyle; Dyle to Escaut; Withdrawal to Dunkirk; Reconstruction in England.

Six months in north-west France during the 'Phoney War', a sprint into Belgium, three weeks of at times bewildering and exasperating withdrawal and finally, amid scenes of disorder and ill-discipline, evacuation from the sand dunes of Dunkirk by craft of every size and civilian calling – not even the dignity of being taken off by the Royal Navy as in previous evacuations from Flanders: this was the regiments' first taste of war as mechanized cavalry.

Between the wars France had poured most of her defence budget into the massive fixed defences on her border with Germany. These, forming the so-called Maginot Line, would have held up almost any ground offensive indefinitely, but they extended only as far as the Belgian border in the north. Expense, besides any other considerations, had prevented further extension. If Germany were going to attack through Belgium again, the French army's mobile troops would be able to concentrate to meet them, their right flank secure on the Maginot Line.

One of the operational plans devised by the French and BEF staffs was for an advance into Belgium as far as the River Dyle in order to conduct a forward defence in cooperation with the Belgian army. The German operational plan *'Sichelschnitt'* ('sickle-cut'), the one which was eventually adopted, envisaged 'fixing' the allies in Belgium and, with a movement resembling that of a scythe, enveloping them in a move through northern France to take the Channel ports and thus the BEF's means of escaping. Belgian neutrality would not permit any allied move across their border until actual German aggression, though there were staff talks at the highest level, so while the German plan could expect to achieve a large degree of surprise and dislocation, the allied plan could only hope for luck in co-operation with the Belgians. The situation did not augur well for coordination, and this was to have the gravest consequences for 15th/19th Hussars in particular.

'Sitzkreig' had at least allowed for some desperately needed collective training as well as completing re-equipment. Neither regiment had been able to do anything other than individual D & M (driving and maintenance), gunnery or signal training before leaving England, and there had certainly been no comprehensive formation-level training. Miller's history of 13th/18th relates that:

> "There were no textbooks on the tactical employment of a mechanized divisional cavalry regiment, so the method adopted was to study the tasks which the Regiment was likely to carry out, then to practise them as a drill, and finally to carry them out as a tactical exercise in the field at which the Divisional Commander was present to criticize and advise."

This was sound enough, and pretty unremarkable. It required the regimental officers to be intelligent and to have a realistic grasp

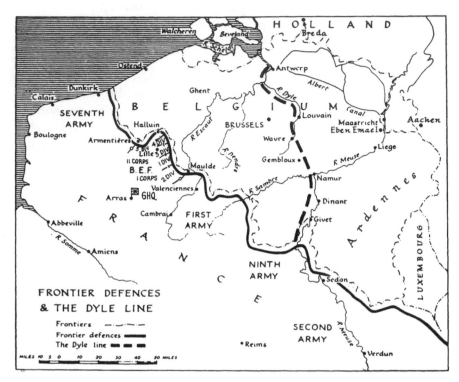

The Frontier Defences and the Dyle Line (*from Official History*).

of the realities of modern warfare – not too much to expect. It also required the divisional commander to be equally equipped and active. In the case of 13th/18th the divisional commander was Major-General (later Field-Marshal) The Honourable H.R.L.G. Alexander. He was a fine tactician, and, no doubt, the regiment's training was well directed. Miller says, "In the spring Major-General Alexander held a seven-day exercise near the Somme. This showed that the Regiment had attained a high degree of efficiency and learned many lessons." No doubt this is true – up to a point. An official regimental history will not be over self-critical. Courage's history of 15th/19th relates much the same picture, though not quite so blandly.

Yet there were real problems. Nigel Hamilton, Field-Marshal Montgomery's most comprehensive biographer, writes of the GOC 3rd Division's training at this time: "Bernard [Montgomery] was particularly dissatisfied with the performance of his cavalry regiment, the 15th/19th Royal Hussars [sic], who to his mind attached more importance to billets and messes than to organized rehearsal for battle." The second-in-command was sacked and they were made to repeat one particular exercise.

But just as things were being sorted out a major change in grouping was ordered: in April it was decided to group the BEF's seven reconnaissance regiments into two reconnaissance brigades for specific operations. In principle there was obvious merit in this but it required a proper establishment for brigade headquarters and time to train. There was neither. The purpose of these brigades was the coordination of reconnaissance for each of the two corps headquarters, with regiments changing their command status from their parent division to the recce brigade as required. Reconnaissance at BEF level was provided by the armoured car regiment, the 12th Lancers, which reported direct to GHQ. The (Bartholomew) Committee of Enquiry into the BEF's operations subsequently described the armoured recce brigades as "a wash-out".

After the months of waiting, most of the BEF heard the news of the German invasion of Belgium on 10 May, 1940, from the BBC. The order for the move to the forward line on the Dyle arrived soon afterwards: 13th/18th and 15th/19th left their billets in La Verderie and Lannoy near the border and set off across Belgium in the early afternoon in the wake of the Lancers who were already sprinting for Louvain. The move was about eighty miles in a hostile air situation, and both regiments had an early taste of dive-bombing and machine-gunning. However, the main bodies reached the Dyle between 8.00 and 10.30pm largely unscathed, surprised that neither sabotage nor refugees had held them up.

As planned, 1st Corps was to deploy on a two-division front (1st and 2nd Divisions) on the right, and 2nd Corps on a one-division front (3rd Division) on the left. The intention was for the divisional reconnaissance regiments to hold along the Dyle until relieved by the infantry brigades, then for them to relieve in turn the Lancers who were watching the approaches to the bridges some eight miles to the east of the river. The occupation of the Dyle line went well, with the 4th/7th Dragoon Guards covering 2nd Division on the right (French) flank, 13th/18th in the centre covering 1st Division, and 15th/19th on the left (Belgian) flank. By 1.00 pm on 12 May the regiments had been relieved on the river line by the infantry, and had moved forward to the screen line beyond, the 12th Lancers having then pushed further east to gain contact with the Belgians.

The BEF's defensive position was a relatively strong one. Its weakness was inevitably the flanks. The right flank was theoretically secure in that the French 1st Army was to take up positions on the same stop line. The left was not nearly so secure: it relied on the Belgian army, conducting a fighting withdrawal from the border, coming onto the open flank. It would have been a difficult manoeuvre in any circumstances.

The BEF's problems began even before their deployment was complete. The French 1st Army's advance to the Dyle was very slow; in fact it was never completed, and in effect the BEF's right flank was open from the outset. The existence and extent of this gap was never fully recognized by GHQ, a fundamental failure of reconnaissance.

On 13 May the regiments learned of the rapid withdrawal of the Belgians to their east and that contact with German ground forces was therefore imminent. The *Luftwaffe* were active throughout the day. Contact was made around midday in 13th/18th's sector: a motor-cycle recce group was engaged by one of the screen troops, with good effect, but three armoured cars followed up, against which the Mark VI's machine guns made no impression. The German recce patrol, having established the presence of the screen, withdrew.

That night and the following morning recce patrols continued to probe, particularly around 13th/18th's right flank. 4th/7th had retired closer to their crossing points on 13 May and this had left the regiment's southern flank less secure. The divisional commander had delegated authority to 13th/18th's commanding officer to withdraw west of the Dyle, so when it appeared that the enemy were exploiting the flank gap Stirling ordered the withdrawal of the regimental screen at midday on 14 May. 15th/19th withdrew at the same time to conform. It was a pity that this general retirement took place since it gave the enemy a free run up to the river. It emphasized the need for careful flank coordination, but it at least showed that 13th/18th and 15th/19th were talking to each other.

This giving ground was nothing compared with what was happening elsewhere, however. On 12 May Rommel had crossed the Meuse and in the north the Germans had reached the Zuider Zee. Two days later the *Panzers* were at Sedan, having slipped through the Ardennes which were considered by the French high command to be impenetrable to armour, and the 'sickle-cut' was underway. That evening, 14 May, the Dutch capitulated, the terror-bombing of Rotterdam having finally knocked all fight out of them. Prolonged defence of the Dyle looked increasingly pointless; orders were received for a general withdrawal to the River Escaut on the night of 16/17 May, to be complete in forty-eight hours.

The gap on the BEF's right flank was now causing growing concern. The 2nd Division had had to withdraw on 16 May in order to reduce the risk to the flank which was in effect only being covered by the 1st Armoured Reconnaissance Brigade with its two Yeomanry regiments. This forced 13th/18th to adjust to cover the 1st Division's southern flank. At the same time 15th/19th were doing likewise on the BEF's northern flank, since it was anticipated that the Belgians might withdraw north-west rather than south-west on to the open flank. The 5th Inniskilling Dragoon Guards (the 'Skins'), who up until this stage had been under command HQ 2nd Corps in a coordinating role, were put into the Dyle screen, and HQ 2nd Armoured Reconnaissance Brigade was activated to coordinate the actions of the two.

13th/18th, under tight control and clear direction from 1st Division throughout the withdrawal to the Escaut, were able to carry out their rearguarding and flank-screening on 18 May in a textbook manner. By 4.00pm they were west of the River

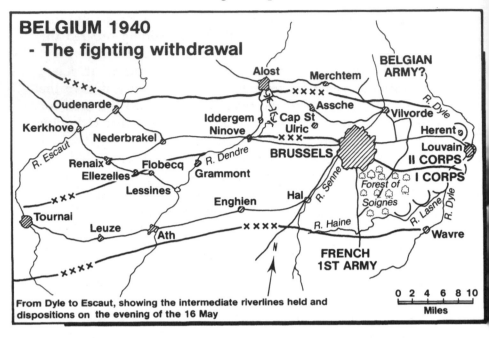

BELGIUM 1940
- The fighting withdrawal

From Dyle to Escaut, showing the intermediate riverlines held and
dispositions on the evening of the 16 May

Dendre, halfway to the Escaut, on which 1st and 2nd Infantry
Brigades were dug-in. 15th/19th, who had still seen no action,
were soon to pay an enormous price for being on a disintegrating
flank and under new and less than satisfactory command arrangements. In fact, in the fighting on 18 May, while 13th/18th were
managing to withdraw in orderly bounds, 15th/19th ceased to
exist as a reconnaissance regiment.

Towards evening on the 17th, 15th/19th had been ordered
to take up a position in the western suburbs of Brussels with
their left flank well forward to maintain contact with the
Belgians. Despite extensive patrolling, however, no contact
with the Belgians could be made. At 8.45am the regiment were
ordered to withdraw to a line north-south through the town
of Assche, eight miles to the west. Regimental Headquarters
moved back to Assche at once where 2nd Armoured Recce
Brigade's commander emphasized to 15th/19th's commanding
officer, Lieutenant-Colonel D.S. Frazer, that the regiment could
only withdraw from this position with his express permission

– time had to be bought for the infantry on the Dendre to complete their occupation. He could not give the commanding officer any information, however, on the enemy, the Belgians or the promised supporting machine-gun battalion and artillery observers. All the brigadier *could* do was to confirm that certain roads were exclusive to the regiment, as agreed with the Belgian staff.

The regiment was sceptical about this exclusion, especially the main road Vilvorde-Alost on the northern flank, so a troop was sent along it to make contact with the Belgians. It was badly shot up after running into German armour: the troop leader was killed, and only the troop corporal managed to get back to report what had happened.

The squadrons never had a chance to occupy the Assche line. They arrived with the Germans on their tails, but worse, by that time the Germans had got between them and the Dendre by motoring straight down the main road on the open flank. Without the machine-gun battalion's support properly coordinated, and the gunners unable to fire because Assche was out of arc, the regiment was in a critical position.

C Squadron on the left flank came under heavy pressure immediately they halted, and 2nd Troop Leader was killed almost straightaway. Later in the morning, when B Squadron arrived having covered the regiment's withdrawal from Brussels, the depleted C Squadron was sent to secure a withdrawal route to the Dendre and B Squadron took over that flank and forward left. 'A' Squadron was ordered to cover the forward right and flank but immediately ran into trouble as it deployed to do so. The squadron leader, Major C. Cockayne-Frith, was killed as his Mark VI entered Assche; only one troop was to escape from A Squadron's fight.

B Squadron had also begun to take casualties. A complete troop was destroyed having been told to rear-recce a route to an intermediate position. Its troop leader was Second-Lieutenant J.S. Livingstone-Learmonth whose father, a 15th Hussar, had been killed in the Great War. B Squadron Leader, unaware of the troop's contact, moved down the same road a little later and ran straight into an anti-tank ambush. Severely wounded, he was taken prisoner.

The situation was rapidly approaching disaster. No contact could be made with the Skins to the regiment's right (they had in fact withdrawn) and communications with brigade headquarters were poor. At 1.00 pm permission was finally given to withdraw east of the Dendre, but by then it was too late. All communication with the squadrons had been lost, in part due to a major jamming effort by the Germans, and it was becoming clear to the commanding officer that total encirclement was imminent. He therefore ordered RHQ to move back to the Dendre by side roads.

They only got half a mile. Anti-tank guns and an armoured car destroyed RHQ in minutes, Colonel Frazer being thrown from his Mark VI badly stunned. Less than twenty-four hours later all RHQ officers, the RSM, signallers and drivers were 'in the bag'. All, that is, except the Adjutant, Captain A.D. Taylor, who had paused while RHQ was getting moving in order to send written orders to A and B Squadrons by despatch rider. As he set off he came across B Squadron Leader who told him that the road down which RHQ had moved was blocked. B Squadron Leader then asked him to lead his squadron column down another side road since he was now the lead vehicle. This he did, but the column ran into the enemy, although Taylor soon got the better of them and pursued them through a village. At this point his Mark VI's steering clutch failed. The remainder of B Squadron (now only three tanks) swept passed and Taylor and his crew were promptly captured. He escaped a few days later and made his own way back to England in a truly remarkable escapade for which he was awarded the Military Cross; the story is related in full in Courage's history.

B Squadron's three Mark VIs became bogged soon afterwards and their crews dispersed to make their way back on foot. Major W.R.N. Hinde, who had assumed command of the squadron a few hours earlier, was wounded in the neck and arm but managed to swim the Dendre, whence he was evacuated to England. Hamilton sums up the day from Montgomery's viewpoint:

"Thus while Bernard's 3rd Division waited intact behind the Dendre for the next phase in the defensive battle on 18 May, it was forced to watch impotently as its vital armoured mobile cavalry screen was thrown away."

All that were able to rally west of the Dendre that night were five officers, five mounted troops, a dozen or so dismounted crewmen and the echelon. Major Sir Henry Floyd took command. It seemed a strange irony of history that the descendant of the 15th Light Dragoons' youthful riding master, John Floyd, the man who had subsequently raised the Nineteenth, should at this moment take charge of the remnants of the 15th/19th Hussars after the biggest disaster in the regiment's history. It was not to be an independent command, however, for that evening he received orders to come under command the Skins.

That same evening 13th/18th (less A Squadron) came under command 1st Corps and were ordered back to their old billets at La Verderie in France. A Squadron's own return to France was via some sharp fighting under direct command of Headquarters 1st Division while covering the withdrawal of one of their infantry brigades. The whole regiment managed nevertheless to concentrate at La Verderie on the morning of 21 May. They had had remarkably few casualties although they had lost sixteen Mark VIs and twenty-four carriers. Regrouping into two strong squadrons was now necessary, however.

By 21 May 15th/19th were also back across the French frontier, at Mouveaux, where they remained for three nights, resting and 're-kitting'. The Germans had destroyed two of the BEF's Territorial Army divisions, and part of 2nd Panzer Division had reached the coast at Noyelles at the mouth of the Somme. On 21 May itself the BEF's heavy tanks made a partially successful counter-attack south into the German flank at Arras but were eventually forced to withdraw. The following day, the *Panzers* began their determined drive for the Channel ports.

On 23 May the Commander-in-Chief, Lord Gort, took the decision to save the BEF. It was not a straightforward decision since it meant withdrawing unilaterally from the allied command at a time when continued French resistance was still being taken for granted in France and, to an extent, in London too. Gort realized the French army was finished and he now saw it as his simple duty to save his force. His many critics would say that it was the only service he performed for the BEF. But if the decision were difficult, it was nothing compared with its execution. The *Luftwaffe* were managing to inflict casualties at a worrying rate. Refugees, both civilian and Franco-Belgian military, were crowding the roads. The *Panzers* were looking likely to sweep right up the Channel coast, and the naval operation to take off the force would be touch-and-go even without the *Luftwaffe*.

Dunkirk was decided on as the point of evacuation. A 'box' would be formed into which the troops would withdraw to be taken off either from the harbour itself or over the beaches. Since the absolute priority was men – British, French and Belgian – no heavy equipment would be taken off. Thus all transport and fighting vehicles were to be destroyed at the Dunkirk perimeter defences.

The immediate problem facing the BEF on 23 May was the strong pressure building up against the southern flank of the box either side of St Omer on the Aire River. Two ad hoc groups were therefore formed to counter this – 'Macforce' and 'Polforce'. 13th/18th went to the former and 15th/19th, still under command the Skins, to the latter. After thirty-six hours, during which there had been some sharp exchanges, though the Germans did not press home their attacks, the regiments were withdrawn. 15th/19th moved back to Armentières to be ready to support the defences on the Lys Canal, and 13th/18th concentrated at Ploegsteert, forever 'Plugstreet' to the earlier generation which had fought in the Ypres battles.

Breakdowns, with no recovery or spares, had further reduced 15th/19th to two Mark VIs and seven carriers. On 26 May they were stunned when ordered to hand over these remaining fighting vehicles and to come under command of the 4th/7th, who likewise were ordered to hand over their vehicles to the Skins, and for 15th/19th and 4th/7th to form a composite mobile infantry reserve. The following day they moved to Estaires to hold the bridges over the Lys Canal. They were ordered to defend them 'to the end' against the anticipated German attack at first light on the 28th.

Meanwhile, early in the afternoon of the 27th, 13th/18th had been ordered to support a counter-attack by a company of the Black Watch and a composite company of Royal Engineers fighting as infantry: the Germans had got across the Ypres-Comines Canal and the eastern point of the BEF's ninety-seven-mile semi-elliptical box looked like being penetrated. The Germans had not at that stage succeeded in getting any heavy weapons across the canal so the Mark VIs were able to do considerable damage. By nightfall the bridgehead had been destroyed and the canal bank re-occupied. This was to prove crucial in order to buy time for the general withdrawal, which was by then moving apace. This time was not bought cheaply, however: the regiment took twenty-two casualties, including B Squadron Leader, Major J. Hawker, killed.

At dawn on 28 May the 125 men of 15th/19th, dug-in around the Lys bridges at Estaires with nothing heavier than a few Bren guns, were stood-to awaiting the German assault. It never came. And to their further astonishment they were relieved in place by French troops, then ordered to destroy all transport less that for essential stores, and told to march to Dunkirk, thirty-five miles away. Fortunately, the acting second-in-command had a map torn from a railway guide – shades of 1914 again.

That morning 13th/18th were once more re-grouping: one squadron was formed from the remains of A and B; all surplus equipment was destroyed and the 'shut-out' crewmen were sent to Dunkirk under the former C Squadron Leader. RHQ and the composite squadron came under command 50th Division in order to cover their withdrawal through Ypres, and by first light were in position. Contact was made almost immediately and continued throughout the morning. The division moved via two major bounds back to the Dunkirk perimeter, covered very skilfully by the squadron, and in the early hours of 30 May they managed to break contact and get inside the perimeter defences. During the fighting there were several more casualties, including the squadron leader, who was wounded too badly to move from the dressing station whence he was captured.

On 30 May both 15th/19th and 13th/18th were taken off from the harbour mole. They had both suffered badly, though 15th/19th's losses were truly appalling: 7 officers and 27 other ranks killed, 4 officers and 22 other ranks wounded, and 6 officers and 100 other ranks taken prisoner. Two fathers and one uncle of future commanding officers clambered on board the ships that day.

* * *

After the fall of France, Britain stood totally alone. She had done so before and the Channel and the Royal Navy had been her saviours. This time, however, there was the air dimension. Neither side's naval forces could operate without air superiority. The *Luftwaffe* therefore had to gain mastery of the Channel airspace before a German invasion fleet could risk crossing. Conversely, the RAF had to deny it them. This was what the 'Battle of Britain', from July until the middle of September, 1940, was all about.

If, however, the Germans had succeeded in making any landings, by sea or air, Churchill had said, "We shall defend our island, whatever the cost may be, we shall fight on the beaches, we shall fight on the landing grounds, we shall fight in the fields and in the streets." The Army, though badly bruised and with almost all its heavy equipment destroyed or abandoned in France and Belgium, had to reorganize and re-equip rapidly to these ends.

On 12 June 13th/18th moved from their recovery area in Gloucestershire to Bovington to form part of the 1st Armoured Reconnaissance Brigade, with the rôle of guarding the coast between Poole Harbour and Corfe. Their armament comprised the rifle and fifty rounds per man. A few weeks later the regiment received some Standard motor cars: these were roofless, with a little armour around the front and sides, and equipped with either a Bren gun or Boys anti-tank rifle. They were known as 'Beaverettes'. At the beginning of July, with seventy-two of these Beaverettes, they moved to Essex under command 12th Corps as *the* mobile reserve for the eastern counties. Here they remained for the next four months with a good view of Number 11 Group's Battle of Britain north of the Thames estuary.

15th/19th's reconstitution was, of course, more difficult. Regimental Headquarters was set up at Bovington in early June, but, with the rest of what remained of 2nd Armoured Reconnaissance Brigade, they moved north a fortnight later to Rawmarsh in South Yorkshire. Here the brigade was to re-form to be a 'Motor Machine-Gun Brigade'.

Few will not know where Rawmarsh is. But only those Light Dragoons from that particular part of the regiment's recruiting area will know its character. At that time it would first have appeared to 15th/19th as a large, grimy village in the coal and steel belt of the Don Valley. There were no barracks, so billeting was arranged – something hardly seen in Britain for a hundred years. The regiment had a few rifles and pistols but no transport or cooking equipment, though each man did have a blanket. Though the local miners and steelworkers were on overtime, they were hardly well-off. The small, terraced houses, with two or three bedrooms at most, were owned by the local council or the coal company. There was no indoor sanitation or bath. Two or three men of the regiment were billeted in one house. It was a recipe for disaster.

In the event it was far from a disaster. Instead, the regiment enjoyed a full month of astonishingly generous hospitality. Without equipment little purposeful training was possible, so much time was given to helping in the township with odd jobs. It proved very difficult even to have parades after the morning muster since every house had a different time for meals. Squadron officers and sergeant-majors found even kit inspections difficult, so protective of 'their' soldiers were many housewives!

At the end of June the regiment's transport arrived, including seventy-two Austin 10hp cars. With these, too, came the Vickers medium machine guns which made the regiment officially operational. The MMG regiment's establishment was relatively small and this, together with officers returning from duty elsewhere, and new drafts from the training regiments, meant that 15th/19th was restored to the order of battle in July. Lieutenant-Colonel W.R.N. Hinde, who as B Squadron Leader had been evacuated, wounded, after swimming back across the Dendre in Belgium, returned to command the regiment and a new RSM arrived, Mr Reynolds, from 13th/18th.

Rawmarsh, and the surrounding area, was not suitable for training, so the brigade moved at the end of the month to north Staffordshire, but the community had made a most positive impression on the regiment at a particularly desperate time. Some twenty-five years later, South Yorkshire, together with the East Riding, became 13th/18th's recruiting area and it continues to be the southern half of the Light Dragoons' area today. After training, 15th/19th moved to Northamptonshire in November, 1940, where they became a mobile reserve for the 4th Corps.

In the same way that the threat of Napoleon's invasion was finally removed by Nelson's defeat of the combined fleets at Trafalgar, the RAF's defeat of the *Luftwaffe*'s summer offensive removed the real threat of a German invasion. There would always be, of course, concern about raids or sabotage, so vigilance could not be relaxed totally. Nevertheless, when both regiments went into winter quarters in Staffordshire their sights were set on early conversion to armour for action in the Middle East or for the liberation of France. Many long months, turning to years, would pass before either regiment was to see action, however. When they finally did so their performance was in marked contrast with the faltering operations in the BEF. It was a triumph of organization, training and, above all, leadership in the preceding three years. In the thrill of the actual events of 1944 and 1945 it would be easy to overlook this achievement.

CHAPTER 15

Normandy to the Baltic

"Technically and strategically the landing in Normandy was a brilliant achievement of the first magnitude. It showed . . . the courage, at any rate in the technical field, to employ a multitude of devices hitherto untried in action."

ROMMEL

13th/18th and 15th/19th training in Britain 1943–44; Normandy Landings; the Breakout Battles; Advance to the Rhine; the 'Final Swan'; Victory in Europe.

Dieppe, 19 August 1942: 6,000 Canadian and British troops, with thirty of the new Churchill tanks, crossed the sixty miles of the Channel to descend on this small French port. Serving with Number 3 Commando was a young 13th/18th officer, Jasper Selwyn, and the news that he had won the MC during the raid was a boost to morale. Raiding, the embodiment of the offensive spirit, always raised morale. This raid's primary purpose, however, was to test the defences of what was later to become known as the 'Atlantic Wall'. Specifically, the question to which Lord Louis Mountbatten's Combined Operations Staff needed an answer was *could a port be seized and held in order that a large invasion force might be landed quickly?*

Only 1,600 men returned from the raid, and no tanks. Half the tanks never got off the beaches. News of the disaster was played up by Goebbels' propaganda machine in Germany, and played down at home: the War Office could hardly announce in mitigation that valuable lessons had been learned for their invasion plans. But that is exactly what had happened – *invaluable* lessons in fact – though, as John Keegan points out in his study of national fighting characteristics *Six Armies in Normandy*, this was like saying that the loss of the *Titanic* held valuable lessons in passenger liner safety: it was of no use to the victims.

It probably seemed of no direct concern to 13th/18th and 15th/19th at the time. Together in 9th Armoured Division, they were continuing with a training programme which had taken them all over the country, but without any apparent future operational purpose. They had been equipped with the wretched Covenanter 'cruiser' tank, mechanically unreliable, under-armoured and under-armed. To make matters worse, large drafts of trained crewmen were taken periodically from both regiments as battle casualty replacements for the Middle East. It was an intensely frustrating and disappointing time.

Towards the end of the year there was more divisional reorganizing, and 13th/18th together with the 4th/7th and the East Riding Yeomanry (ERY), the other regiments of 27th Armoured Brigade, left the 9th Armoured Division and came under command 79th Armoured Division. The 79th's commander was arguably the Army's leading tank expert – 'Hobo', Major-General Percy Hobart, stern, uncompromising, austere, practical. He came to inspect the regiment in November, for which days of special spit-and-polish preparation took place. He passed down the line of the first squadron's immaculate tanks, crews front: "Very nice," he said, "now start them up." What followed would have inspired a Bateman cartoon had it not been so serious: only seven tanks started. The squadron leader was sacked.

The move to 79th Armoured was no more than routine regrouping at the time, but in March the following year Hobart was instructed to make his division the centre of specialized armoured devices and techniques for the invasion. In the months following Dieppe the lessons of the raid had been carefully drawn. "The Lesson of *Greatest Importance*," wrote the operation's naval commander, in capitals and italics, "is the need for overwhelming fire support, including close support, during the initial stages of the attack." Specifically, the infantry needed the intimate support of tanks on the beaches in the first minutes of an assault. This meant, among other things, amphibious armour.

Hobart was the perfect choice to create an experimental formation. He was an innovative thinker and had commanded the experimental tank brigade in the 1930s. He had subsequently raised and trained both 7th and 11th Armoured Divisions. Before D-Day 79th Armoured were to develop bulldozer tanks to clear beach obstacles, 'bobbin-tanks' to lay trackway on loose sand and shingle, 'flail-tanks' to beat pathways through minefields, tanks which could hurl explosive charges against concrete fortifications, turretless tanks which acted as ramps for other tanks to scale sea walls, bridgelayer tanks, flamethrower tanks and, most innovative of all, amphibious or DD (Duplex-Drive) tanks which could swim ashore under their own power.

13th/18th were told in April, 1943, that they were to train as a DD regiment along with 4th/7th and the ERY. The Canadians were also intending to form DD regiments, but the Americans were not interested at first. The DD was not a British invention, however: it was the brainchild of the Hungarian-born engineer, Nicholas Straussler. His demonstrations of the principle using converted Valentine tanks convinced the War Office but not initially the Admiralty. Hobart took over five DD Valentines and soon established that the equipment could be adapted to the Sherman hull, the principal tank in the Allied armoury. In July, 1943, therefore, the War Office placed orders for the conversion of 900 Shermans but the Ministry of Supply was reluctant to divert manpower and materials to the production of experimental equipment in which the Navy had no confidence. Output was consequently so small that six months later Hobart doubted that there would be enough of these tanks to use *en masse* on D-Day as Montgomery, the operational commander, wanted. On 27 January, 1944, the DD was demonstrated for the first time to the Supreme Allied Commander, General Dwight D. Eisenhower. His American number two, also to be commander of the US ground forces during the landings, had watched 13th/18th's training in the Solent two weeks before and was already convinced. The result of these demonstrations was that the Americans became sold on the value of DDs. Consequently the production difficulties were rapidly overcome: on 28 January a British engineer flew to Washington with the blueprints and within a week American factories were at work on the project. Within two months 300 converted Shermans were being shipped to Britain.

Prior to these demonstrations 13th/18th had been training intensively. The tank itself, whether Valentine or Sherman, got its buoyancy by a rubberized canvas screen attached to the hull deck. The screen doubled the tank's height and had to be collapsed quickly once ashore for the gun to be used. The movement of the tank's tracks in the water produced a certain amount of headway but not enough to make real progress in anything other than the calmest water. Two propellers were therefore fitted at the rear of the tank. These were driven by off-takes from the rotating tracks, hence 'duplex-drive', giving a speed through water of roughly one hundred yards per minute. Sluggish steering was provided by a tiller.

Normal conversion training to the Sherman was carried out during the spring and summer of 1943, including brigade training at Thetford. It was only in November, once sufficient Valentines had been received, that the regiment began their specialized training amidst great secrecy at Fritton Lake in Suffolk.

The key element in this training was safety, in particular the action to be taken if a tank were to sink. This was a very real danger since the canvas was easily damaged and, with a freeboard of only two feet, in rough weather there was severe risk of swamping. Each crewman therefore wore a modified Davis Submarine Escape Apparatus (DSEA), a rudimentary underwater breathing device. It was probably better than nothing, but its effectiveness required luck in addition to rigorous training. The culmination of this training was an escape from a 'sawn-off' tank, complete with turret and driver's compartment, at the bottom of a forty-foot well at the Naval establishment in Gosport in Hampshire. Into this truncated tank climbed the full crew of

56. *"Useful indirect fire support."*(*p.261*) 13th/18th Shermans provide 'battery fire'
for US troops at Geilenkirchen in November, 1944.

57. *"Resistance began to stiffen perceptibly when the approaches to the River Weser
itself were probed."*(*p.265*) A Comet tank of A Squadron 15th/19th Hussars at
Petershagen, April, 1945.

58. *"In close country they should in theory have closed down hatches and fought the tanks through the periscopes. The regiment just did not believe that was practicable."(p.265)* Trooper Lyons, a 15th/19th Challenger (the forerunner of Centurion) wireless operator during the 'Final Swan', although for the regiment this meant fighting virtually every inch of the way to the Baltic.

59. *"Their hardest battle of the war".(p.266)* Three weeks before the War's ending, 15th/19th Hussars had to fight a costly battle to take the crossings over the River Aller at Winsen. In two days' fighting the regiment had twenty-two killed or severely injured. The photograph shows Sergeant J Finlinson receiving his MM ribbon, which he won as a lance corporal during the battle, from Field-Marshal Montgomery.

60. *"As a result of the killing [of the High Commissioner] all future VIP escorts became the responsibility of the armoured car regiments."(p.279)* 13th/18th Hussars, Malaya, 1952.

61. *"Countryside prone to flash-floods and land slippage in the Monsoon season."(p.281)* An incident in December, 1956, where a Saracen of C Squadron 15th/19th Hussars was swept over the edge of a 200ft drop into a flooded river, killing Corporal Wells and Trooper Walker. The rest of the convoy had a lucky escape.

62. *"An exemplary action by a junior NCO."* (p.282) Corporal P Conlon, 15th/19th Hussars, leads his patrol out of the jungle after a successful opportunity-action resulting in the capture of a 'CT', January, 1955.

63. *"The dynamic General Sir Gerald Templer . . ."* (p.279) Churchill's appointment of Templer to the combined position of High Commissioner and Director of Operations proved the turning point in the campaign. 13th/18th furnished his escort for almost two years. He is here photographed talking to Sergeant Clegg.

five dressed in overalls with the DSEA adjusted at the ready. Hatches were shut down, the sluice gate was opened and water gushed in. When it reached chest height the crew applied nose clips and started breathing through the mouth pieces. When the well was full, at the given signal, they opened the hatches and left in the correct crew sequence, adjusting their rate of ascent by a control valve on the DSEA. No one failed to break surface during this preliminary training, but the Chief Petty Officer's remark "Rather you than me, mate!" summed up the depth of confidence in the procedure.

After this, and a little cruising on Fritton Lake, the regiment moved to Gosport to get used to working in tidal waters. Twice every twenty-four hours the Valentines would go out in 'Landing Crafts (Tanks)' – LCTs – which would embark them at Stokes Bay, cross the Solent and launch them into Osborne Bay off the Isle of Wight. This training proved what many sceptics had predicted, that manoeuvring in the open sea, with its choppy water, tides and currents, was extremely difficult. Though the War Office was still convinced, and now the Americans, no one doubted the difficulties and dangers for the crews. The next phase of training was to be critical, and in January, 1944, the brigade (27th Armoured) moved up to Scotland, to Fort George on the Moray Firth.

The Moray Firth in winter was thought to be a reasonable test, and intensive training with the other elements of the landing force continued here for the next three months. The beaching areas proved remarkably similar to those eventually to be encountered on 'Queen' Beach. By April it had been finally established that the theory was workable, but the test had not been without cost to the regiment. In the early morning of 1 March the DDs were launched in the Firth as usual. The wind was rising at the time and when the tanks were halfway inshore a severe snowstorm broke. The sea became very rough and two tanks of A Squadron were swamped and sank. Miraculously, all the crewmen were picked up except one of the drivers, Corporal Underhay. This proved to be the only fatality the regiment suffered throughout DD training, however. It was a remarkable record – and against the odds since five tanks in all sank during this period.

After the regiment got back to Gosport the Shermans started to arrive. The flotation apparatus on these was much better. The canvas screen was raised by inflating rubber pillars from compressed air bottles rather than manually by elbow-jointed struts, and could be dropped with equal speed and with the crew under armour. When swimming it had a good three feet of freeboard, although, being heavier than the Valentine, it actually sat lower in the water (the top of the turret was level with the surface of the water). It really had only one disadvantage – its late arrival. Indeed some tanks only arrived a few days before the regiment set sail for France. The regiment's orbat had finally been fixed at two DD squadrons, A and B, with C as the non-DD wading reserve in which was concentrated the 'Firefly' Shermans with the 17-pounder gun, too long for a DD hull.

Throughout this time 15th/19th had continued intensive individual and collective training, increasingly on the new Cromwell tank. There were great hopes for the Cromwell: it was well armoured and had a good gun. At last it seemed the British were capable of producing an effective battle tank. But the regiment still had no news of any future operational role. It was getting to be unbearably frustrating, but wartime Britain was a totally different place: everywhere 'security' and often petty officialdom. There were also constant shortages. Economists and soldiers alike scoffed in later years at the sight of whole divisions of the Red Army taking to the collective farm fields of the Soviet Union each harvest time. From October until Christmas, 1943, however, 15th/19th had to provide 300 men daily to help lift the sugar beet crop in Norfolk and Lincolnshire. It was not popular, even as a break from intensive training.

15th/19th in 1944 were an exceptionally well-trained regiment. Their brigade, 28th Armoured, was an exceptionally well-trained brigade. Frustration at being apparently left out of the *OVERLORD* (Normandy landings) order of battle was therefore intense, and remained so for many months. It was only in June, 1944, when Operation *OVERLORD* was already underway, that the regiment learned that it too was to convert to DD Shermans to become what by that time was termed a 'Water Assault Regiment'. Under command now of 79th Armoured, they went through precisely the same specialized training at Fritton and Gosport, and subsequently sea training at Lee-over-Sands in Essex. They were unable to practise launching from LCTs because these were all committed to the build-up in France, but in all other respects the regiment completed the conversion programme remarkably quickly and without losing a single man or tank. At the end of July they then moved back to Suffolk to await arrival of the new Shermans.

At this stage they had still not been told where it was intended they were to operate. There was plenty of speculation – a landing in the Pas de Calais to destroy the V1 launching sites, southern France to open a second operational front, even the Far East. The V1 rocket, the 'doodlebug', would do considerable damage to London and the south-east. A strategic raid on the recently dis-covered launch sites would be of immense value if successful, but virtually suicidal too. The regiment never did learn where it was meant to be, for during the evening of 12 August, while carrying out yet more regimental training at Thetford, they received orders to proceed to France in forty-eight hours' time. There they would take over the Cromwells of the Northamptonshire Yeomanry to become 11th Armoured Division's armoured re-connaissance regiment. This was 'flexibility' *par excellence!*

* * *

13th/18th's ordeal during the previous two months had at least followed much as planned. The cold, windy conditions which had occurred during most of their training had given way to the better weather of early summer, and the sea had improved accordingly. The regiment embarked for operations on 3 June at Portsmouth. No sooner had they done so than a sharp breeze got up. It looked as though the weather was breaking. In fact a severe summer storm was setting in, forcing Eisenhower to postpone the landings for twenty-four hours. Although a lull was predicted for the following morning, it was far from certain that there would be any real improvement. Meanwhile all his forces were embarked in appallingly cramped conditions. It does not take much to imagine the scenes, with little shelter from the rain, nauseating diesel fumes, the rolling motion of the flat-bottomed LCTs in the swell, the vomit. Some craft were already sailing from ports on the west coast of England to marry up with those due to sail from the south coast ports. The top secret packages of orders, maps and air photographs had been opened and everyone briefed, for the first time, on their exact objectives, so there was no question of disembarking the troops even if it had been technically feasible. They would all now have to endure these conditions for at least another twenty-four hours.

Early in the morning of 5 June (the original D-Day), with the chief meteorologist still predicting the lull required to give the landing craft a chance to do their work and for the RAF to provide air support, Eisenhower made his decision to begin the landings the following day. The order reached the regiment at about midday on the 5th and their LCTs set off almost at once, passing the boom of Portsmouth Harbour at 2.00 pm.

On opening the sealed orders it had been revealed that the regiment's task was to support the assault of the 8th Infantry Brigade of 3rd Division on the 'Sword' group of beaches on the extreme left of the Allied landings. The regimental plan was for the two swimming squadrons, B left, A right, to touch down at H minus 7½ minutes (H hour being the time the infantry hit the beaches) and, remaining at the water's edge, to subdue all local opposition not destroyed by the preliminary naval and air bombardments. Subsequently they were to provide conventional close support for the infantry as they moved inland. RHQ and C Squadron would land at H plus 45.

The sea that night seemed to be getting rougher. The crews bedded-down on the open decks of their landing craft as best they could and at about midnight the last self-heating tins of soup were produced. Dawn broke in the Channel grey, misty and showery. Without doubt, though, the sea was calmer. But it

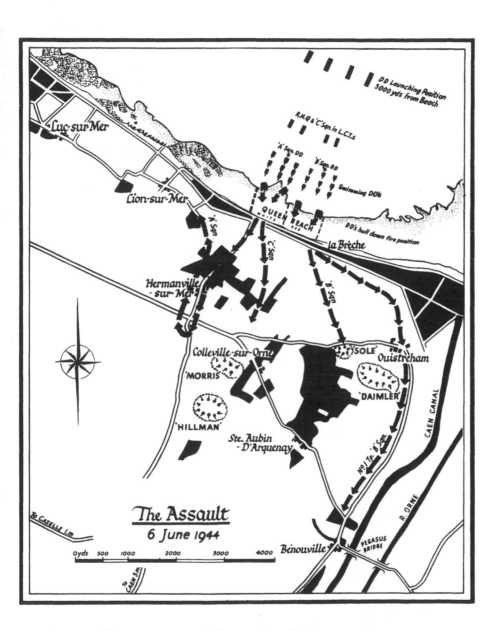

The Assault
6 June 1944

From Miller's *History of the 13th/18th Hussars 1922–47*

remained to be seen whether it would be calm enough to launch the tanks. Launching time was set at 6.02 am and 30 seconds, impressive precision and necessary in order to coincide with the naval bombardment programme. In the event the ramps were lowered just after 6.16 am, exactly five thousand yards from the Normandy shore. This was a welcome two thousand yards closer than planned, the result of the bad weather's inhibiting a German counter-bombardment.

The DDs rolled down the ramps to the accompaniment of ear-shattering fire from the Royal Navy, each in John Keegan's words "plopping off the ramp into the waves like toads from the lip of an ornamental pond". Thirty-four of the forty tanks were able to launch but one tank foundered immediately, succumbing to the long-feared danger of being washed back against the ramp and rupturing the flotation screen before it could engage its propellers. It sank like a stone but the crew was able to escape and stay afloat in their aircraft dinghy, which all the DDs carried, until rescued by the LCT crew.

The DD's rate of advance, one hundred yards in the minute, meant a swimming time of at least 50 minutes. This was a long time to be pushing through a rough sea under the gaze of a hostile shore but it began well, the squadrons picking up their pilot boats and getting into column with relative ease despite the waves whipped up by the Force 5 winds. The heavy seas made the DDs' progress slower than calculated, however, and the second wave of LCTs carrying specialist mine-clearing tanks was soon bearing down on them. A swimming tank in that heavy swell was difficult to spot, let alone avoid, and there were some near misses. One DD was rammed by an LCT about eight hundred yards from the shore and sank. None of its crew surfaced, in spite of their DSEAs and 'Mae West' life jackets, except the officer commanding the tank, Captain Noel Denny, who was thrown into the water by the collision, tank commanders having to stand on the engine deck to steer. He was picked up after swimming for thirty minutes. It had been Denny's tank, too, which had sunk during training in the Moray Firth, drowning the driver. A second tank was rammed and sunk four hundred yards from Queen Beach but all the crew were saved.

The drill for 'touch down' was very slick. When in about five feet of water, the commander got into the turret and the driver took over the direction-keeping by means of his periscope. Because the tracks were going round to drive the propellers, the tank made headway on the sloping beach as soon as it touched down. The order was then given to 'break struts' and the elbow-jointed struts holding the screen up would be broken by hydraulically-operated plungers. The air was let from the pillars by valves and the screen fell to the deck enabling the gun to be brought into action. Thirty-one DDs reached the shore but a number were then overcome by breakers and the rapidly rising tide which swamped their engines. Nevertheless, these too remained in action, even with the turrets flooded, the crews only baling out when the guns themselves were almost awash. The scene is vividly described by one of the tank commanders, Corporal Pat Hennessy:

"75, HE, Action Traverse right, steady, on. 300 – white fronted house – first floor window, centre."
"On."
"Fire!"
Within a minute of dropping our screen we had fired our first shot in anger. There was a puff of smoke and brick dust from the house we had aimed at, and we continued to engage our targets. Other DD tanks were coming in on both sides of us and by now we were under enemy fire from several positions which we identified and to which we replied with 75mm and Browning machine-gun fire.

The beach, which had been practically deserted when we had arrived, was beginning to fill up fast. The infantry were wading through the surf and advancing against a hail of small arms fire and mortar bombs. We gave covering fire wherever we could, and all the time the build-up of men and vehicles continued. Harry Bone's [driver] voice came over the intercom:

'Let's move up the beach a bit – I'm getting bloody wet down here!' We had landed on a fast incoming tide, so the longer we stood still the deeper the water became. As we had dropped our screen, the sea was beginning to come in over the top of the driver's hatch and by now he was sitting in a pool of water. The problem was that the promised mine clearance had not yet taken place, so we had to decide whether to press on through a known minefield, or wait until a path had been cleared and marked.

Suddenly, the problem was solved for us. One particularly large wave broke over the stern of the tank and swamped the engine which spluttered to a halt. Now, with power gone, we could not move, even if we wanted to. Harry Bone and Joe Gallagher [co-driver] emerged from the driving compartment, soaking wet and swearing.

More infantry were coming ashore, their small landing craft driving past us and up to the edge of the beach. There was quite a heavy fire fight in progress so we kept our guns going for as long as possible, but the water in the tank was getting deeper and we were becoming flooded. At last, we had to give up. We took out the Browning machine guns and several cases of .3-inch belted ammunition, inflated the rubber dinghy and, using the map boards as paddles, began to make our way to the beach. We had not gone far when a burst of machine-gun fire hit us. Gallagher received a bullet in the ankle, the dinghy collapsed and turned over, and we were all tumbled into the sea, losing our guns and ammunition. The water was quite deep and flecked with bullets all around us. We caught hold of Gallagher, who must have been in some pain from his wound, because he was swearing like a trooper, and we set out to swim and splash our way to the beach. About half way there, I grabbed hold of an iron stake which was jutting out of the water to stop for a minute to take a breather. Glancing up I saw the menacing flat shape of a Teller mine attached to it; I rapidly swam on and urged the others to do so too.

Somehow, we managed to drag Gallagher and ourselves ashore. We got clear of the water and collapsed onto the sand, soaking wet, cold and shivering. A DD tank drove up and stopped beside us with Sergeant Hepper grinning at us out of the turret. "Can't stop!" he said, and threw us a tin can. It was a self heating tin of soup, one of the emergency rations with which we had been issued. One pulled a ring on top of the tin, and miraculously it started to heat itself up. We were very grateful for this, and as we lay there on the sand, in the middle of the battle taking turns to swig down the hot soup, we were approached by an irate Captain of Royal Engineers who said to me:

'Get up, Corporal – that is no way to win the Second Front!'"

The heavy seas delayed touchdown by 15 minutes and the assault on 'Queen' Beach developed into a running fight. The regiment silenced many strongpoints that morning, enabling the infantry to gain their beach-heads, and then pushed on inland. One troop, taking a wrong turning, found themselves reinforcing the hard-pressed airborne troops holding the legendary 'Pegasus Bridge' over the River Orne on the left flank.

The regiment was the only one to launch as planned. There is no doubt that, as predicted, where tanks were not on the beaches quickly the infantry had a harder time. The terrible losses on 'Omaha' Beach were in part due to the US DDs either being unable to launch or foundering during the approach: thirty-seven out of the thirty-nine tanks launched in one regiment sank. 13th/18th attributed their success to the training in the heavy seas of the Moray Firth.

By the end of the day 8th Infantry Brigade had secured all its objectives and the regiment was able to leaguer-up. Casualties had been lighter than anyone had dared hope – twelve killed and twelve wounded, though during the course of the launching and beaching seventy-eight had been registered 'missing'. All were to rejoin within a few days, but the figure serves to indicate the real nature of the regiment's D-Day: it was very much an individual crew battle.

"If only because success speedily dimmed the inherent danger of the enterprise," wrote the war correspondent John North in his *North-West Europe 1944–5*, "it is well to record that no military operation in history has faced such unpredictable hazards as those that attended the opening of the Second Front in Europe." With a certain nonchalance 13th/18th marked it musically by adding eight bars of 'A Life on the Ocean Wave' to the regimental march. They also commissioned Charles Cundall, whose well known and definitive painting of the Dunkirk beaches haunted a generation, to paint the regiment's DDs launching – the return match so to speak. Sadly, the distinguished Royal Academician was unable to capture this scene quite as well, but it remains nonetheless a grand reminder of this epic of the 13th/18th Hussars' history.

Rommel was right: *OVERLORD* was a strategic, tactical and technical surprise to the Germans. Their strategy, ultimately ordered by Hitler though opposed by many of his generals, was to hold forward on the beaches. The fact that by nightfall on 6 June the Allies were ashore and able to hold against any local counter-attacks meant that D-Day, itself a separate battle, had been emphatically won. It now remained to be determined by how quickly each side could reinforce.

* * *

The Allied plan was relatively simple. They had chosen the more difficult Channel crossing to Normandy because the beach defences were not as tough a nut to crack as those opposite the shortest crossing in the Pas de Calais. The German high command remained convinced, however, that the main effort would be in the Pas de Calais, and continued to believe it for several crucial days even after 6 June. They were given every reason to do so by the brilliant Allied deception plan *FORTITUDE* which convinced the German intelligence staff that there was yet another army in southern England (under Patton) waiting to cross. Breaking out from Normandy was, however, the price for going for the easier beaches. Montgomery's plan, therefore, was that the British, on the left, would push down the Caen-Falaise plain, apparently threatening to break out towards Paris by the most direct route, with the Americans on their right covering their flank and rear. This push would, however, be a feint. After the Germans had concentrated all their armour against it the Americans would break out, turning westwards to take the Brittany ports and Cherbourg which were vital to the Allies' logistics. All four Allied armies would then turn eastwards to advance on a broad front so as not to expose a flank to a

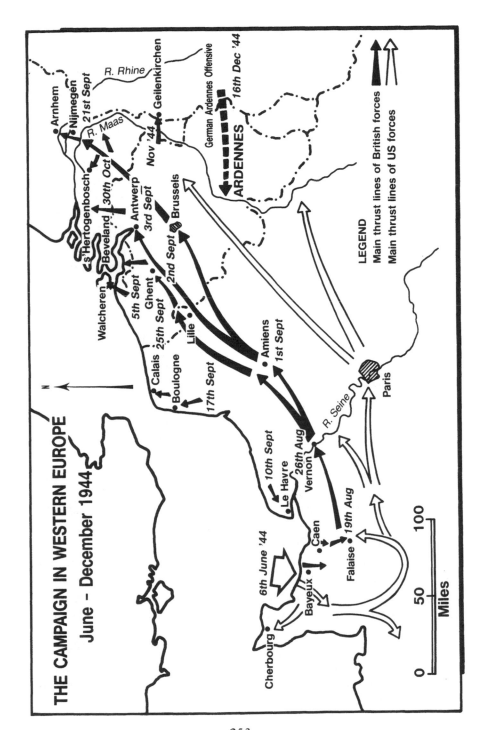

THE CAMPAIGN IN WESTERN EUROPE
June – December 1944

Cherbourg

6th June '44

Bayeux
Caen
Falaise
19th Aug

Le Havre
10th Sept

R. Seine
Vernon
26th Aug

Paris

Boulogne
17th Sept
Calais
25th Sept
Lille
Ghent
2nd Sept
5th Sept

Walcheren
Beveland
5th Sept
's Hertogenbosch
30th Oct
Antwerp
3rd Sept
Brussels

Amiens
1st Sept

R. Maas
21st Sept
Arnhem
Nijmegen
Geilenkirchen
Nov '44

R. Rhine

German Ardennes Offensive
16th Dec '44

ARDENNES

LEGEND
Main thrust lines of British forces
Main thrust lines of US forces

N

Miles
0   50   100

253

German counter-attack. There was no fixed timetable but the Allies expected to be at the River Seine by D plus 90 days.

13th/18th, now back under command 27th Armoured, fought a number of actions during these 'Breakout' battles, including the bloody and faltering Operation *GOODWOOD*, and crowned their achievements in a spectacular little action at Mont Pinçon which in John North's words "knocked out one of the last key rivets in the Normandy gate".

These achievements were not won cheaply, though. The RAF had established virtual air supremacy over Normandy, but the Germans' artillery and mortars were rarely silent and their tanks were tenacious in probing and harassing. Only ten days after D-Day 13th/18th's commanding officer, Lieutenant-Colonel R.T.G. Harrap, was killed by tank machine-gun fire. Like 15th/19th's commanding officer he had been adjutant during the retreat to Dunkirk and, again like Taylor, he had been second-in-command until relatively recently.

The regiment did not have a central role in Operation *GOODWOOD* – it was 8th Corps' battle and 13th/18th were in 1st Corps. But this strong push south out of the Orne bridgehead would have exposed 8th Corps' left flank, so 1st Corps was tasked with its protection. During the operation the regiment had to fight its way forward on a number of occasions, and casualties again began to mount – in one instance from misdirected ('friendly') night bombing. *GOODWOOD* lasted from 18 to 20 July but fighting on the 1st Corps flank continued sporadically for over a week afterwards. 13th/18th were withdrawn on 27 July to learn that 27th Armoured Brigade was to be broken up. The brigade had never been expected to remain operational beyond D plus 2 days, but the losses had been mercifully light. The regiment would now replace 24th Lancers, who were being disbanded, in 8th Armoured Brigade (30th Corps). It was these reorganizations, in the wake of the Breakout battles, which brought 15th/19th to France, for 11th Armoured Division had taken a considerable battering during *GOODWOOD* and their armoured reconnaissance regiment, 2nd Northamptonshire Yeomanry (2 NY), were to amalgamate with 1 NY.

The breakout had not been achieved, however, because *GOOD-WOOD* had made only limited progress. *COBRA*, a mirror-image operation in the American sector, began on 25 July while the newly constituted 1st Canadian Army renewed the attack towards Falaise in the British sector. The American attack, against lighter opposition, succeeded in making a break-through at Coutances at the western foot of the Cherbourg peninsula.

A major push was now needed in the British sector to take advantage of the American success. Part of this push was Operation *BLUECOAT* by 8th and 30th Corps to secure the dominating ground of Mont Pinçon. The operation started on 30 July, hardly giving time for 13th/18th to find its feet in 8th Armoured. During the first few days of the operation they supported several infantry brigades but the overall progress was slow and 30th Corps commander was dismissed on 2 August. Along with him, in a 'clean sweep' by the army commander, Dempsey, inspired in part by Montgomery, went the commander of 7th Armoured Division, the famed 'Desert Rats', together with his artillery commander and chief of staff. Also removed was Brigadier W.R.N. Hinde who had been 15th/19th's second-in-command in France in 1940 and then, having recovered from wounds, had pulled the regiment back together after Dunkirk. He had subsequently commanded 22nd Armoured Brigade with great distinction in North Africa and Italy. Chester Wilmot, probably the finest of all the war correspondents, says in his masterly book *The Struggle for Europe*, "Hinde's fearlessness had long since earned him the nickname 'Looney'." Max Hastings recounts in *OVERLORD*, one of the most readable books on the Normandy battles, the eccentricity in Hinde which also contributed to the nickname:

> "Brigadier 'Looney' Hinde drove up to his tank positions in a scout car, and began to give his officers their night orders for withdrawal, covered by the exhausted infantry of the Queen's Regiment. Hinde had won his nickname in the desert, both for courage and eccentricity. Now, he suddenly broke off in mid-sentence and peered fascinated at the ground. 'Anybody got

a matchbox?' he demanded in excitement. Under the acute strain of the battle, Lieutenant-Colonel Carver of R.T.R suggested that this might not be a good moment to worry about nature. 'Don't be such a bloody fool, Mike!' exploded Hinde. 'You can fight a battle every day of your life, but you might not see a caterpillar like that in fifteen years'!"

Hastings is wrong about two things, however: first, the caterpillar was on the branch of an apple tree; secondly, Hinde's nickname was earned much earlier in the hunting field where his fearlessness had been remarkable even among the hard riders of the day. He had represented Great Britain at polo in the 1936 Olympics and, in the spirit which might be expected, he soldiered on despite the sacking, rising to major-general and being knighted for his performance in Kenya in the Mau Mau campaign in the 1950s. His and the other dismissals were strongly resented throughout the division. Many commentators have written that by this time 7th Armoured had lost their will to fight, feeling they had done their 'bit' in the Desert and Italy. But Field-Marshal Carver points out that the sackings were the result of the commanders actually taking too optimistic a view and leading off with the armoured brigade in conditions (the bocage) in which it would have been more appropriate for the lorried infantry brigade, with tank support, to have done so.

The dismissals now brought to command of 30th Corps a real star, the incomparable Brian Horrocks. Lieutenant-General B.G. Horrocks was an infantrymen of immense experience. He had been in action continually since 1940 until wounded in North Africa in command of 10th Corps. He was still not fully recovered but Montgomery wanted him in Normandy urgently. Horrocks, in addition to his intense professionalism, had the cavalryman's jauntiness and exuded confidence. His impact on 30th Corps was immediate. By 5 August a determined attack was being made on Mont Pinçon from the west. After defying attacks by the infantry for twenty-four hours the heights fell to a resourceful dash by six tanks of A Squadron the following day. Horrocks, never a one for understatement, recalls in his racy memoirs *Corps Commander:*

"The weather was hot, the country damnable, and the Germans in the Mont Pinçon area even more bloody-minded than usual. Battle groups based on a couple of Tiger tanks were proving particularly obnoxious. I began to wonder how we would ever capture the formidable objective in front of us.

As I drove back to my H.Q. on 6 August, I was met by a jubilant Pyman [chief of staff], who, even before we reached him, shouted out, 'We've got it! – Mont Pinçon!' I could hardly believe my ears. Apparently Captain Denny, commanding the leading group of tanks of the 13th/18th Hussars, had found a narrow track, seemingly unguarded, leading to the top of the mountain. Showing great initiative . . . he had led two troops up the track, which was so narrow that one tank came off it and had to be abandoned. Now they were on the top, but a thick fog had come down and they could hear German voices all round them. Denny added somewhat plaintively on the R.T. that they were 'feeling rather lonely'. Pyman assured me, however, that the already battle-weary 4th Wiltshires were being led to the top by Lieut.-Col. Luce, their C.O. They reached the summit under cover of darkness and next day repulsed a somewhat half-hearted German counter-attack. So the most formidable feature in Normandy, which had been pointed out to the troops over and over again on models of the area during training, had been captured by seven or eight tanks – thanks to the initiative and courage of one young officer of the 13th/18th Hussars and his Commanding Officer. The effect on morale was tremendous. Mont Pinçon had been the cornerstone of the enemy defences in Normandy. With it now in our hands, the position was reversed. We could overlook them, not they us."

The capture of Mont Pinçon was probably the turning point of the breakout in the British sector. The regiment had several more days' fighting and were then withdrawn to rest and re-fit. Since 17 July they had lost five officers and fifteen other ranks killed, and seven officers and forty-two other ranks wounded. Eleven tanks had been 'brewed-up'.

* * *

The Germans in Normandy were now being enveloped by twin Allied advances forming the famous 'Falaise Pocket'. German armour, artillery and transport, in the press to move east, presented concentrated targets for the swarms of rocket-firing Typhoons which circled Normandy on a virtually continuous basis. The blackened sky and scenes of destruction would be mirrored on the road from Kuwait at the end of the Gulf War, but in Normandy it was on an enormous scale – only twenty-four tanks and sixty guns escaped to be ferried east across the Seine.

On 21 August Montgomery issued one of his periodic messages *to be read out to all troops*:

> "Having brought disaster to the German forces in NW France, we must now complete the destruction of such of his forces as are still available to be destroyed. After knowing what has happened to their armies in NW France, it is unlikely that these forces will now come to us; so we will go to them."

It was into this semi-euphoria that 15th/19th were pitched in the early hours of 18 August. They had arrived in France only two days before and had collected their Cromwells, and the 17-pounder variant Challenger, from the armoured delivery organization. After little time to sort things out the tanks were loaded on to transporters for the sixty-mile journey up to 11th Armoured Division, the commanders having gone on ahead. By mid-morning on the 18th they were operational with the division as it led 30th Corps' advance to the River Seine. Few regiments can have had such an extraordinary introduction to active operations. It was certainly no time to hesitate, for by 23 August the Corps had closed up to the river and the regiment had had its baptism of fire, although the divisional commander, Major-General 'Pip' Roberts, was clearly trying to break them in gently. 11th Armoured were now pulled back to allow 43rd Wessex Division, predominantly infantry, to mount an assault crossing of the river at Vernon, and 15th/19th were put under their command for the operation.

The Seine at this point was about two hundred yards wide,

with a fast current. Bridging was going to be difficult even once the infantry had secured the far bank. The crossing started at 7.00 pm on 25 August, with supporting fire by the regiment's tanks on the high ground overlooking the river and from the water's edge. The infantry managed to establish a bridgehead and during the night of 26/27 August the regiment started ferrying its tanks across by raft, alternating troop by troop with the 4th/7th.

Once the bridgehead had been firmly established, and Bailey bridges built, 11th Armoured resumed the lead and 15th/19th reverted to its command. The crossing had not been heavily opposed and there had been no serious fighting during the move up. Nevertheless the regiment had suffered one officer and five other ranks killed and three officers and eight other ranks wounded since arriving in France only a fortnight before. But the Seine was both a physical and a psychological barrier: its crossing meant a further boost to the Allies' morale. So the following week saw the remarkable advance of 11th Armoured from the Seine to the Scheldt at Antwerp, a distance of 340 miles in six days - what one hard-pressed RASC platoon commander described as the 'petrol stakes'. 29th Armoured Brigade led throughout, with 15th/19th providing left flank protection, squadrons leap-frogging in bounds of five miles. Responsibility for keeping the division's centre line clear also rested with the regiment and this accounted for several skirmishes with anti-tank guns and Panther tanks which periodically tried to cut the line. For the most part, however, the difficulties were limited to dealing with prisoners, keeping supplied and keeping in communication.

On 9 September 11th Armoured moved out of Antwerp, which they had entered to scenes of wild celebrations, to protect 30th Corps' right flank some twenty miles east of Louvain on the Albert Canal. The regiment was in action the following day across the canal as the Guards Armoured Division edged its way north towards the Dutch border. On the 14th they were in some very sharp fighting in the tiny bridgehead over the Meuse-Escaut Canal held by 32 Guards Infantry Brigade. There was very little space to manoeuvre and some strong counter-attacks were made by German armour and infantry throughout the day. Since the advance from the Seine, three officers and thirteen other ranks had been killed and four officers and twenty-five other ranks wounded: over sixty casualties, a third of them fatal, had been taken in the first month's fighting – the best part of a squadron's worth of crewmen.

Next came the magnificent gamble to 'bounce' a crossing of the Rhine in a standing-start from behind the Dutch frontier – Operation *MARKET GARDEN*. The concept was simple enough: the British 1st Airborne Division would seize the bridge over the Lower Rhine at Arnhem. The intermediate bridges over the Waal at Nijmegen and the canals at Eindhoven would be seized by the US 82nd and 101st Airborne Divisions. 30th Corps would advance up the main road, over the 'airborne carpet', to expand the Arnhem bridgehead. Once across the Rhine, the North German Plain and the Ruhr could be rapidly penetrated and the end of the war hastened – possibly to as early as the end of 1944.

There is no doubt that it was a glorious enterprise, and it very nearly came off. Both regiments played a part – not a major one, although 13th/18th came frustratingly close to reinforcing the perimeter into which 1st Airborne had withdrawn after being pushed off the Arnhem road bridge. 15th/19th's role was initially to protect the centre line, the main road itself, as far as the 82nd's perimeter around Nijmegen. This meant they would come under command 101st US Airborne itself. The regiment saw some sharp fighting in the 101st's sector. It was particularly difficult for them, too, since this was their first contact with American troops, and procedures were far from standardized. It is evident they did extremely well by the immediate award of the DSO to the commanding officer, Anthony Taylor, for this operation.

When Guards Armoured's advance was halted at Nijmegen and 43rd Wessex Division was pushed through, 13th/18th, moving with 130th Infantry Brigade, managed to leave the main road and reach Driel opposite 1st Airborne's perimeter. But by this time, 23 September, it was too late. All that could practically be done was to assist with harassing fire and to take part in the deception measures covering the withdrawal across the Rhine of the remnants of 1st Airborne during the night of 25/26 September.

The attempt to rush the war to a close had failed. On 16 October, Montgomery ordered that offensive operations by his 21st Army Group be suspended, with the exception of those to clear the Scheldt estuary so that Antwerp could be opened as the alternative to carrying supplies over the long distances from Cherbourg and Dieppe. The regiments therefore went into a period of rest and maintenance. This was sorely needed for odometers were by this time reading 1,000 miles or more. 15th/19th were told that they were to receive the new Comet tank, an up-gunned and up-armoured Cromwell, and they lost no time in organizing a gunnery training camp in Belgium. Trickle leave began and both regiments made the most of the warm reception they received in their Dutch and Belgian quarters. Balaklava and Sahagun days were celebrated in great style: the regiments had danced with French girls in 1939, with English girls for the next four years, and now in 1944 they danced with Belgian and Dutch girls. Balaklava celebrations at Nijmegen were attended by some 300 girls who had not danced since 1940: it must have been some party!

13th/18th's respite was broken in early November by a brief but busy operation at Geilenkirchen where the Americans had made a small dent in the 'Siegfried Line', the German defences on the Dutch border. Having given some useful indirect fire support over the border they were back in their concentration area around Nijmegen by the end of the month. No further operations were expected until the new year, but on 16 December the Germans counter-attacked out of the Ardennes. The offensive achieved total surprise and the Americans, in whose sector the main attacks fell, were hard-pressed at first to contain it. 13th/18th were stood-to for the defence of Maastricht, but in the event they were not required. After some extremely bitter fighting the Ardennes offensive, Hitler's last throw, was brought to a halt by Christmas.

It now remained to bring the war to a close as swiftly as possible and on the most favourable terms to the western allies. The broad policy for the occupation of Germany had been decided at the Yalta Conference the previous year: the Russians would mount their major offensive towards Berlin which they themselves would take, though the city would subsequently be governed by the four principal allies. The Russian limit of exploitation was the River Elbe, but the British and Americans were not convinced that they *would* limit themselves given the chance. The offensive during the final phase of the war was therefore to be three-pronged: a rapid thrust for the Elbe, an envelopment of the Ruhr, the German industrial generator, and a thrust into southern Germany to prevent any resistance in the 'national redoubt' of which there had been rumour.

First, however, the Rhine had to be crossed. And before that the west bank had to be cleared. Both regiments were to pay heavily in this operation to which they were committed in early February. The Reichswald Forest, Goch, Cleves, Udem – these were names which meant hard fighting and many casualties. 13th/18th lost ten tanks in the battle for Goch alone. At Udem 15th/19th had eleven men killed and twenty-four wounded.

Having helped to clear the west bank in Operation *VERI-TABLE*, the regiments were withdrawn for repair and reinforcement before taking part in Montgomery's thrust for the Elbe. They were not required for the assault crossing of the Rhine itself: this was achieved on 24 March at Wesel in a well-coordinated operation involving airborne and commando troops, DD tanks and both British and American divisions. The bridgehead was developed over the next five days and by the 29th it was thirty-five miles deep and twenty wide. That night (28/29 March) the thinning German cordon snapped and breakout was at last possible.

On the morning of the assault crossing 13th/18th had moved up to the river in reserve. Progress was slow because of the sheer volume of traffic. During one of the halts they heard

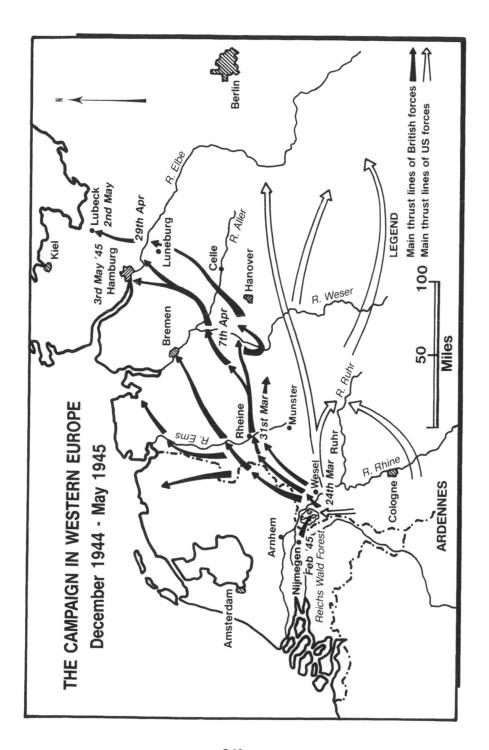

THE CAMPAIGN IN WESTERN EUROPE
December 1944 - May 1945

Berlin

N

Kiel

Lubeck
2nd May

29th Apr

3rd May '45
Hamburg

Luneburg

R. Elbe

Celle

R. Aller

Hanover

Bremen

7th Apr

R. Weser

LEGEND

Main thrust lines of British forces
Main thrust lines of US forces

100

Miles

50

Rheine

31st Mar

Munster

R. Ems

R. Ruhr

Ruhr

24th Mar

Wesel

R. Rhine

Cologne

Amsterdam

Arnhem

Nijmegen

Feb '45

Reichs Wald Forest

ARDENNES

263

on the BBC the news that Churchill had already been over the Rhine on 30th Corps front. The regimental history says that the news cheered and reassured the regiment: they would have been particularly cheered had they known that the Prime Minister had fulfilled a long-cherished ambition by peeing into the Rhine from the east bank!

15th/19th, now firmly back under command of 11th Armoured and having just received their Comets, moved across on 29 March. 11th Armoured Division was 2nd Army's reserve for the breakout across the North German Plain and would be expected to seize any opportunity to exploit weaknesses in the scattered German defences. By this time the regiment was used routinely as both the division's reconnaissance unit, having a squadron's worth of scout cars as well as three tank squadrons, and as an armoured regiment to support the division's infantry brigade. And while 13th/18th had a relatively easy time on the northern route through Hengelo, Lingen and Cloppenburg to Bremen, where their war finished, 15th/19th still had some hard fighting on the axis Wesel, Osnabruck, Petershagen, Luneburg, Bad Oldesloe.

They had a particularly tricky time through the Teutoburger-wald, the thick-forested ridge beyond the Dortmund-Ems Canal. It was ideal country for infantry to slow down an armoured advance. It was in any case the site of an earlier destruction of a force which had dared to cross the Rhine: almost two thousand years earlier (9 AD) Arminius Germanus, a German tribal leader, had lured the forces of the Roman governor into the Teutoburgerwald and utterly destroyed three legions (15,000 men). The triumphant statue to 'Herman the German', as he was known later to most British soldiers, dominates the surrounding countryside to this day.

Now the Wehrmacht were hoping to repeat the success. Equipped with the *Panzerfaust* hollow-charge bazooka, and with good local knowledge, they could expect to do so. The approach to the ridge also favoured the defenders since much of it was water meadow and marsh. Fortunately the bazooka parties were not backed by heavy anti-tank guns, so although progress was slow it was at least progress. *Panzerfaust* shooting was also surprisingly bad: again and again projectiles from the same firer would burst harmlessly on the road behind a speeding tank, the principle of aiming-off simply not being mastered even at these very short ranges.

But it was hot work for the tank crews. In close country they should in theory have closed down hatches and fought the tanks through the periscopes. The regiment just did not believe this was practicable so fought with the commander 'head-up'. This of course attracted fire, and there was some spirited fighting from the turrets with small arms and grenades in the absence, for most of the time, of close-support infantry. During the fighting in the *wald* on 2 April the regiment killed or wounded probably 150 Germans, many of them high-grade officer and NCO cadets, under their instructors, from a training school in Hanover. Many prisoners were taken that day too, some no more than boys. Amazingly, in all this close-quarter and confused fighting the regiment took only one casualty – a troop leader, Lieutenant R.F. Leslie, who was shot in the leg during attempts to recover one of his bogged tanks. The day's fighting opened up the Weser Vale for the rest of 11th Armoured Division and was reported in some detail on the BBC war news. All now looked set for what promised to be the 'final swan'.

When the regiment resumed the lead a few days later it still looked as though the advance was to be no more than a mopping-up operation, but resistance began to stiffen perceptibly as the approaches to the River Weser itself were probed. The *Luftwaffe*, virtually swept from the skies by the RAF save for some dazzling but brief and largely ineffectual appearances of their new and noisy rocket-powered planes, now put in a series of determined attacks. One of Recce Squadron's Dingo scout cars was hit and set on fire. *Panzerfausts* were about again too, this time with more accuracy.

Nevertheless a divisional bridgehead was established around Petershagen and the regiment was over and pushing on to the River Aller by 12 April. That day a curious event occurred which showed the utter confusion beginning to beset the *Wehrmacht* during their fighting withdrawal. The local German commander approached 11th Armoured under a white flag to ask for a temporary ceasefire. Some miles to the north was an internment camp containing 60,000 political and criminal prisoners, he said. Typhus had broken out in the camp and there was a very real danger that if the division continued on its presumed axis the prisoners would escape and spread the dreaded disease over a wide area. The German commander added that, of course, the *Wehrmacht* had known nothing about this camp: it was run by the *SS* at an obscure railhead called Belsen. *Would the British allow the local German forces to disengage and withdraw well north of the camp?* In return the division would be able to take the crossings over the River Aller at Winsen unopposed.

In the event the precise terms could not be agreed. This was to cost the regiment dearly, for on 13 and 14 April they had to fight their hardest battle of the War to gain those same crossings. The attacks were supported by 1st Battalion The Cheshire Regiment and rocket-firing Typhoons. It was close-quarter battle again, this time against both determined and skilled opposition from, amongst others, German marines. Lord Rathdonnell, B Squadron Leader, won the MC for his part in directing the battle on the first day. During the following day's fighting Sergeant J. Burton won the DCM for quite exceptional leadership despite being badly wounded in the head. His troop lance-corporal, J. Finlinson, won the MM. Lance-Corporal A. Chambers won the MM for continuing to fight his tank and directing the troop's fire though his own tank had been hit no less than five times by an '88'. His driver, Trooper Fellows, was mentioned in despatches which described him, surely with monumental understatement, as having been "partially stunned"!

By nightfall on the 14th the town had been taken but at a cost of six killed and sixteen badly wounded. So close to the end of the war it seems a particular tragedy, but here and there were well-sited pockets of determined German resistance which simply had to be overcome. The '88' accounted for a number of Comets during that battle, but a further indication of German determination was their willingness to improvise equipment as the standard issues dried up: one '88' was found in fact to be a 75mm gun bored out to 88mm, consequently with a smooth bore, and firing a hollow-charge projectile. Accurate only up to about 500 yards it was nevertheless lethal. It and other examples of ingenuity gave substance to the *graffiti* threatening 'no surrender' – *Kapitulaterein? Nein!* – seen increasingly on the walls of buildings in the worst hit towns and villages. If no one doubted the ultimate result it was nevertheless chilling to see such threats.

When news of the German unconditional surrender *was* received, during the evening of 4 May, 15th/19th were just short of the Baltic. A few days later they reached the sea at Kappeln, twenty miles from the Danish border. They had covered 500 miles in six weeks and very little of this had been 'swanning'. As the end of hostilities approached the atmosphere had been particularly tense. Horrocks paints the scene vividly:

"On 3 May I was told confidentially that the Germans were negotiating surrender, but this was not to be communicated to anyone else. I was determined that, with the war so nearly over, no lives should be lost unnecessarily. So, as I went round the different formations, instead of urging them on, as was my normal practice, I invented all sorts of excuses to make them postpone the next day's offensive operations. I could see them looking at me with astonishment, and no doubt after I had departed they must have shaken their heads sadly and said, 'The old man has lost his nerve at last.'

I had often wondered how the war would end. When it came it could hardly have been more of an anti-climax. I happened to be sitting in the military equivalent of the smallest room, when I heard a voice on the wireless saying, 'All hostilities will cease at 0800 hours tomorrow morning, 5 May.'

It was a wonderful moment – the sense of relief was extraordinary; for the first time for five years I would no longer be responsible for other men's lives."

Both regiments' sense of relief would have been no less profound. The battle honours awarded chart the very progress of

Montgomery's 21st Army Group: *Normandy Landings, Caen, Mont Pinçon, Seine 1944, Nederrijn, Geilenkirchen, Rhineland, Aller, Bremen* and many others. And those six long years are summarized with stark simplicity in the two campaign honours *North-West Europe 1940*, and *1944–45*. But there were now the realities of occupation duties to face and, for 15th/19th, a sudden and unexpected move, for Palestine was becoming the first of Britain's post-war 'trouble spots'.

CHAPTER 16

The Empire Recedes

"In 1945 the British Army found itself in occupation of a larger part of the world than ever before . . . a vast army of three million men found itself scattered across the face of the globe. The army had been raised to fight the powerful Axis war machine. Clearly it would soon be redundant, or so everyone thought."

MICHAEL DEWAR
Brush Fire Wars

Germany 1945; 15th/19th in Palestine and Sudan; 13th/18th in N. Africa; 13th/18th and 15th/19th in Malaya. 13th/18th and 15th/19th in Aden and Muscat.

Britain had not had to shoot her way into the Baltic since the Napoleonic Wars, and never from landwards. Now the 15th/19th Hussars were occupying Kappeln and finding it a very decent billet. Only days before they arrived, however,

"the roads running northwards out of Schleswig-Holstein were crammed with German transport escaping into Denmark. That Dönitz might still try to make a temporary stand there and in Norway, to give himself some bargaining power, was not quite beyond the bounds of possibility."

So writes Robert Kee in his detailed study of the war's aftermath *The World We Fought For*. Grand-Admiral Carl Dönitz had become *Reichsführer* on Hitler's death on 1 May. Rather than fighting on he set up a putative German government at Flensburg on the Danish border, hoping that the Allies might somehow deal through him. Although this rump of the Third Reich immediately proved powerless it was nevertheless embarrassing that it should be seen to be tolerated in the Western Allies' territory: "Only extreme political blindness can excuse this parody of government," exclaimed the *News Chronicle*. "The harm done to our relations with Russia can easily be seen by anyone who takes the trouble to study the Soviet press in the past week." Something had to be done, and quickly.

Flensburg is only twenty miles up the road from Kappeln so it was not surprising that on 23 May 15th/19th took part in Operation *BLACKOUT* to arrest the 5,000 or so *Reichsministers*, senior officers, civil servants and guards constituting the 'government' and *OKW – OberKommando Wehrmacht*. Remarkably, perhaps, not a shot was fired and the operation was complete inside a few hours with every *Nazi* target captured – the sole exception being the navy's commander-in-chief who took poison. Damp squib though it was, important symbolic action it was too – and a tricky and potentially dangerous one at that. With it the last vestiges of *Nazi* authority were destroyed.

For the rest of the regiment's, and 13th/18th's, time carrying out the business of military government it was largely a matter of refugee control and supervision of the German agencies and bureaucracies which ran local services on their behalf. The German army itself was still in being and was given certain administrative responsibilities. This led to some bizarre, some would say obscene, instances of cooperation though none so appalling for the regiments as the occasion in Holland quoted by Kee, where the German commander borrowed ten rifles and 100 rounds of ammunition so that his disarmed troops could shoot for desertion five of his men who had attempted to make off home.

The sense of having survived was particularly marked. Perhaps it was the sheer scale of the disaster as much as anything, for the full horrors of the concentration camps and the effect of allied bombing were now becoming clear to everyone. This sense of survival is usually expressed by the British soldier in a brief, but moving, commemoration of his dead comrades. The regimental padre steps forward and, as he probably did before battle was joined, speaks on behalf of all ranks: in the intervening period he has been with the dead, the dying and the wounded in the regimental aid post. But for the British soldier, almost uniquely, life in its fullest sense then goes on. It is very much a British characteristic. Where else but in Britain (and *The Times*) would such a letter be found:

"Sir,
    Truly we are an odd race. Having read that churches would be open on VE Day for thanksgiving, I went to St Paul's Cathedral at 2 p.m. on Tuesday and found the entrance steps thronged with people listening to a Guards band seated below who at that moment were giving a spritely rendering of 'Roll out the Barrel'. Excusable, perhaps, but hardly the place even on VE Day."

Roll out the barrel, literally and metaphorically, was precisely what the two regiments now did. It takes little imagination to picture the canteens, cinemas, sight-seeing, sport and a host of other diversions at their disposal. The first tentative steps towards contact with the civil community are recorded, rather coyly, by Miller:

"Very strict orders were at first issued with regard to fraterniz-ation by the troops with the German inhabitants, but, as time went on, these were somewhat relaxed and German girls were allowed to attend the dances and other entertainments."

Horses soon re-appeared for sport and recreation. They were, however, properly 'brought onto strength', fed with government rations and bedded down on government straw. They, their rations and bedding came from the Germans – and sometimes their grooms too. Both regiments had riding schools up and running within a few months of VE day and held horse shows

271

in the autumn. 15th/19th had so many horses, including three international showjumpers, that 'D Squadron' was formed to tend them. The *Wehrmacht* had never given up horses. They had in fact increased their reliance on them as the war had drawn on. Although many were big artillery and transport animals there were some fine light ones too: several reconnaissance regiments were still horsed even at this time. On too many occasions during the advance from Normandy to the Baltic the regiments had found themselves having to dismount to despatch badly wounded horses, a job which the wartime crewmen were particularly pleased to leave to their pre-war regular colleagues.

It wasn't a bad life in Germany that summer, but for 15th/19th it came to an end abruptly the day after their horse show. Some weeks beforehand the regiment had been warned that it was to come under command of 3rd Division which was soon to move to Palestine. There they were to re-equip with light vehicles as the division's reconnaissance unit. The date of embarkation was brought forward, however; home leave was cancelled and they set sail in October, many officers and men in the various specified age groups having been sent to other regiments and new drafts having hastily arrived in their place.

If it were possible to explain succinctly the background to the Palestine problem then perhaps there would have been no problem in the first instance, let alone one which has continued for so long. It is fashionable to trace the late twentieth century regional troubles to the Balfour Declaration of November, 1917, but it would be fairer to start as early as 1200 BC with the collapse of the Hittite Empire followed by the infiltration of Semitic and non-Semitic tribes. It is a problem as intractable as that of Ireland. Nevertheless, the Balfour Declaration (so named after the Foreign Secretary at the time) attracts blame because it bound the British to establishing a national home in Palestine for the Jews.

After Allenby had ejected the Turks in 1917 the League of Nations had entrusted Britain with the 'Mandate' for Palestine. As post-war Jewish immigration increased in accord with the Balfour Declaration the Arabs rose in rebellion. By 1939 the rebellion had been put down with the help of seventeen British battalions, but throughout the Second World War there had been trouble with Zionist gangs challenging the British Mandate to demand a true Jewish homeland. After the War the gloves finally came off as far as the gangs and the moderate Jewish Agency were concerned, and a general Jewish rebellion looked likely. The British Government was in a dilemma: almost any quota imposed on Jewish immigration would be unacceptable to the increasingly powerful Zionist element and equally unacceptable to the Arabs, who saw their place in Palestine inevitably threatened by almost any continuance of immigration despite the promises of the Balfour Declaration to protect their interests. In these circumstances British troops were expected initially to restore the situation, then, as the scale of the problem became fully apparent, to hold the ring while the newly-formed United Nations sought a political solution.

Two divisions were already in the region, 1st Infantry and 6th Airborne, as part of the Middle East Reserve. 3rd Division's arrival would allow two divisions to be operational in Palestine at any time while a third could be resting and training in the Suez Canal Zone. In late October 15th/19th collected their vehicles from the ordnance depot at Tel-el-Kebir, 124 Humber scout and armoured cars and Universal Carriers, and 99 'soft-skin' vehicles together with six two-pounder anti-tank guns. They then deployed to northern Palestine, just south of Haifa, and for the next seven months carried out the sort of internal security tasks which were to become the routine for armoured reconnaissance regiments throughout the Empire during the next twenty-five years – road checkpoints, patrols, cordons, escorts, convoys, searches, observation posts and quick-reaction forces.

In June, 1946, the regiment moved back to the Canal Zone where they spent the rest of the year in training and 'R & R'. As they did so, the troubles in Palestine began escalating in violence: the infamous blowing-up of the King David Hotel in Jerusalem, which housed the British military and civil headquarters, took place in July, so when the regiment together with the rest of 3rd Division went back for its second tour in January, 1947, the situation was significantly more dangerous. This next tour was spent in southern Palestine amidst much tighter security, the predominant activity being searches in support of the Palestine Police. The tour was short-lived, however: although, as the end of the Mandate approached, violence was actually increasing, with the various Jewish factions trying to maximize their strength prior to independence, withdrawal of British troops began early. The tour came to an end in November but with a posting to the Sudan, not back to England as expected. The Governor General of the Sudan had asked for an armoured presence of some sort, so the regiment spent a pleasant but uneventful eighteen months just outside Khartoum, the city which the Nineteenth had so nearly relieved sixty-three years earlier. Indeed the only action seen on this tour involved the legendary post-war RSM, John Laing, who instructed the prowler guards to open fire on an intruder fleeing from the sergeants' mess. This took some explaining away!

Also in North Africa by this time were 13th/18th. They had resumed their reconnaissance role in 1947 and, having staged through Aldershot, moved to Tripolitania and Cyrenaica, both Italian colonies whose future was still being debated by the UN (they became the 'United Kingdom of Libya' in 1951).

Each regiment was also experiencing the same turbulence in manpower at this time. The demobilization of wartime conscripts and volunteers had proceeded very quickly, their places taken by a trickle of regular recruits and a flood of National Servicemen. For the first time in British history (except for a few months in 1939) there was National Service in peacetime. Opinions on National Servicemen vary: Correlli Barnett, for instance, maintains that "especially when they became non-commissioned officers or junior officers, [they] brought all the talents and diversity of the nation into the forces"; others maintain that while the concept was very good for the nation, it very nearly ruined the Army. The merits are obvious; the problems lay in motivation (many National Servicemen were deeply resentful of conscription) and in boredom among the regulars who had to train successive intakes of conscripts – although the problem was arguably no greater with two-year National

64. *"It was hot and frequently dangerous work."*(p.287) A patrol from A Squadron, 15th/19th Hussars outside the Government Guards fort at Themir, a halting point for convoys on the Aden-Dhala road, May, 1957.

65. *"An operational commitment almost unparalleled in its geographical scope."*(p.288) B Squadron 13th/18th Hussars relieved the 15th/19th squadron and were given responsibilities throughout South Arabia. One of the squadron's ferrets is photographed here in Aden.

66. *"That constant of British military history, Ireland, was making demands."(p.305)* The regiments' first time back in (Northern) Ireland since the 1922 amalgamations was in 1957 when 15th/19th Hussars were based in Tyrone. Patrolling the border proved tiring and uncomfortable, if not as dangerous as in later years.

67. *"To vehicle-borne troops, however, the mine was always the biggest worry."(p.308)* Both regiments had their share of such incidents. In this instance Troopers Metcalfe and Felton were lucky to escape serious injury after their Ferret had been blown thirty feet into the air, March, 1976.

68. *"They arrived . . . into the worst violence since the 1920s [following the announcement of internment]."(p.307)* Trooper Stark, 15th/19th Hussars, keeps watch in the Ardoyne, Belfast, August, 1971.

69. *"Detachments in Rhodesia following the 1979 settlement."* (p. 290) Again, mines proved the major hazard to vehicle-borne troops. Sergeant Lawson and Corporal Drewery (13/18H) were lucky to escape fatal injuries when their Landrover detonated a mine in the remote Rhodesian bush, although Corporal Drewery sustained serious injuries. One officer and thirteen men from the regiment joined the Commonwealth Monitoring Force in the highly successful Operation *AGILA*.

70. *"Families put down roots in a number of places."* In 1982, Prince Abdullah bin Hussein, eldest son of King Hussein of Jordan, received a short-service commission in the 13th/18th after training at Sandhurst and Bovington. His father took the salute at a regimental parade in Wimbish the following year.

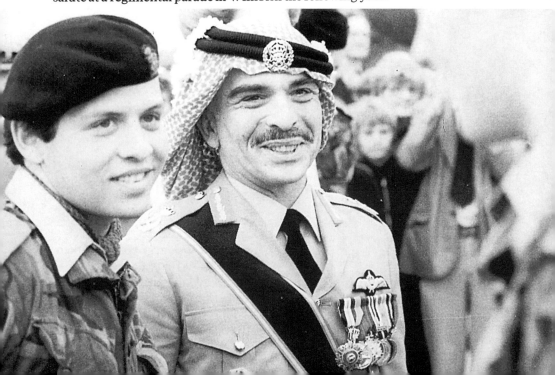

71. *"English towns and cities do not bestow their freedoms lightly . . . first Newcastle in 1973. . . ."*(*p.310*) A Chieftain of 15th/19th Hussars lowers its gun in salute to the Colonel-in-Chief, Princess Margaret, and the Lord Mayor of Newcastle, on the Freedom Parade.

72. *". . . then Barnsley in 1979."* The Commanding Officer, Lieutenant-Colonel George Stephen, escorts the Mayor of Barnsley, Councillor Harry Fish, in the review of 13th/18th Hussars' crews at the freedom ceremony.

Servicemen than in a regular army with a large turnover of 'three-year men'. The problems of training and assimilating National Servicemen were smaller in 'family' regiments, and both 13th/18th and 15th/19th believed that their policy of treating National Servicemen and regulars alike paid dividends. Whatever the complaints, the fact is that the country's post-war military obligations were largely met by National Servicemen until the institution ended in 1962.

Over and above this turbulence was the post-war re-allocation of regular officers from the many regiments which were contracting, reverting to the Territorial Army or disbanding. And just as this upheaval was beginning to settle there came a second wave of 'dispossessed' officers, this time from the Indian Army whose regiments were totally 'Indianized' when India and Pakistan became independent in 1947. During this time of immense upheaval, however, the two regiments appear to have retained their style and character to a remarkable degree. Horses remained very much part of the scene, and other aspects of pre-war regimental life began to revive: regimental property, including the messes' pictures and silver, re-emerged from wartime safekeeping and the bands, who had not been with the regiments since 1939, rejoined. In many respects North Africa and the Sudan became reminiscent of the regiments' time in India before the war. Some chill winds of change were beginning to blow around the Empire, however.

* * *

John Strawson, in *Gentlemen in Khaki*, says of the Army's colonial policing role at this time that "most of it was done with a view to handing power over to those who were generally thought of as 'nationalists'. Many of the leaders of these so-called nationalist movements had communist leanings." In Malaya, however, there was no question of any handover to men with communist leanings: twelve years of determined struggle were to be spent in resisting just such armed demands, during which time both regiments operated in what was to become the classic role of armoured car regiments in counter-insurgency operations. Their three tours also spanned the three main campaign phases of the 'Emergency'.

The Malayan Communist Party had been formed in 1930. When Russia and Great Britain became allies in 1941 the MCP was instructed to give all possible help to the British against the Japanese, including waging guerrilla warfare in the jungle behind the enemy's lines. The 'Malayan People's Anti-Japanese Army' (MPAJA) was formed as a result and fought well, but when it was disbanded in late 1945 after the Japanese surrender, 4,000 of its members kept their weapons.

Malaya in 1945 had a population of about five million, of whom 49 per cent were Malays, 38 per cent Chinese and 12 per cent Indians. The other 1 per cent were the indigenous tribes (the Malays themselves are thought to have immigrated from the continental north) and Europeans. The British connexion had been established through the East India Company which had begun trading there in 1785. The legendary Stamford Raffles had founded the port of Singapore in 1819 and by mid-Victorian times both Malaya and Singapore had effectively become British colonies.

Malaya was a guerrilla's paradise. The peninsula was covered in thick jungle, either 'primary', where the virgin tree canopy shut out the light, or 'secondary', where trees had been felled thus stimulating dense growth on the jungle floor. In these forests lived a few primitive tribes, but the Malays themselves were on the whole terrified of the place – the jungle was where evil spirits lurked. Throughout the peninsula vast rubber plantations, owned and run largely by British settlers, covered areas of cleared jungle. And on the jungle fringe lived the Chinese squatters, many of whom had fled from the towns when the Japanese had invaded, eking out a living from land to which they had no title.

Trouble started in earnest in June 1948. The MCP, almost exclusively Chinese and led by the seasoned fighters of the MPAJA, began a campaign of terror against the European settlers and the Malayan Police. On 18 June a national state of emergency

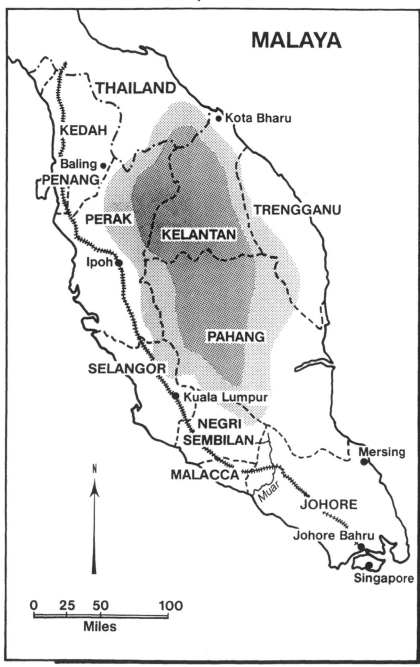

MALAYA

THAILAND

KEDAH

● Kota Bharu

Baling ●

PENANG

TRENGGANU

PERAK

KELANTAN

Ipoh ●

PAHANG

SELANGOR

● Kuala Lumpur

NEGRI
SEMBILAN

● Mersing

N

MALACCA

Muar

JOHORE

Johore Bahru ●

Singapore ●

0   25   50   100
Miles

was declared, and the self-styled 'Malayan People's Anti-British Army', numbering about 5,000 and led by Chin Peng OBE, the decorated veteran of the war against the Japanese, took to the jungle.

The first phase of the Emergency lasted from 1948 to 1950 and was in effect a holding operation by the British garrison and the Malayan Police. Despite their intense campaign of violence, however, the communist terrorists, known as 'CTs', failed to 'liberate' any areas during this time – as required by their Maoist revolutionary war theory. Nevertheless they were still managing to increase the pressure by the skilful manipulation of the Chinese squatters who provided information, food, money and auxiliaries. The second phase of the Emergency, the real start of the campaign, began in 1950 when General Sir Harold Briggs was appointed Director of Operations and drew up a plan which, among other things, hit at the very core of the CTs' support. His bold plan involved the re-settling of half a million squatters into new villages protected by newly raised home guard units, and it was at this point that 13th/18th arrived in June, 1950.

The only armoured corps regiment in the country during the first phase were the 4th Hussars who had been increasingly stretched to satisfy all the demands for escorts and patrols. The arrival of a second meant that the 4th could be concentrated in the north of the peninsula while 13th/18th provided the escorts and patrols in the southern half, the half in which Resettlement was to begin.

The squadrons were operational in a little over a month and were dispersed throughout Johore, Negri Sembilan and Selangor. Headquarter Squadron was disbanded in order to reinforce the sabre squadrons, who were to be wholly self-administering and who also needed extra manpower in the sabre troops, GMC armoured personnel carriers, in place of two-men scout cars, providing the immediate 'infantry' back-up in case of ambush or the need for an impromptu foot patrol. The regiment were to make several jungle forays in the early days and, although self-confessed amateurs by comparison with the in-fantry, who understandably guarded intelligence closely, they claimed some successes: in two separate ambushes in December the regiment killed three CTs and wounded and captured two.

Operations continued throughout 1951. In one contact, on a pitch-black night in September in pouring rain, a young troop leader was killed by 'friendly fire'. This as much as anything illustrates the degree to which the regiment was committed to more than just escorts. But escorts were vital – in the literal sense: in October the High Commissioner, Sir Henry Gurney, was killed in an ambush. He was being escorted by police at the time and as a result of the killing all future VIP escorts became the responsibility of the armoured car regiments.

As a change, B Squadron had suddenly to up sticks from Johore and get their widely separated detachments in an overnight move to Singapore. Widespread rioting had broken out there following Moslem demonstrations over a court decision on the future of Maria Hertogh, a girl of Dutch-Indonesian parentage; the police had had to call for Army assistance. In an eminently successful operation the Squadron cleared the cathedral square, the centre of the trouble, and then patrolled further afield dealing with minor skirmishes. A potentially serious situation had been nipped in the bud.

1951 was a particularly bad year in the Emergency: although nearly 1,500 CTs were killed or captured, over 500 civilians were murdered, and as many members of the security forces, and the High Commissioner's death probably marked the low point of the campaign. In the following year, however, the dynamic General Sir Gerald Templer was appointed both High Commissioner and Director of Operations. Given extensive powers by Churchill, who had been returned to Downing Street after the defeat of the post-war Labour Government, he reinvigorated the flagging Briggs plan. For 13th/18th the pattern of operations remained much the same but more intensive. In September, 1951, B Squadron had been sent to Hong Kong to patrol the border between the New Territories and China and at one stage it looked as though the whole regiment would be sent there: plans were changed, however, and B Squadron rejoined in March the following year.

In July, 1953, the regiment handed over its operational commitments to the 11th Hussars. In its three years in Malaya it had covered three and a half million vehicle-miles, escorted over 4,000 food convoys and provided over 400 VIP escorts without loss of life, food or vehicles. It had been involved in 146 'incidents', killing four CTs, capturing three and wounding fourteen. Two soldiers had been killed by enemy fire, nine wounded, one seriously; one officer and two troopers had been killed in accidents during operations and, as described earlier, a subaltern had died from friendly fire in a jungle contact. The regiment's six months' in England prior to returning to Wolfenbuttel, which they had left for North Africa in 1947, were both welcome and well-deserved.

* * *

During the early years of the Emergency 15th/19th had occupied a succession of stations in north Germany as a divisional armoured car regiment. In 1954 they sailed to Malaya and took over responsibility for the northern half of the peninsula from the 12th Lancers. Their pattern of activities was very similar to 13th/18th's but the demands on the regiment for escorts, of both convoys and VIPs, was particularly heavy. The tour took place during the turning phase of the Emergency: by this time Templer was able to implement vigorously the far-sighted plan which was, almost uniquely, to win a counter-revolutionary war outright.

In Templer both civil and military authority was combined. He intensified the battle to isolate the guerrillas but also introduced a civil aid programme. Most significantly he promised political independence, with full citizenship rights for the Chinese population. His operational plan was the very antithesis of the MPLA's: areas were systematically cleared of CTs, declared 'White' and therefore free from curfews and other restrictions, and garrisoned so that there could be no CT resurgence. From these White areas further operations were mounted to clear neighbouring 'Black' areas. The concept had a self-increasing momentum but demanded an immense number of police, troops and local defence forces – a quarter of a million at the height of the Emergency, including 25,000 British and Ghurkha troops and even more from Australia, New Zealand, East Africa and Fiji.

The weekly quota of convoy escorts for 15th/19th was about thirty, often with convoys of up to eighty trucks and round trips of 200 miles. Like 13th/18th, the sabre troop was reorganized to include two APCs, the GMC being phased out during the tour and the Saracen replacing it. When a VIP was escorted through a dangerous area he was transferred to a specially converted armoured car fitted with a dummy gun barrel to allow more space and comfort inside. 15th/19th even had the distinction of escorting Chin Peng himself on one occasion: after the 1955 elections, when Tunku Abdul Rahman's party won all but one seat, the CTs were offered an amnesty and the regiment escorted their leader under a flag of truce from the Thai border to the talks at Baling. The talks came to nothing, however, and he was returned to Thailand.

During this three-year tour the regiment's vehicles clocked up a total of four million miles. Such a high mileage could not be without accidents, especially in countryside prone to flash floods and land slippage in the monsoon season, although perhaps a total of seven fatalities is comparatively light for such exceptional mileage. There were many more near-misses, however. On one such occasion Lieutenant I.R.E. Gow's scout car turned over, only saving him from death or severe injury by ending up balanced on the two Bren guns. Ian Gow left the regiment on its return to England, though he continued as an active reservist officer for many years, subsequently becoming Member of Parliament for Eastbourne and Parliamentary Private Secretary to Prime Minister Margaret Thatcher. He was murdered at his home by the IRA in 1990.

The regiment's operations included regular 'harassing shoots' into the jungle with the intention of keeping CTs on the move. How cost-effective this speculative fire was is impossible to judge, but unboxed ammunition could deteriorate rapidly in that climate and this was at least a purposeful way of disposing of ammunition coming to the end of its 'shelf-life': 3,500 rounds of two-pounder and 125,000 rounds of machine-gun ammunition were fired into the jungle in total.

Some of this was from time to time in support of specific operations which led to the death or capture of CTs, but the regiment's ironic boast was "four million miles and one bandit", 'bandit' being the original term used by the Malaya administration until the real nature of the insurgency was admitted. If figures like this mean anything it is worth noting that William Jackson, in *Withdrawal from Empire*, says that 1,600 patrol-hours were required to kill a CT and 1,000 to capture one. 15th/19th's CT was, however, killed in an exemplary action by a junior NCO. On 21 January, 1955, Corporal P. Conlon was leading a dismounted patrol of seven men in the jungle in Pahang state. It was just beginning to get dark when the patrol spotted a fire burning. Being a proscribed area this meant CTs. Conlon decided that, rather than attacking at once and perhaps losing the CTs in the dark, he would wait until first light. The patrol put in its attack the following morning and found four CTs, one of whom was captured though the other three escaped. The capture live of a CT was of great intelligence value, and no easy business. Conlon thoroughly deserved his subsequent Mention in Despatches.

The danger of jungle fighting is not always appreciated by those who have never stepped inside a rain forest. Close-quarter battle is a high-risk business at the best of times and in the middle of thick jungle it has its particular dangers. Just as 13th/18th lost a subaltern to friendly fire in a jungle skirmish, so 15th/19th lost one of their most experienced NCOs when Sergeant Cyril Thompson, who had been in the regiment for twenty-four years, was killed in his own ambush.

The tour, like that of 13th/18th's, had been accompanied, although this meant only by the wives of the officers, senior ranks and the regular junior ranks. It came to an end in May, 1957. By this time the MPLA had been all but broken, and 60 per cent of the peninsula had been declared White. The final phase, from 1957 to 1960, was essentially a mopping-up operation. Independence Day came on 31 August, 1957, and a general amnesty for all CTs was announced. There was no mass surrender but several key MPLA officials in south Perak gave themselves up and then cooperated to an astonishing extent, in exchange for money, and in this way gradually the whole of the cell structure of the south Perak region was destroyed. A similar 'super-grass' accounted for most of the CT commanders in Johore State. The military commitment was scaled down accordingly and by 1958 there was only one British armoured car regiment in the peninsula, the Malayan army itself having raised its own armoured car units. 13th/18th had helped to train one of the original squadrons which later became the 2nd Regiment Federation Reconnaissance Corps and with whom a formal alliance was made with the regiment which continues still with The Light Dragoons.

13th/18th began their second tour as this final phase was beginning, arriving in the country in the middle of September, 1957.

The bulk of the regiment deployed to Ipoh in Perak State where the remaining troubles were at their worst. One squadron was able to move permanently to Singapore island in January, 1959, after the whole of Johore had been declared White, having taken part in the final operation to clear the last twenty CTs from the south of the state. The rest of the regiment, however, was always on stand-by for internal security duties in the teeming city of Singapore and this meant periodic practice exercises involving a round trip from Ipoh of a thousand miles.

In 1959 there were only twelve terrorist incidents and twenty-seven contacts by the security forces in the peninsula. By the end of the year there was only one British infantry battalion, The Loyals, operational. On 31 July, 1960, restrictions ended everywhere except in a few zones on the Thai border, on the other side of which a handful of hard-core survivors had taken refuge, including the redoubtable Chin Peng. 13th/18th were able to leave the country in December for England. Like 15th/19th they had had their share of 'jungle bashing', but the role of an armoured car regiment in counter-insurgency operations is essentially one of keeping open the roads. Without freedom to use the road network transiting forces and logistic elements must either use helicopters or take to the 'ulu'. The former is extremely expensive and therefore limited; the latter is impossibly time-consuming. The regiments' contribution to the Malaya campaign may have been unglamorous but it was certainly significant. The convoy escort was required not only to ensure that supplies got through but to ensure that they did not fall into the hands of the CTs. As in the Boer War, the guerrillas thrived on windfalls from the security forces, and again as in that war, this became particularly the case once Resettlement had removed the primary source of supply.

The Emergency had also been tackled, at the contact level, by National Servicemen as much as by Regulars. A contributor to *The Lilywhite*, 13th/18th's journal, perfectly captures the atmosphere of Malaya, the convoys and the blend of conscripts and regulars – his account could equally have been written by 15th/19th:

"The road is hard, hot and dusty. For an hour they have sat there, some on the hard floor, the lucky ones on a cushion or groundsheet, absorbing the bumps, the heat and the drowsy monotony of the jungle streaming by on either side. Tall trees, creepers, bushes, ferns, grass and swamps.

Eight men in a GMC, eight individuals united as a crew, training, working and enduring as one. They are taking a convoy to a village up the road, sixty miles of dangerous road, there might be a bandit on every corner.

The driver, a National Serviceman, who never dreamt he should come to see and do the things he does now. The Crew Commander, a Regular NCO of several years' service, still thinking of when he soldiered in the comparative luxury of Germany or the Middle East. The operator, another National Serviceman, whose time is nearly up, still doing his job as well as the rest. The Bren Gunner, by the rear door and his Number Two are Regulars. The Bren Gunner can remember Barce [Libya], but the other had only just arrived.

Throughout the crew a mixture of Regulars and National

Servicemen – mixed like an alloy that is stronger than its components.

None have ever been in action before and they wait for the sound of bullets cracking by and the sight of wrecked and burning vehicles.

Mile after mile, every man looking, waiting.

The Commander gives an order, the driver changes gear and the convoy speeds up. Now a cool breeze is blowing but with it come the first unwelcome spots of rain. Soon it falls like hail, stinging and blinding the driver and commander, soaking everything and everybody. Water runs down the barrels of their guns and trickles out of the breech, the grenades lie in puddles on the floor. Then, as quickly as it started, the rain stops and once more the way is hot and hard.

Now the most welcome time of all. A halt to rest and have a smoke. "Halt", "Dismount", "Sentries Out". Oh! what a relief to stretch one's legs, to be able to relax for a minute or two.

"Start Up", "Advance" and on the convoy goes again.

Another score of sleepy miles pass by. Now! This is the dangerous part. The crew watch closely, every bush and every dip may hide a bandit – waiting.

Crack! Crack! There it is. The hurried message over the wireless "Ambush Right. Rifle fire and Bren." The driver speeds up to get clear, smoke rises from a smoke grenade thrown to mark the spot. There is still firing but now it is our own. The Bren Gunner sprays the bank, each rifleman picks a spot and fires. The Commander fires, watching the lorry behind to see that it is still alright. And then another burst of shots on the road in front of them. The driver speeds up still more, cursing the hot empty cases bounding down his back.

Then quiet once more. The convoy halts, the sentries are posted. Check-up, no casualties, a few bullet holes in the cab of a lorry. Report to control. On again! the bandits want the food in our lorries and the convoy must get through.

A patrol will soon be out to search the area.

No more incidents and soon the convoy rolls into the village and halts. The crew unloads, dismounts and smokes.

Another escort finished, another job done."

* * *

The East India Company, or rather one of its legacies, was to make one further appearance in the history of The Light Dragoons. British involvement with Muscat, on the Arabian peninsula, dates from the earliest days of the Company. In the nineteenth century in particular the Company, and then the British Government, found it convenient to collaborate with the Sultan of Muscat in the suppression of piracy on the sea route to India: the 'Trucial Coast', in the lower Persian Gulf, was indeed called at this time 'The Pirate Coast'.

Aden, at the south-western end of the Arabian peninsula, had been ceded by the Turks to Britain under diplomatic pressure in 1839 and had developed as the principal coaling station on the new steamship route via Suez to Bombay. In 1937 it had become a British Crown Colony including 100,000 square miles of the hinterland. On its north-western border was Yemen, independent from the Turks since 1918 but increasingly unstable in the 1950s. As unstable too was the eastern side of the peninsula after the discovery of oil in Saudi and the lower Gulf after the Second World War. British involvement in the region was therefore complex, based on sovereign possessions, formal treaties and 'guarantees', all seemingly important for control of the Suez Canal and the maintenance of the supply of Gulf oil, not least from Kuwait which had been independent since 1914 but was still a British protectorate. Instability was endemic, and when the Egyptians nationalized the Suez Canal in 1956, and Anglo-French forces intervened only to be withdrawn after U.S. pressure, the region was primed with a mixture of nationalism and opportunism in very volatile proportions.

The order to send a squadron to Aden in May, 1957, came as a complete surprise to 15th/19th, who at the time were preparing to hand over in Malaya to the King's Dragoon Guards. But after a few Saracens had been drawn from the base depot in Singapore, together with the new Ferret scout car, A Squadron were soon operational in Arabia with two troops in Aden itself and the remainder of the squadron in Mukalla in the East Aden Protectorate. The Aden half-squadron's task was essentially the

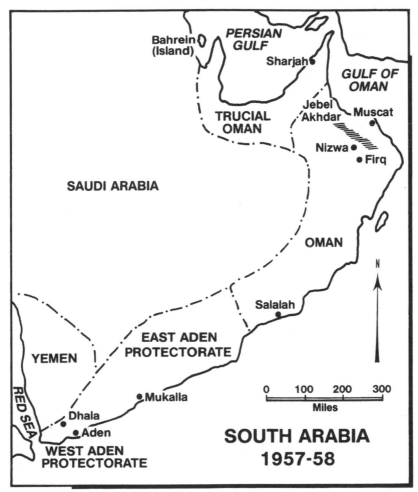

protection of convoys along the road from Aden to Dhala,
the town from which the garrison troops and Aden Levies
patrolled the Yemeni border in order to prevent incursions by
increasingly dissident Yemeni tribesmen and soldiers. It was
hot and frequently dangerous work, not unlike that in Malaya
though in much more mountainous and rugged terrain.

The half-squadron in the EAP soon had a different problem
to face, however. Fighting broke out in Muscat and Oman in
July when factions hostile to the Sultan, aided and abetted by

Saudi Arabia and Egypt, destroyed the best part of the Oman Regiment of the Sultan's Armed Forces. The Sultan immediately appealed to Britain for military assistance. Within a month two companies of The Cameronians were flown in from Bahrain, two squadrons of the Trucial Oman Scouts (Omanis from the Trucial States under British officers) were moved into the country and one troop from A Squadron was flown in from the EAP under Captain J.S.F. Murray. An operation was quickly mounted against the rebel strongholds in the small towns of Firq and Nizwa during which the Ferrets gave some spirited fire support with their Brownings. After the devastatingly accurate cannon and rocket fire of the Venoms from RAF Salalah the operation was soon over, the rebels who fled taking refuge in the almost impregnable *massif* of the Jebel Akhdar.

The 15th/19th detachment stayed on in Muscat until October when they sailed home to England with the rest of A Squadron. They were relieved by B Squadron 13th/18th from Neumunster in north Germany who were now given an operational commitment almost unparalleled in its geographical scope. Distances in Arabia are misleadingly vast: from Aden itself to the Yemeni border varies between one and two hundred miles only, but the EAP was almost as large as France, while the distance from the Colony to central Oman, via the air route through Bahrain, is roughly that of London to Moscow. B Squadron's operational rôle was support to the infantry units on the Yemeni border, convoy protection and escorts not just between Aden and Dhala but throughout the Western Aden Protectorate, support to the Bedouin Legion in the maintenance of law and order in the EAP, *and* support to the SAF! And in the first six months the squadron's strength never exceeded 137 until they were reinforced by two troops from The Life Guards. Of its eventual eight troops, seven were detached – truly a troop leader's dream. When eventually the squadron was relieved it was by The Life Guards, complete less one squadron, tacit acknowledgement that B Squadron had been hopelessly over-committed.

No less awesome than the operational commitments was the supply problem. The detached troops were largely dependent on air supply and the only source of arms, ammunition and technical stores was the base at Aden. These had to be drawn, packed and consigned by squadron headquarters under the full rigours of peacetime accounting.

B Squadron's dispersed troops frequently saw sharp action during their year in Arabia. On several occasions when patrolling the Aden-Yemeni frontier, Second-Lieutenant Mark Barty-King's troop was attacked by heavy machine-gun fire. Each time he and his troop forced the Yemeni to evacuate their sangars, whence they ran into the fire of supporting weapons and suffered heavy casualties. This repeated gallantry and skill in using ground, fire and manoeuvre won Barty-King the MC. Sergeant Douglas Steel won the MM for his gallantry in an ambush in a bare and precipitous wadi. The action lasted in all some thirteen hours during which Steel on four occasions dismounted under fire in the open to assist the wounded and recover equipment.

The climate and terrain were no less hostile than the dissident inhabitants and although they had only a few casualties from enemy action the squadron lost two dead from sickness and one in an accident. In such operations an accurate tally was impossible, but intelligence reports showed that the sabre troops probably accounted for fifty enemy casualties in their thirty-three separate engagements.

The containment of the Oman rebels to the fastnesses of Jebel Akhdar was largely due to the two troops operating there. The following January the Jebel was to be cleared with the help of 22 SAS in a spectacular scaling of the mountain approaches, but by then B Squadron had handed over to The Life Guards. They were picked up by the remainder of 13th/18th from Neumünster, sailing for the final stint in Malaya and bringing the squadron's wives with them.

13th/18th paid one more, brief, visit to Aden. When in 1967 the British Government decided to withdraw, it was at the end of what General Strawson describes as a campaign "doomed by lack of political will, [resulting] at length in a hesitant and humiliating relinquishment of colonial rule". In order to assist with this withdrawal, which looked as if it would be a fighting one every inch of the way, a composite squadron under C Squadron headquarters was sent from England in a dismounted role to guard Khormaksar airfield. Though they did not in the event see action they proved their worth by relieving the infantry for forward patrolling.

As the Empire receded there were other trouble spots – notably Cyprus and Borneo, but neither regiment was committed. Throughout the 1960s, '70s and '80s elements of the regiments were involved in residual and generally peaceful post-colonial commitments across the world: a troop in Belize, a squadron in the Sovereign Base Areas or with UN forces in Cyprus, an exercise in Singapore and Malaya, detachments in Rhodesia following the 1979 settlement, but while the 'brush fire' wars were where the action was, the eyes of the world, and the bulk of the British Army, were concentrated on north and central Germany and on fighting the 'Cold War'.

CHAPTER 17

Fighting the Cold War

"In the later 1950s manoeuvring in Germany reached a new pitch of extravagance and extensiveness. Several armoured divisions at a time would 'swan' across the Hanoverian plains, fighting each other in mock battles of unparalleled severity, making or breaking the reputations of aspiring commanders, and almost exhausting the patience of the Westphalian farmers."
                    JOHN STRAWSON *Gentlemen in Khaki*

13th/18th and 15th/19th in Germany, England and Northern Ireland 1946–1989.

The Germans' defeat had been total and utter, their surrender unconditional. In May, 1945, most of them simply wanted to salvage what they could and get on with living – which for many meant little more than merely surviving. There were some, however, whose defiance was still quite marked. There was even a touch of arrogance.

A few suggested that the western allies should join with what remained of the *Wehrmacht* to push the Russians back to their pre-war borders. The idea was of course preposterous: it came from such places as the *Kriegsmarine* which, since it had not been defeated at sea, was still not totally bowed, or from units such as the *Gross Deutschland Brigade* which carried out its administrative duties in 15th/19th's area with a notable haughtiness. Yet within a short time Russia began to behave like the menace and Germany looked like a defenceless ally. There was indeed soon to be a remarkable transformation

291

in international relations. Some of the western allies' leaders, notably Churchill, had foreseen that *the* post-war issue would be Russia's hegemony in eastern Europe rather than German resurgence, but others had not. Nevertheless, Roosevelt, Stalin and Churchill had agreed from as early as 1941 that Germany should be disarmed, demilitarized and the Nazis removed. In the event only the last of these objectives was to be followed through, for the threat of communism soon regained its former pre-eminence and Germany became the bulwark against its spread in western Europe. It is ironic that Franz Josef Strauss, the conservative politician who became one of Germany's first ministers of defence only a few years later, could say in 1947, "May every German hand wither that touches a gun again."

The advancing Red Army had ensured communist control of Poland, Hungary, Romania and parts of Germany and Austria, although this had in any case been virtually guaranteed by the various agreements at the allies' conference at Yalta in February, 1945. In Yugoslavia and Albania the local communists seized control, while Greece was only saved by swift British action. In 1948 the communists seized power in Czechoslovakia too. An "iron curtain of silence", in Churchill's words, had fallen across Europe.

Against this dismal background the British Army of the Rhine carried out its functions as an army of occupation. 13th/18th handed over their Shermans and took over armoured cars and the 'Chaffee' light tank to become once again a reconnaissance regiment, moving to Northampton Barracks, Wolfenbuttel, in April 1946. This was to be a case of 'first in, last out' since these excellent barracks were taken direct from the *Wehrmacht* and then, nearly half a century later, handed over to the *Bundeswehr* when 13th/18th left them (for the third time) at the formation of The Light Dragoons.

By the time 15th/19th returned to Rhine Army, in October, 1949, the situation had markedly changed. During 1946 and 1947 alarm had been growing throughout western Europe, where post-war disarmament had been quick, over the continued presence of huge Russian forces in the heart of Europe and the building up of 'satellite' armies under Soviet control. In March, 1948, a defensive alliance, the Brussels Treaty, a rudimentary Western European Union, was formed by Britain, France and the Benelux countries. Militarily this was hardly a sufficient counter-balance to the Soviet and satellite armies, and from the outset United States' support was sought. Traditionally reluctant to become involved in a European alliance in peace-time, the US demurred at first but overcame their isolationism when a number of threatening moves were made by the So-viet Union, including support for the Czech coup, pressure on Norway and Finland and the blockade of West Berlin. In August, 1949, the US and Canada joined with the five Brussels allies and with Italy, Norway, Denmark, Iceland and Portugal in setting up the North Atlantic Treaty Organization. NATO's first Secretary-General, Lord Ismay, unofficially summed up the Alliance's purpose as being "to keep the Russians out, the Americans in and the Germans down". After the com-munist attack in Korea in 1950 an integrated military com-mand structure was set up with a Supreme Headquarters Allied Powers in Europe (SHAPE) initially near Paris but moving to Mons in Belgium when France left the integrated command (but not the Alliance itself) in 1966.

From 1949, therefore, both regiments' position in Germany became progressively less that of occupying troops and in-creasingly that of Alliance defence forces on the borders of the democratic west and the communist east. The location of 13th/18th close to the IGB – the Inner German Border – had an obvious operational purpose but that of 15th/19th, at Lubeck, was forty miles from the nearest British unit. Its operational rôle was in fact singular: it was the armoured car regiment for the Norwegian Division, which included a Danish brigade, whose mission it was to defend Schleswig-Holstein in the event of Soviet aggression. This was a gloriously straightforward rôle which would have meant in reality covering the division's with-drawal across Schleswig-Holstein, over the Kiel Canal and up into Denmark: memories of events in 1940 cannot have been comforting. 15th/19th moved to Neumunster in November,

1951, a little nearer the Kiel Canal, and stayed there until 1953 when the Norwegians went home, leaving the Danish brigade covering this sector.

Life for both regiments at this time was uncomplicated and sometimes incongruously grand. The families in particular frequently lived in splendid comfort: the married quarters were all requisitioned houses in the best part of town, rent free. It was not unusual for a senior NCO, his wife and one child, to live in a six-bedroomed house with a large garden, and the services of a nanny and domestic, again free of charge. Once a week the army ration truck would arrive to deliver the entire week's rations which, for a family of three, came to about £2. And all this on a sergeant's pay of eight shillings (40p) a day plus three shillings marriage allowance!

In August, 1949, the first post-war German national elections were held and Allied military government ceased. It was not until 1954, however, that Germany regained full sovereignty and not until 1955 that the western Allies gave up their rights as occupying powers (except in Berlin). Allied forces remained thereafter in western Germany by agreement and from that year were formally joined in NATO by the Federal Republic whose new army, the *Bundeswehr*, had already started to take shape. The Soviet Union immediately arrayed its satellites into the Warsaw Pact, a purely political gesture in response to the admission of the Federal Republic to NATO since to all intents and purposes the Red Army and the satellite armies had been one military system for several years. The Cold War battle lines began to harden.

Exercising over the German countryside was a unique experience. Until 1954 there was absolute right of free manoeuvre anywhere, at any time and without compensation for training damage. After 1954 these manoeuvre rights were curtailed but this meant little in practice initially since once an area had been agreed by the German authorities to be *ein übungsraum* under the 'Schedule 443' system training could carry on as before. A '443 area' required permission being sought (and a nominal sum paid) before entry to buildings and also provided compensation for damage to crops, roads and fences, but since there was no shortage of welcoming farmers, especially near the Border, nor of money to compensate for damaged crops, grand 'schemes' (or 'FTXs' – field training exercises – as they would later become known) could still be played out on the north German plains. Nevertheless, 1954 was something of a watershed as far as the size of the scheme was concerned: in 1984 Exercise *CRUSADER* attracted considerable media coverage since it involved the whole of 1st (British) Corps, but thirty years earlier no less than three army corps – British, Dutch and Belgian – under HQ Northern Army Group, swept across northern Germany in Exercise *BATTLE ROYAL*.

As late as 1961, however, some Germans clearly thought that the British Army still possessed quite remarkable training rights over the countryside. On one exercise near Hanover the equivalent of the borough engineer came across a 15th/19th support troop placing dummy charges on a bridge over the River Leine. In halting English the engineer asked what was happening. The NCO in charge replied that they were blowing up the bridge. Very concerned, and probably with a low expectation of cooperation, the engineer then said, "Would it be possible to find another bridge? This one was only completed a week ago"!

Armoured cars on exercise were one thing, tanks quite another. Both regiments converted to armour in the 1960s, 13th/18th rather quaintly referring to their Centurions as 'remounts'. Almost symbolically after this change to the 'heavy cavalry' rôle, guidons reappeared. The 15th and the 18th Light Dragoons had relinquished theirs on becoming hussars, and the remaining regiments of light dragoons had given them up in 1832. The drum banners of the kettle drums, which had replaced the guidons as consecrated emblems, were phased out with the official passing of drum-horses themselves, and 13th/18th received their first guidon at a parade in 1961, 15th/19th having received theirs two years earlier. Queen Mary had died in 1953 and as her place as Colonel-in-Chief of 13th/18th had not yet been taken, the guidon was presented by The Duke of Gloucester. He, as a 10th Hussar, had served with 13th/18th in England in the 1920s while the Tenth were in India. 15th/19th's guidon was presented at the regiment's bicentenary parade at Barnard Castle in 1959 by Princess Margaret who had become their Colonel-in-Chief the previous year. This appointment had been unfilled too since the death of Queen Alexandra in 1925. 13th/18th had to wait, however, until 1989 when the Queen appointed The Princess of Wales to be Colonel-in-Chief.

While map reading, radio and independence were the characteristics of professional life in a recce regiment, gunnery was everything in an armoured regiment. 15th/19th appear always to have taken their gunnery particularly seriously: in 1944/45, for instance, it was noticeable that firing practices were arranged whenever there was a lull in the battle. Nevertheless it must have been especially satisfying when in 1965, after their first firing camp as an armoured regiment, they received the following letter from the CRAC – Commander Royal Armoured Corps – HQ 1st British Corps:

> "You will be delighted to learn that a recently wheeled regiment, accustomed to the light 76mm Ordnance of the Saladin, can acquire tanks, convert and shoot on the ranges so well that it emerges unofficially graded third best in the Corps by the range staff (and then only by a fraction). This is a truly splendid achievement and confirms what I always thought of 15th/19th. I do congratulate you."

It was perhaps not surprising that the regiment was soon chosen to represent UK in 'CAT' – the Canadian Army Trophy. This NATO tank gunnery competition later achieved such prestige that national industrial reputations came to be at stake and the atmosphere in which it was conducted became little short of frenzied. Fortunately for everyone, in 1985 the 'authorities' remembered that the defeat of the potential enemy, the Warsaw Pact, was of more importance than the defeat of fellow NATO regiments in tank gunnery, and the competition was suspended. By that time it had in any case become a contest between fire-control computer programmers; in the 1960s it was still 'real shooting'. 15th/19th shot extremely well in their Centurion tanks during the final practice for the 1967 competition but then came second to the Canadian team in the actual shoot after being plagued by misfires and stoppages. This was the greatest pity since they would otherwise have completed a 'hat-trick' for the UK, 13th/18th having won the competition the previous year. That victory, with its all-time highest score, was in fact to be the last occasion on which the UK was to win. The troop leader of that team was the young Lieutenant Roddy Cordy-Simpson, whose father had clambered onto one of the evacuation ships at Dunkirk as a squadron leader having organized area-cleaning parties on the beach beforehand! 'John Cordy' commanded the regiment during the first tour in Malaya and was Colonel from 1968 to 1974. His son went on to command the regiment in the early 1980s and at the time of the publication of this history was selected for command of 1st Armoured Division.

This was very much a time when family strengths and connections were renewed all round, a number of other regimental sons rising to command. Lieutenant-Colonel Stewart Balmain, whose grandfather had served in the Fifteenth in the Great War, whose uncle had fought back to Dunkirk with the regiment and whose father had commanded in Palestine, became 15th/19th's commanding officer in 1985. Lieutenant-Colonel Robert ffrench Blake, whose father had been the mainstay of 13th/18th's polo team between the wars and who had been killed in North Africa while commanding the Lothian and Border Horse, commanded from 1981 to 1983 and subsequently became regimental Colonel. Nor was the family tradition confined to officers. In 15th/19th three generations of Wellings have served since the war, following forebears who served in the nineteenth century. In the 1980s there were no less than five Thompson brothers serving in the regiment at the same time, an RSM's nightmare.

* * *

For the first few years of NATO's existence the US had an effective nuclear monopoly. It was not surprising therefore that the strategy for meeting the Soviet threat relied essentially on atomic weapons. Indeed the British, French and Americans together could raise only four divisions at this time, against as many as 175 Russian divisions. The Russians had tested an atomic device, however, so it was only a matter of time before NATO's reliance on nuclear weapons would no longer be credible. It was also the time of the North Korean invasion of South Korea. This example of communist expansionism persuaded the US of a real threat to western Europe and thus brought a fuller commitment of ground troops to Germany than originally intended. From 1949 to 1954, when the hydrogen (thermo-nuclear) bomb was developed, NATO military planners sought to match Soviet strength in what they believed would be a long conventional-style war, and Alliance force goals set a target of no less than ninety-six divisions. In the early 1950s, therefore, both regiments found themselves training for operations reminiscent of the last war.

In 1954 this conventional concept was dropped (only fifteen divisions had in any case been deployed in Germany) and reliance returned to nuclear retaliation – *Massive Retaliation*. For the next three years NATO's strategy was for ground forces to be little more than a 'tripwire' which would trigger thermo-nuclear strikes by the United States' long-range bomber force deep into Soviet territory. There was a shift of emphasis in ground force deployment from a war-fighting stance, which required defence in depth and therefore giving up ground when militarily expedient, to one of forward deployment to the IGB itself. Spending on Rhine Army was cut back to a level appropriate to this military burglar alarm, and the armoured corps Territorial Army was virtually wound up.

After 1957 Massive Retaliation appeared increasingly to be a less than credible strategy. The Soviets' successful launching of the *Sputnik* signalled the vulnerability to nuclear strike of the US itself, and therefore brought into question America's readiness to trade Detroit for Hamburg. The 'tripwire' turned gradually into a 'shield', a concept requiring twenty to thirty mobile divisions to hold up a conventional attack to provide a breathing space in which negotiations could take place. *Shield* saw a return to defence in depth and the regiments again became as familiar with the Weser as they had previously been with rivers nearer the IGB. But the shield was never made of tempered steel: at best, parts of it were cast-iron but other bits were little more than *papier-maché*. Barely twenty in-place divisions, including seven from the Federal Republic itself, could have been mustered in 1960 and there was therefore a growing reliance on 'battlefield nuclear weapons'.

The *Shield* concept evolved into *Flexible Response*, the NATO strategy which for all its "intellectual incoherence", in General Sir Hugh Beach's words, applied from 1968 and eventually saw the collapse of the Warsaw Pact itself. As the name suggests, it required a balance of strong and capable force across the spectrum – conventional, battlefield nuclear (or 'theatre nuclear') and strategic nuclear, the latter provided largely by the US but also by UK and, to an indeterminate extent, by France.

Allied to this strategy, and also because of understandable German reluctance to surrender any territory without a fight, the doctrine of *Forward Defence* rigorously applied and thus the two regiments saw their operational areas, especially as recce regiments, move back once again to the IGB. *Forward Defence* and *Flexible Response* also placed the highest emphasis on 'readiness' which in turn shaped the lives of both 13th/18th and 15th/19th in the 1970s and '80s.

A comfortable but demanding pattern of life in BAOR emerged, the essentials of which were to be able to deploy lock, stock and barrel into the field at a moment's notice, and dedication to maintaining the highest standards within the 1st British Corps' annual training cycle. These together meant that manning levels had to be kept high at all times, many hours had to be spent on the tank park in order to maintain a high level of vehicle serviceability, and a virtually non-stop routine of training had to be followed – individual training during the winter months, troop training and 'CPXs' (command post exercises) in the spring, and squadron and regimental training in the summer ready for the big brigade and divisional FTXs in the autumn. A whole generation of soldiers would talk in

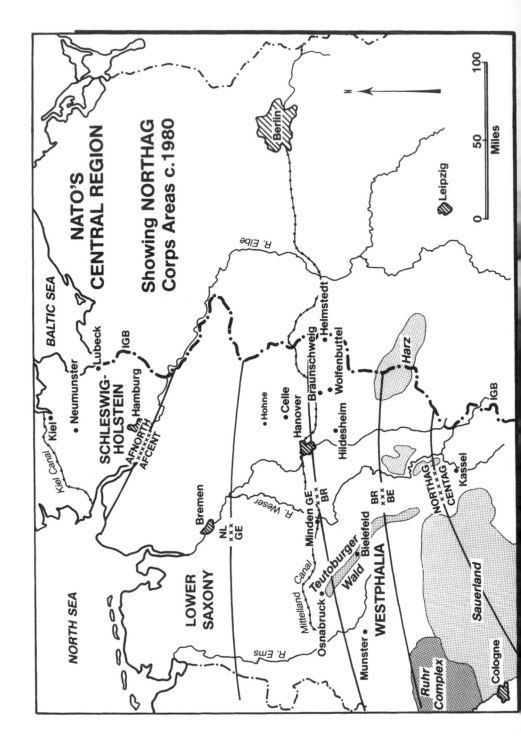

NATO'S
CENTRAL REGION

Showing NORTHAG
Corps Areas c.1980

a sort of BAOR code – *Quick Train, Active Edge, Summer Sales, Eternal Triangle*, and many more, were alert practice and FTX nicknames known to every trooper. And whether recce or armoured, the regiments would in addition have to carry out their 'Annual Firing', on which the regiment's grading by the Lulworth and Hohne gunnery instructors – the influential 'IGs' – would make or break a commander's name.

Yet against this background of sometimes frenzied activity, a great deal of equally frenzied non-military activity took place. At times, especially in the early years, it was downright sleazy, such as the almost ritual journeys to Hamburg. Simon Raven, in his novel *The Sabre Squadron* describing cavalry life in the Rhine Army of the late fifties and early sixties, sets the scene:

"The Oo-Woo Stube was something of a surprise. Daniel had been led to believe that it boasted a bar for the sale of drink and women and an inner room in which, roulette being forbidden in Hannover, some variant of Boule was played; and he had wondered why Giles Glastonbury [the squadron leader], who took an educated interest in his pleasures, should have thought such a place worth a special visit. He now found out. Beyond the gambling room was another bar, champagne only, and a tiny theatre, in which one could watch, at intervals of half an hour and for a charge of fifty marks a time, a selection of ingenious and obscene cabaret acts. Giles, the perfect host, had paid a lump sum and arranged that members of his party should be admitted to the theatre as and when they chose throughout the evening.

'It's a hangover,' Giles explained to Daniel, 'from the gay days just after the war. They'll stop it any time now. Any minute, I wouldn't wonder."

In the main for the officers, however, it was skiing, hunter trials, polo and shooting. For the unmarried soldier it was less glamorous. Better paid because of the LOA (local overseas allowance) he should have been set fair to enjoy his continental posting. Often, however, unless a soldier were a real self-starter or a 'gladiator', there wasn't *quite* enough money to make a big enough difference, and life, especially in the big, isolated, self-contained garrisons such as Hohne, could soon become a matter of booze and *bratwursts*. Squadron bars flourished in the sixties and seventies, and did much to maintain cohesion and control excesses, but they largely died out in the eighties as standards of living accommodation improved and social patterns changed. The system of three- or four-man 'flats' encouraged, perhaps, more responsibility and pride, and expensive stereo and television systems would be as much a feature of the later accommodation as stimulating but artless pictures on the walls were of the earlier barrackrooms. However, through the generous official and regimental subsidy of downhill and cross-country skiing many soldiers were introduced to these sports, often with notable success. Indeed throughout this period 'adventurous training' was widely developed and well supported financially, adding much to the quality of life for all ranks as well as to their experience of remote parts of the globe. The concept was the envy of many other armies who recognized its military value in leadership and self-sufficiency development too.

Relations with German civilians underwent some interesting changes during these four decades. The pendulum swung from non-fraternization in the immediate months after the war to enthusiastic mutual embracing in the 1950s and '60s. It then swung back as the Federal Republic's self-confidence returned, settling at a position of rest in the 1970s and '80s, trembling a little one way or the other in different parts of Germany since. In the early years the Germans themselves often made the running. There seemed to be three broad categories: those old German families who felt they had the same values and interests as British officers, and who to an extent disdained contact with their own *bourgeoisie*; those middle-class Germans who wanted to distance themselves from the old order which had brought the country to its ruin, and finally, those with no particular political or social views who simply saw pleasant relief from the sheer austerity of post-war Germany in contact with free-spending officers and soldiers (and even better if American). There were 'mixed marriages' in all categories. Perhaps the most interesting examples of the first category were the *Gelbe Kreisen* – the Yellow Circles, associations of former German cavalry officers and their families, many from proud Prussian stock dispossessed of their estates in East Germany. Their hospitality was generous.

There were closer and more personal contacts. Lieutenant-Colonel 'Dag' Rugge-Price, commanding 13th/18th in Neumunster in the late 1950s, records: "The inhabitants were for the large part friendly farmers all of whom kept horses for show jumping. . . . The considerable body of German nobility living in the neighbourhood were hospitable though it was clear that they refused to mix with the townspeople or take part in political activities. Many owned large estates and shooting invitations were numerous. . . . Another family who deserve mention for their hospitality to the Regiment were the von Bethmann Hollwegs whose nephew Alec did his National Service with 13th/18th." Theobald von Bethmann Hollweg had been the German Chancellor throughout most of the Great War.

The 1970s and '80s saw a distancing between the officers and the civil population. Besides growing German social self-sufficiency, cheaper air-travel, the European motorway network and the tax-free GTi brought London and the shires much closer to Munster and the other garrisons. There were some mixed marriages, often to pretty girls from old families, sometimes rich ones, but always to girls who spoke impeccable English. Since few officers bothered to learn German this was not surprising. The NCOs and troopers often set a far better example in this, and the mixed marriages in these messes were usually far more 'democratic' about which was to be the language used at home. In the late 1980s there was a concerted effort at the highest level to make officers learn German, but without spectacular success. Besides any in-built British reluctance to learn languages, the sheer turbulence in officers' lives did not help. In this respect other ranks had a somewhat better opportunity.

Breaks from the high-intensity training and social life in BAOR were always welcome. The regiments' postings home, whether as an RAC training regiment or with the former 'Stratco' – Strategic Command – allowed a little more freedom of action at all levels, though 'FTXing' was limited. In theory the Manoeuvre

Act gave the Army the same training opportunity that it had in Germany under the 443 system, but in practice the Act was never invoked. Training other than on the MOD's own land had to be by laborious negotiation and goodwill, the latter being sometimes in short supply. In 1989 13th/18th made the national news when one of its exercises introduced *Maneuverschaden* (exercise damage) to the West Country. And despite even more care when training later in the year in East Anglia the commanding officer received a letter complaining of inconsiderate behaviour, ending: "I shall put a curse on All Queen Mary's Own officers. For this season you will all miss even low partridges and pheasants and all your horses will be unsound and you will kill no fishes. The curse will lift next August." The gamebook for that season is the emptiest it has ever been and the regiment lost to the Navy in the finals of the Inter-Regimental Polo at Windsor in front of the Queen.

From these home postings there would often be a squadron detached to the Cyprus Sovereign Base Areas or to the United Nations troops on the island, but after a while there would be itchy feet and a desire to get back to where the serious business of armoured soldiering was – BAOR. Certainly the regiments never developed better cohesion and morale than when sharing the testing demands of a Corps training season, especially if it included a stint at BATUS – the British Army Training Unit Suffield, in Canada. This massive prairie training area had been leased in the early 1970s after armoured training in Libya was stopped following the republican coup in 1969. 15th/19th pioneered this outstanding live-firing training in 1973 and an armoured regiment's performance on these testing exercises soon became one of the touchstones of prowess.

Ironically, it had been in Libya, in 1967, that British armoured troops had come closest to action in these later years. C Squadron 15th/19th (known as 'The Legion' from the years following 1922 when it was the 19th Hussar Squadron) was training in Libya as part of the 1st Battalion Devonshire and Dorset battlegroup when the second Arab-Israeli war erupted. The battlegroup was split two ways: the infantry element was deployed to Benghazi

304

for internal security duties, while the squadron activated the tank stockpile at the El Adem RAF airbase under the command of Major R.A. Coxwell-Rogers, later to be the last Regimental Colonel of 15th/19th. The threat (from Nasser's Egypt) failed to materialize, however, and the squadron enjoyed several months' operational soldiering in the Middle East.

* * *

While the regiments were engaged in the varied battles of the Cold War, that constant of British military history, Ireland, was also making demands. Independent since 1921 and formally constituted a republic outside the Commonwealth in 1949, Roman Catholic Eire's population at around three million was twice that of the predominantly Protestant north whose six counties had elected to remain part of the United Kingdom. But the IRA, the instrument of the original resistance to British rule in the south, was wracked by internal dissent and embroiled in the intense in-fighting during the early days of the Irish Republic. During the Second World War Eire had remained neutral, though many of its citizens had joined the British services, and the IRA had been little more than a shadowy dormant threat in Ulster itself. In 1954, however, the IRA mounted a campaign of cross-border raids to stir up feeling against partition. These became increasingly violent though they never threatened to be seriously de-stabilizing because the RUC managed to maintain a strong grip on the border areas.

15th/19th arrived in the Province from Malaya, Aden and Muscat in 1957. They took over two camps, the main one at Lisanelly in Omagh, County Tyrone, and a secondary base at Castle Archdale on the banks of Lough Erne some twenty-five miles away in County Fermanagh. It was meant to be a normal peacetime rotation, but the IRA raids made other demands and the regiment frequently found itself in its Daimler scout and armoured cars on security patrols along the 200 miles of border.

The regiment managed to spend its two years there with an enjoyable mixture of operational excitement, worthwhile training

and unabashed good fun, similar in many ways to their time in Malaya, and uncannily like the experience of both regiments in Omagh twenty years later: the stories of inadvertently crossing the border, deliberately crossing the border, hunting, shooting, fishing, point-to-pointing and soldiers' humour could be the same. But although the IRA campaign in the late '50s could be brutal at times, it was nothing like as sophisticated or dangerous as the later campaign. It also lacked popular support among the Ulster Roman Catholics and in 1958 the government of Eire brought it effectively to a close by the internment of all the suspected leaders and operators in the south.

The campaign which began in 1969 was a different matter. Skilfully harnessing itself to the Roman Catholic civil rights movement, the IRA gained a strong popular base in the north. Violence escalated alarmingly and the Province began absorbing troops on emergency tours like blotting paper. The Infantry were not able to meet all these demands so other arms were looked to. In July, 1971, 15th/19th group under Lieutenant-Colonel J.S.F. Murray (dubbed 'The Black Hussars' as it included two RTR

73. *"Prepared to fight its own particularly cold war north of the Arctic Circle in Norway." (p.310)* A Scorpion of D Squadron 13th/18th Hussars with the Allied Command Europe Mobile Force on winter training, January, 1990.

74. *"There would often be a squadron detached to the Cyprus Sovereign Base Areas or to the United Nations troops on the island."(p.304)* A patrol from B Squadron 13th/18th Hussars in Nicosia, September, 1989.

75. *"13th/18th had to wait, however, until 1989 when the Queen appointed the Princess of Wales to be Colonel-in-Chief."(p.296)* She is photographed here arriving at the 1987 Guidon Parade. With her is the Colonel of the Regiment, Major-General Stuart Watson, who went ashore with the regiment on D-Day and held the colonelcy for eleven years until 1990.

76. *"Who serves as a soldier at his own expense?"* (*1st Corinthians, Chap 9, vs 7*). An RSM's uniform, officer pattern, is traditionally paid for by the officers. Much of the soldier's ceremonial dress is paid for by himself or from regimental funds. Band full dress, instruments and sheet music are paid for by the regiment. At amalgamation, the expense of changes to uniform is met almost entirely by individual officers, soldiers and regimental funds. RSM S.P. Davies at the 1987 Guidon Parade.

77. *"On 10 November 1989, literally, 'people power' forced open the Berlin Wall."* (p. 311) A Chieftain and crew from D Squadron 15th/19th Hussars, with the Brandenburg Gate and the wall in the background, the day before the border was opened. The regiment's Chieftains were the last British tanks to garrison Berlin.

78. *"Sadly, the fact of amalgamation meant that one of the two royal Colonels-in-Chief would in effect be standing down. The Queen took an early decision on this question and it was announced that the Princess of Wales would assume the appointment."(p.315)* The Princess emerging from the turret of a Scimitar after live-firing on Salisbury Plain, 1988. (Photograph by William Curtis).

79. *"On the day itself [1 December, 1992] all ranks could parade in the new identity of The Light Dragoons."(p.316)* The two regimental guidons about to be marched onto parade at Hohne, Germany. In due course a new, unified guidon will be presented to the regiment.

80 *"You cannot make war in white-painted vehicles."* (p.322) D Squadron Scimitar loading into an RAF Hercules for deployment to Bosnia, 1994.

81 *"You cannot make war in white-painted vehicles."* Unless in snow? C Squadron Scimitars patrolling in the depths of a Bosnian winter, 1994.

82 *"The Regiment became known as 'the Bosnia Hussars'."* (p.322) Scimitar of 1st Troop, C Squadron, under NATO command (and therefore no longer white painted), Blagai, Bosnia, 1998.

83 *"The role gives a young officer an unrivalled opportunity for independent command."* (p.326) C Squadron troop patrols near Sipovo, Republica Srpska (Bosnia), 1998.

84 *"Colonels-in-chief are important."* (p.327) HRH The Princess of Wales with the commanding officer, Lieutenant-Colonel Robert Webb-Bowen and members of the Association, Hohne, 1995.

85 *"It was, though, really a homecoming."* (p.328) HRH Princess Margaret, resuming the colonelcy-in-chief, with the commanding officer, Lieutenant-Colonel Tim Checketts, Hohne, 1997.

86 Top: "*The King's credentials were, of course, impeccable.*" (p.328) HM King Abdullah on his first visit to the regiment, at Swanton Morley, on appointment as colonel-in-chief.

87 Above: "*But there was unfinished business in Iraq.*" (p.329) After a gap of the best part of a century, the regiment patrols in Baghdad again (2003), mounted…

88 Right: "*Insufficient troops to keep order…*" (p.329) … and dismounted.

89 *"Then in May 2005 The Light Dragoons deployed as a unified regiment..."* (p.330) The commanding officer, Lieutenant-Colonel Robin Matthews, with his Orders Group, Al Muthanna, Iraq, 2005.

90 *"The early months of this far-flung deployment almost defy description."* (p.331) RV in the desert: CO's Rover Group links up with C Squadron.

91 *"Troops regularly operated on their own..."* (p.331) 2Lt Nick Binnington briefs his troop in anticipation of counter-foreign-fighter operations, 2005.

92 *"All rather reminiscent... of Beau Geste."* (p.331) A Squadron patrolling the Iran-Iraq border.

93 "*Responsibility for the urban areas…*" (p.331) B Squadron patrolling the outskirts of As Samawah, 2005.

94 "*Everything matters.*" (p.332) Lieutenant Will Jelf bowling to a soldier of the Australian task group, Al Muthanna, Iraq, in 'the Desert Test' series (Gentlemen vs Players, evidently), 2005.

95 *"The amalgamation should be outstandingly happy and successful from the outset."* (Colonel-in-chief's foreword) Retired officers from both sides of the amalgamation forming up as one for the march-past at Cavalry memorial Sunday.

squadrons) became the first RAC regiment to deploy on an 'Op *BANNER*' (unaccompanied) tour. They arrived just as the Roman Catholic population had openly turned against the Army (initially the Army had been seen as protectors from extremist Protestant elements) and into the worst violence since the 1920s. This was precipitated by the controversial internment operation in August, 1971, in which the regiment took part. Subsequently they were given tasks as widespread as Belfast, Lurgan and South Armagh. They quelled riots, had fire-fights on the border, searched, arrested, guarded internees – and patrolled extensively, the fundamental activity of internal security operations. They were four months of sometimes chaotic and continuously dangerous work but the only award was a well-earned OBE for the commanding officer: honours were harder-won in the early days of the emergency.

The first visit by 13th/18th to the Province came in the following year, 1972, and was spent guarding the internment camp at Long Kesh, better known later as HMP The Maze. A second Op *BANNER* tour by 15th/19th followed in 1973, largely in Armagh and Tyrone and mirroring the first tour in its scope of operations. A well-earned MM was awarded to Lance-Corporal W. Stuart for two incidents, the first of which was the capture of a senior IRA member and the second, three days later, his reaction to an ambush on the patrol of which he was in command, despite being badly wounded in the arm by a sniper's bullet. That tour in fact won an MBE and two 'mentions' in addition to Stuart's MM.

In 1974 the regiment went back one more time, back in fact to their old haunt of 1957, Lisanelly Camp in Omagh, now refurbished almost beyond recognition. The families were able to enjoy a large measure of normal life in this corner of Tyrone but the squadrons were kept routinely busy, including responsibility for patrolling the length of the border. The routine was not without incident, however. Most infantrymen, who have borne the brunt of the long 'slog' in Ulster, pass the months of their Op *BANNER* tours, and even the years of their resident tours, without firing a single shot at the enemy.

During the night of 20 January, 1975, however, a patrol led by Captain John Gillman came by accident upon a party of IRA who had hijacked a bus near the border at Kinawley. Gillman was a Bisley rifle-shot. A short-range gun battle followed which resulted in the death of one terrorist, the wounding and capture of another and a Mention in Despatches for the patrol commander. It was an impressive business and proof, if proof were needed, that there could be equally aggressive action from a cavalry regiment as from anyone else. Sadly, three weeks later, again in an action at night in the same area, Sergeant W. Robson was killed in another fire-fight with an IRA patrol.

To vehicle-borne troops, however, the bomb was always the biggest worry. 400 lbs of explosive in a culvert blew a Ferret scout car thirty feet into the air later that year. Both driver and commander survived, Trooper Metcalfe not badly injured though Trooper Felton was subsequently invalided out of the Army.

The tour ended in May, 1976, and the regiment moved to Tidworth to convert to the new CVR – Combat Vehicle Reconnaissance – series of vehicles, essentially the Scorpion (tracked) and Fox (wheeled) variants. CVR(T) had in part been designed with a view to counter-insurgency operations: one of the operational requirements of the original staff specification was that it should be able to manoeuvre between rubber trees on standard Malayan plantations. It was never deployed in Northern Ireland, however, where the favoured patrol mix was two Ferrets escorting two landrovers, the latter each with a crew of four men.

13th/18th also had a busy time of it in North Armagh in late 1975. They had deployed in a purely infantry role after intensive training throughout the summer and were regarded as the equal of most infantry battalions which had run that 'patch', especially the close recce troop whose work was of such a high order that the troop leader, Lieutenant Charles Nutting, was mentioned in despatches. As a further mark of esteem their commanding officer, Lieutenant-Colonel David Edelsten, was subsequently on promotion appointed deputy commander of

3rd Infantry Brigade, the brigade responsible for the most active part of the border. The regiment's last full-strength commitment in Ulster (B Squadron had a stint of Maze guard duty in 1985) was from 1978 to 1979 as the Province armoured reconnaissance regiment. Based in Omagh as 15th/19th had been, with Ferrets and Foxes, they too saw a great deal of the Province and particularly of Tyrone and Fermanagh.

The pattern of operations and off-duty life was also much the same. Kinawley was again a scene of action when, in March, 1979, 1,000 lbs of explosive in a horse trailer was parked outside the police station guarded by C Squadron. The massive explosion which followed all but destroyed the elevated sangar from which Trooper Scott had raised the alarm. Scott was somewhat shaken but, remarkably, unscathed. He had recently returned to duty from a stint in the officers' mess. When the commanding officer, George Stephen, saw him later that evening and asked him how it felt coming so close to oblivion he delivered a reply the equal of W.C. Fields' "On the whole I'd rather be in Philadelphia" – Scott believed it to be on the whole "Better than serving gin and tonic, Colonel!"

Although the RAC's performance in the Province had been generally effective, there were doubts as to the wisdom of asking cavalry and RTR regiments to undertake tours in an infantry role because their manpower establishment did not permit them to meet the minimum manning strength laid down by Headquarters Northern Ireland. It had also been decided, for several reasons, that patrolling in armoured cars was unacceptable, and the tours were in any case having their effect on BAOR standards of training. 13th/18th were the last RAC regiment to serve in Northern Ireland until 1990 when the changing threat and sheer pressure of commitments worldwide led to the reappearance of RAC regiments in a dismounted role in the Province.

* * *

Although fighting the Cold War in the 1970s and 1980s seemed at times to be simply a business of alternating between, on the one hand, operational over-commitment and, on the other, over-exercising but under-training, they were in fact years of increasing stability in regimental life. Families put down roots in a number of places, not least in some of the garrisons in Germany. The regiments too put down roots. Until 1958 the cavalry had recruited nationally in contrast to the Infantry who since the nineteenth century had recruited territorially. In this year the RAC was put on to the same recruiting basis. 15th/19th had enjoyed a special association with Northumberland since being stationed there in 1942: in 1947, for instance, they were affiliated to the Northumberland Hussars, so it was natural that when territorial recruiting was introduced these links were formalized and Durham included too. 13th/18th were given South Yorkshire and the East Riding as their recruiting area. When small 'Home Headquarters', analogous to the infantry regiment's depot but comprising only a retired officer and a clerk, were established for 13th/18th in York and 15th/19th in Newcastle, the territorial links rapidly strengthened. English towns and cities do not bestow their freedoms lightly, so it was a considerable mark of this strengthening when first Newcastle in 1973 then Barnsley in 1979 gave these freedoms to the respective regiments.

General Strawson adds to his commentary on fighting the Cold War, which heads this chapter, "But the real action was elsewhere." It certainly was, and both regiments had good tastes of it, but the substantial effort had been with NATO's forces facing the Soviet bear and her Warsaw Pact allies. By 1989 15th/19th were back in tanks again, ageing Chieftains (which had replaced Centurion in the early '70s) in Paderborn, although conversion to the Challenger was expected soon. 13th/18th had completed ten years as a reconnaissance regiment and were based in Tidworth in support of the United Kingdom Mobile Force whose war role was in Danish Zealand or Schleswig-Holstein, and with one squadron committed to the ACE (Allied Command Europe) Mobile Force prepared to fight its own particularly cold war north of the Arctic Circle in Norway.

By 1988 there were signs that the Warsaw Pact was no longer the homogeneous alliance it had once appeared to be. Hungary and Poland in particular were taking some robustly independent decisions. In Czechoslovakia there were similar signs. In East Germany the hard-line government was under pressure for reform although it seemed there was little chance of it being made. In President Gorbachev's Soviet Union some remarkable statements were being made under the doctrines of *Glasnost* ('Openness') and *Perestroika* ('Restructuring'). The sheer expense of maintaining the old communist system and its massive arsenal, in particular nuclear weapons, was beginning to cripple the economy and the Soviet leadership appeared willing to consider substantial arms reduction proposals. But in the statement on the defence estimates for that year, Her Majesty's Government was warning against premature celebration, that, in Churchill's words, "the cause of disarmament will not be obtained by Mush, Slush or Gush. It will be advanced steadily by the harassing expense of fleets and armies."

Fortunately the expense was to prove even more harassing for the Warsaw Pact. The command economies and totalitarian societies of the Soviet Union and her satellites could not in the end bear the stresses and strains of economic forces and the increasing demands for democratic reform, especially when exacerbated by strong feelings of nationalism. Christopher Donnelly, NATO's principal adviser on Soviet military matters, often repeated what he had heard senior Soviet officers describe as the Red Army's "cast-iron morale", pointing out that the key characteristic of cast-iron is that it is immensely strong under even pressure but extremely brittle when struck by a sharp blow. This now seemed to apply to the Soviet Union as a whole, whose system had withstood immense pressure for seventy years but which was now fracturing under a series of blows it was powerless to parry.

The blow, and signal, which probably meant the most occurred on 10 November, 1989, when, literally, 'People-Power' forced open the Berlin Wall. It was the most tangible sign that the West had won the Cold War, a remarkable achievement and one for which the United Kingdom could take a major share of the credit. So too could the Army and especially the Royal

Armoured Corps whose very *raison d'être* throughout had been to counter the quite staggering numbers of armoured vehicles which 3rd Shock Army of the Group of Soviet Forces Germany arrayed against 1st (British) Corps. And both the 13th/18th and 15th/19th Hussars were equal shareholders in this achievement, richly deserving of any dividend.

Unlike 1945, however, there was no unconditional surrender from which to dictate terms. The Cold War had been spectacularly and, to many, unexpectedly won but the sheer speed of the Warsaw Pact's collapse presented major difficulties for NATO's strategic planners. The massive monolithic threat from the Soviet *bloc* had gone but the world hardly looked a safer place. The nature of the peace, and its management, appeared to be the fundamental question for the West, and for the West's new 'allies', in the last decade of the century.

CHAPTER 18

No Option But Change

"As we now move to the mid-1990s and beyond, there will therefore be major changes in the nature and scale of the Army's commitments; in our forward contribution to the defence of Europe; in our needs for the direct defence of the United Kingdom. . . It is against this background that we have devised a new structure matched to our defence needs."

TOM KING, Secretary of State for Defence
Britain's Army for the 90s
White Paper Presented to Parliament, July, 1991

"It was only to be expected that as soon as peace in Europe was firmly secured the Army would be drastically reduced." So began Chapter Six which chronicled the aftermath of the Napoleonic Wars. It seems to be a particularly apt beginning to this final chapter, too, but whereas in the immediate years following Waterloo the cavalry escaped the worst of the retrenchment, this time the cuts seemed to fall disproportionately heavily on the Royal Armoured Corps.

Following the collapse of the Warsaw Pact and the beginning of the disintegration of the Soviet Union, the Ministry of Defence carried out a review which it called *Options for Change*. Ministers apparently felt there was no reason for a fundamental review of defence policy, but that it was right to look at opportunities to adjust the defence programme in light of the changed international situation. In July, 1990, the Secretary of State, Tom King, announced to the House of Commons the Government's outline proposals for force levels and structures.

313

Media speculation had been rife as to what direction *Options for Change* would take, and now it intensified as speculation about specific regimental cuts mounted. Particular attention was focused on the Royal Armoured Corps whose very *raison d'être*, as was explained in the previous chapter, had been to defeat the Warsaw Pact's armour. "Even though the emphasis will be on flexibility and mobility," wrote Michael Evans, *The Times*'s defence editor, in April, 1990, "it will not mean the death of the tank. . . The trouble is that no one at the Ministry of Defence has much idea at whom the tanks will be firing." Within twelve months British tanks were firing at Soviet-built Iraqi armour in the Gulf. Herein lay the crux of the planners' problems: where there was previously a clear and quantifiable threat to match in terms of numbers and equipment capability, there was no longer such certainty. Judgements would have to be made as to the size and shape of the new 'capability-based' army in the light of a great many imponderables.

The Iraqi invasion of Kuwait, and the subsequent Operation *DESERT STORM* under United Nations' mandate to re-establish Kuwait's sovereignty, was a powerful reminder of the dangers still lurking in the post-Cold War world. For the duration of the Kuwait operations, *Options* work was put on ice. 1990 and early 1991 was a very uncertain time for the regiments as they awaited news of whether or not they would be caught up in the reductions.

It was subsequently announced that the Royal Armoured Corps would be reduced from nineteen regiments to eleven. This reduction was even greater than had been feared and now placed both 13th/18th and 15th/19th Hussars firmly in line for another amalgamation. The Director of the Royal Armoured Corps had earlier laid down the principles on which the reductions were to take place, these being seniority, proportionality (equal reductions in lancers, hussars, dragoon guards and RTR) and 'like with like'. It only remained to be learned with whom the pairing would take place.

In fact both regiments wanted to amalgamate with each other: the two had always got on well together, their outlook and historical antecedents were very similar and, most important, both had firm roots in the North. A joint approach was therefore made to the Colonel Commandant of the RAC, and the subsequent agreement to the request that the regiments should combine did much to lessen the pain of amalgamation.

Sadly, the fact of amalgamation meant that one of the two royal Colonels-in-Chief would in effect be standing down. The Queen took an early decision on this question and it was announced that the Princess of Wales would assume the appointment. During the subsequent discussions by the joint amalgamation committee one of the major questions was what the new regiment should be called. The two other pairs of amalgamating hussar regiments had chosen to style themselves *Queen's Royal* and *King's Royal* respectively and, being senior to 13th/18th and 15th/19th, had first choice. It was decided not to incorporate the Colonel-in-Chief's title into that of the new regiment, however, in order to be even-handed to both regiments and to have a name with 'bite'. *Light Dragoons* therefore emerged as the name which met all these requirements and which described a new regiment rather than a 'harlequin' one, yet which identified firmly with an illustrious past. Nevertheless there were regrets that 'hussar' would disappear from the title, though the Regiment's full dress and appointments would continue to be the hussar pattern. In this the wheel had turned full circle so that things were back to what they had been at the end of the eighteenth century – light dragoons in name, hussars in style. In February, 1992, the Secretary of State for Defence informed the House of Commons of the new title and soon afterwards it was confirmed that amalgamation would take place on 1 December, 1992, each regiment reducing beforehand, by discharge or transfer, to half its peace establishment in order to make for the most equitable union.

Saying goodbye to half the regiment, many of whom did not want to leave at all, notwithstanding redundancy payments for those on long engagements, was a sad affair for both sides. For those in command who had to make the choices where there were insufficient volunteers, it was a particularly unpleasant duty. Nevertheless there emerged early in the pre-amalgamation discussions a remarkably positive approach. By the time of the actual amalgamation all the details which had caused irritation in 1922, dress, music and the like, had been resolved so that on the day itself all ranks could parade in the new identity of The Light Dragoons, They did so under the command of Lieutenant-Colonel Andrew Stewart, whose grandfather had won the DSO in France with the 18th Hussars in the Great War and whose father had clambered aboard an evacuation ship at Dunkirk as a troop leader with the 13th/18th.

The badge with which they paraded harked back to the earlier regiments of light dragoons whose helmet plate was a cross *formy*, or *pattée* – similar to a Maltese cross – with a roundel bearing the regiment's number, and the whole plate surmounted by a crown. The regimental quick march *Balaklava*, previously 13th/18th's, was retained. It had been a popular tune in the music halls at the time of the Crimean War. In recent years the 'territorializing' of recruiting had also led to the unofficial adoption of several regional songs, most notably *Ilkla Moor ba't'at* and *Blaydon Races*. "Strange how potent cheap music is," says Elyiot in Noel Coward's *Private Lives*. *Denmark*, retained as the slow march, with its association with the Danish Princess Alexandra through the 19th Hussars, was much grander, but, cheap or otherwise, music has been a potent part of both regiments' histories.

The regimental bands have always been at the centre of formal parades and informal celebrations alike, and the trumpeters have long functioned as 'speaking clocks' in the routine of barrack life. The sight and sound of up to a dozen regimental trumpeters, under the Trumpet Major, marching to the centre of the Square mid-morning each day to play the symbolic *Stables* call could not but fail to stir. A similar sight certainly stirred Anne Garland in Thomas Hardy's novel *The Trumpet Major*, set during the Napoleonic Wars: "What is there like the army?" she interrupted, "I like the cavalry better than anything I know; and the dragoons the best of the cavalry – and the trumpeters the best of the dragoons!"

All the more impressive is the fact that each of these bandsmen, musicians, is 'dual trade'. Latterly this second qualification has been as medical orderly, so that on general mobilization the bands join field hospitals and dressing stations. During Operation *GRANBY* the bands of both regiments deployed to Saudi Arabia in this role and won unstinting praise for the way they carried out their task.

At the time of writing this history the future of the line cavalry bands is uncertain. Severe limits placed on Army manpower as a whole, and proportionately on overall numbers of bandsmen too, have questioned the viability of small bands, notwithstanding their demonstrably important operational role as medical orderlies. It has been suggested that 'brigading' bands for hussars, lancers and dragoon guards might be preferable. There is something of a fashion for big bands in parts of the military music Establishment. There are strong arguments for them but to argue exclusively for big bands is to forget the origins and purpose of military music. It is like attending one of the monumental performances of Handel's *Messiah*, with vast ranks of the Huddersfield Choral Society and an augmented Hallé Orchestra thundering out a Victorian expanded score – then forgetting that Handel performed it with an orchestra of only thirty-eight musicians and a chorus of nineteen men and boys from the Chapel Royal. There is no doubt whatever that the regimental preference is for the present system to remain, so potent an element in continuing to foster *esprit de corps* is the band considered to be.

One of the many positive aspects of the amalgamation has been the doubling of the alliances with Commonwealth regiments. It was decided that the existing links would be renewed so the friendships built up over many years could carry on; thus the Royal Canadian Hussars are joined by The South Alberta Light Horse, and the 6th and 19th Lancers in Pakistan likewise. The lst/15th New South Wales Lancers and the 2nd Royal Reconnaissance Regiment of the Malaysian army will continue their alliances, and so too will Skinner's Horse, whose officers carry 13th/18th whips and whose cummerbunds are worn by both Light Dragoon officers and mess staff alike (on formal occasions the mess staff wear the royal livery, a distinction granted the Fifteenth during the Duke of Cumberland's colonelcy). The unofficial alliance with the *4ème Chasseurs* of the French army, which has flourished since Balaklava, also remains.

Finally the already close relationship both regiments had enjoyed with the TA armoured reconnaissance regiment, The Queen's Own Yeomanry (13th/18th with The Yorkshire Hussars Squadron at York and 15th/19th with The Northumberland Hussars Squadron at Cramlington), was further reinforced. Not only would The Light Dragoons share the rôle (only three regiments in this rôle remaining) but Home Headquarters would be in Newcastle, sharing Fenham Barracks with RHQ and HQ Squadron of The Queen's Own Yeomanry.

Both 13th/18th and 15th/19th had spent the majority of the post-war years in the recce role and it is not surprising that they preferred this to armour. Armoured recce is particularly attractive to the junior officer and NCO because of the independence of the troop in the field and for recce's 'reach', whether tactical or strategic. Basil Liddell Hart, in his *Thoughts on War* written in 1944, says, "The soldier serves in small garrisons and exercises in cramped areas, while the sailor traverses the wide oceans and learns navigation as the staple of his craft. For him geography precedes gunnery." For the recce soldier, too, geography precedes gunnery.

There were many and continuing reservations about the shortage of regular armoured reconnaissance in the new order of battle. The House of Commons Defence Committee's review of *Options for Change* brought this concern into sharp focus:

"We are concerned lest the armoured reconnaissance strength envisaged in Britain's Army for the 90s, reduced from five to two Regular regiments, proves too small even in relation to peacetime requirements, including international peacekeeping operations, and may lead to difficulties in ensuring the maintenance of armoured reconnaissance skills. . . . We consider that . . . the possibility of providing a further armoured reconnaissance regiment should not be ruled out at this stage [February 1992]."

At the time the HCDC made this report it could not have been known that an armoured recce squadron of the 9th/12th Lancers (a regiment due later to convert to tanks) would be deployed in war-torn Bosnia by the end of the year, nor that The Light Dragoons' first operational deployment there would be within six months of the amalgamation.

* * *

If there were ever a *Cavalry Spirit* distinct from any other sort of spirit, and many great soldiers have maintained that there was – and *is* – it would include the qualities of independent thought, quick decision and boldness. It would also include a quality which is difficult to define: the French words *élan* and *panache* are close but not precisely appropriate because although in many ways the *Cavalry Spirit* is international, there is an element in the history of the British cavalry which makes them different. Perhaps better is *Swagger*, in the best sense of the word, the sense in which it was applied in the Edwardian soldier's 'swagger stick', and as the Oxford dictionary defines it: "a dashing or confident air or way of doing something, freedom from tameness or hesitancy, smartness". The reputation of the new regiment called The Light Dragoons will be made by the men who serve with that regiment, but there is a character already there: it is what lies behind the paintings in the Messes, the prints and photographs in the squadron lines, the written and unwritten customs, the standing orders – the accumulated memorials of past duty and glory, like those on the walls and in the rituals of a parish church.

What will not be found written down is a special characteristic which 13th/18th and 15th/19th shared – a singularly close and relaxed relationship between all ranks. In 1980 the then Lieutenant-Colonel Tony Wells, on handing over command of the 15th/19th, wrote of this characteristic in his regiment:

"Last but not least it remains a large happy family whose members laugh a lot, help each other and enjoy each other's company tremendously." It is easy to see in the history of the regiments how this came about, how the recce troop leader today in the field, detached for long periods from the close control of the squadron leader and the immediate support of the other squadron officers, finds the exercise of command different from that of the young officer in other types of regiment, and how this echoes through the decades and centuries. This should not be mistaken for any laxness or lack of aggression: things went wrong from time to time, certainly, but Gillespie at Vellore, Logan at Campo Mayor, Barrow and Marshall at El Teb, Garforth at Mons, Taylor near Dunkirk, Denny at Mont Pinçon, Gillman at Kinawley, and legions of others, are testimony to the right spirit – and there will soon be new names to add.

The history of The Light Dragoons' forebears is one of remarkable parallels and cross currents, which this book has sought to highlight. Their former mottos, taken into the new regiment, seem to sum up a robust confidence for the future as well as a great pride in the past:

Viret in aeternum – It flourishes forever
Merebimur – We shall be worthy

CHAPTER 19

The New World Order: a Decade of Operations

"The best regiment in the army at present: consistently the best officered, the best recruited, and all round the most effective."

General Sir Charles Guthrie,
Chief of the Defence Staff, 2001

Germany; the Balkans; Ireland; England; Iraq; Afghanistan?

It all seems so obvious now (and in truth it was obvious to many at the time): the collapse of the Soviet Union would not usher in a period of universal peace; the fall of the Berlin Wall would not herald, in the title of one book, 'The End of History' (1992) – a long, irreversible glide into liberal democracy. Or if it has, the Army could be excused for disbelieving the evidence. The previous chapter gave a taste of what optimists called 'the new World order', and what most old sweats were soon calling instead 'the new World disorder'. Saddam Hussein's Iraq invaded Kuwait, and the former Republic of Yugoslavia (FRY) began imploding. That implosion sucked in troops from all over the World under the flag of the United Nations, and eventually NATO. In 2001, after the al-Qaeda attack on the World Trade Centre in New York ('9/11'), the United States threw its weight behind Afghan warlords to remove the Taliban regime which had made Afghanistan a base for Osama Bin Laden, al-Qaeda's leader. In addition to these legacies of the Cold War there were other places requiring the British army to bare its teeth: Sierra Leone, for instance, saw some of the most intensive hand-to-hand fighting since the Falklands. Only in Ireland, 'that constant of British military history' (indeed 'Ireland' is mentioned no less than forty times in this history) does there seem to have been a resolution of conflict. In the wake of the 'Good Friday Agreement' (1998) and the subsequent faltering steps in the implementation process, the Treasury declared another peace dividend – a cut of 9000 in army manpower. This was later whittled down to 3000 by the General Staff, though still precipitating the wholesale reorganization and reduction of the infantry by mid-2006. Time and a good deal of painful overstretch will show whether this decision was any more judicious than Tom King's disastrous 'Options for Change' cuts a decade and a half ago.

Within six months of the amalgamation, B Squadron was in Bosnia with UNPROFOR, the inaptly named UN Protection Force (the then Brigadier Roddy Cordy-Simpson was already in Sarajevo as UNPROFOR's first chief of staff). In November 1993 the squadron returned and 'C' took its place. In March the following year D Squadron joined them. In May, 'C' was replaced by 'A', and in July a regimental tactical headquarters deployed. And so it went on, throughout 1995 and 1996 – every year, in fact, to 2001. The regiment became known as 'the Bosnia Hussars'. The BBC's Martin Bell, famous for his nightly television reports in his trademark white suit, frequently with gunfire echoing in the background, declared that The Light Dragoons were his favourite regiment: "everywhere I go they're there, and always cheerful and hospitable." Michael Evans, defence editor of *The Times*, has even more cause to hold the same opinion, believing Major Marcus Browell to have saved his life during a mortar attack near Tuzla.

UNPROFOR was not a 'shooting war', the history books will say. CVR(T)s were white painted (UN peacekeeping forces do not deploy in camouflage), and as UNPROFOR's commander, General Sir Michael Rose, memorably put it when being pressed to take on one side or another: "you cannot make war in white-painted vehicles". It was definitely peacekeeping. But it was often peacekeeping where there was no peace to keep. Fighting between the Serbs and Moslems and Croats continued (and even that is a considerable simplification), and UNPROFOR's efforts were increasingly directed towards humanitarian aid for the civil population, though in a civil war the distinction between combatants and non-combatants is never easy to define. And so day-to-day, and sometimes hour-to-hour, car commanders had to take difficult tactical decisions, many of which had strategic implications. They were not helped by the inadequacy of the VHF radios, unsuited to the mountainous terrain. Martin Bell once recounted how astonished he was at the army's poor communications compared with his own, and once lent his satellite link to a troop. But it all reinforced the recce soldier's initiative, independent judgement and capacity to take action. *Not a shooting war*; and yet on one occasion a patrol from B Squadron counted fourteen main-armament (115mm) rounds fired at them by a Serb M84 tank. In Major Ellwood's report on D Squadron's 1994 deployment there is, too, a telling list of, as he put it, "things that stick in the mind" in this so-called peacekeeping: "First Troop being fired at by Moslem forces in Mosevac; a foot patrol led by SSjt Whitehead getting pinned down by Serb sniper fire and the subsequent accurate return fire by LCpl Robson; the SQMS attracting Serb fire in Sniper Alley and the follow-up action by Second Troop with Cpl Dove and LCpl Casterton; SSjt 'Jonah' Barnstaple's troop and the artillery fire which seemed to follow them wherever they went; Fourth troop under Capt Hamilton getting shelled near Doboj; Lt Deakin's vehicle running over an anti-personnel mine near Guce Gora; death threats from a Bosnian security officer following Capt Mayo's exposure of misappropriation of humanitarian aid... Bosnian and Croat hospitality; Bosnian and Croat intransigence; deep snow in March, scalding temperatures in July, and colossal thunderstorms." The list goes on and on. These operations are called, in a wonderful euphemism of army doctrine, 'Wider Peacekeeping'. Wider still and wider...?

The story of the regiment in Bosnia, and indeed of the army, is one of untold, unseen acts of courage, fortitude, devotion to duty, and downright professionalism. Individually the acts may not sound much, but without the qualities of judgement and restraint displayed by men having as it were to make up the script as they went along, 'a little local difficulty' might all too often have become a major incident, deeply embarrassing to the UN. And UNPROFOR was in no position to take embarrassment: it was hopelessly under-deployed, over-mandated (it was for instance the Security Council's declaration of Srebrenica as a UN safe area, but without the troops to guarantee it, that resulted in the massacre of many thousands of Moslem men and boys in July 1995), and it was weakly led at the political level. In such unpropitious circumstances, a car commander's misjudgement could make the international news and set every dove aflutter in the doocots of New York.

Sometimes there were opportunities for distinction. In 1993 the Vance-Owen peace talks with the warring parties were in progress in Geneva (Dr David Owen, former British Foreign Secretary, the EU special representative for Bosnia, and Cyrus Vance the former US Secretary of State). Knowledge of the activities and positions of each side was crucial in establishing the ceasefire conditions, and needless to say both Serb and Bosnian-Moslem accounts were usually inaccurate, fluid and opportunist – mendacious, indeed. B Squadron, deployed in the key 'Posavina corridor', was able to send such accurate and timely information to Geneva (thirty minutes from Scimitar to conference hall) that the warring delegates were frequently 'outflanked' at the negotiating table. And all this intelligence collection was done under fire – frequently heavy shelling. The second-in-command, Captain Arthur Ibbotson was awarded an MBE for his part in it.

Indeed, there can never have been such a time when the regiment has so routinely acquired different campaign medals, let alone decorations (there is a separate 'Honours and Awards' entry in the index of many of the journals during that Balkans decade). Today's ten-year corporal might well be into his second row of ribbons, which could even include the GSM with Northern Ireland clasp, since despite the Balkan pressure the regiment regularly managed to answer the calls for formed-troop reinforcements there. It is, of course, a truism that the work of reconnaissance goes unobserved; it follows therefore that decorations are infrequent and relatively minor. In addition, such is the strict limit on awards, the number ever more tightly regulated, that an independent squadron is unlikely to get its dues. Nevertheless the regiment has been steadily if unspectacularly honoured: no DSOs or MCs (yet), but enough MBEs, MiDs, QCBs, QCVSs and other initials to show that The Light Dragoons have been 'where the action is'. Indeed, as the then colonel of the regiment, Brigadier Tony Wells, put it in his 1996 journal message, these years were "one of the most intense periods of operational soldiering the Regiment has experienced since the Second World War". In addition, command appointments speak eloquently of the regard in which the regiment's officers have been held: the first armoured division commander in the history of either antecedent regiment (Roddy Cordy-Simpson), two armoured brigade commanders (Andrew Stewart and David Rutherford-Jones), command of British forces Afghanistan (Simon Levey, a colonel relieving a major-general), and three-star tactical command of SFOR (Stabilization Force) in Bosnia, the NATO command which succeeded the UN after the ceasefire of December 1995 (Roddy Cordy-Simpson again, who was appointed KBE in recognition of his year's challenge in Sarajevo).

The name Cordy-Simpson is, of course, familiar from Chapter 17. 'Cordy' is now colonel of the regiment, as was his father John before him. This may well be a unique double in the army's history, but to the regiment it just seems the way things are. The continuity amid the change is extraordinarily strong; and it is immensely fortifying. Another officer who went ashore with John C-S on D-Day was Captain (later Major-General) Stuart Watson, Colonel of the 13th/18th Hussars from 1979 to 1990; his son, Angus, takes command of the regiment in 2007. These things defy utilitarian explanation. Do they really matter, asks a quill-driver in Whitehall who has identified a potential saving by knocking away another regimental prop. They do: they are what makes the regiment (even if for a brief moment) in the opinion of no lesser man than the CDS himself the best in the army.

There are other things. One is the regiment's role: armoured reconnaissance, light armour, armoured cars – it can be all three and more. The Recce spirit is the same as that displayed by the Fifteenth at Emsdorff, which set the regiment on its course so dashingly: bold, decisive action, not waiting for orders, every man with a stake (and a part) in the outcome. *Everyone*. The role gives a young officer an unrivalled opportunity for independent command. This consequently places the greatest demands on his troop serjeant. Generals and even politicians may make crucial decisions based on what they learn from a troop corporal or lance-corporal. A driver-mechanic must know how to keep his 'waggon' on the road at all costs, for it may be operating beyond the range of recovery. A gunner-operator must be able to outshoot anything if the worst comes to the worst, and be able to 'stag' for his vehicle commander so that the troop can operate 24 hours a day – which is what generals expect them to do. This is *Recce*. And, dismayingly, the regiment must live with the knowledge that no officer who has not served with Recce seems really to *understand* Recce! "We few, we happy few, we band of brothers..."

Occasionally the closeness of that band is as painful as it is sustaining. There are sometimes casualties. John Ruskin, the nineteenth-century author and critic, put it well: "The soldier's trade, verily and essentially, is not slaying, but being slain... and the reason the world honours the soldier is that he holds his life at the service of the state." Peacekeeping in FRY was, sadly, not all the near-misses that Major Ellwood's report suggested. There were 'fatalities', as the MOD casualty-reporting form calls them – more properly, men killed on operations; *On Active Service* in the old parlance. On 28 January 1996 one of C Squadron's Spartans (CVR(T)) was destroyed by that dread of all armoured troops, an anti-tank mine. The crew of three were killed instantly: Lieutenant Richard Madden, his gunner-operator Trooper Andrew Ovington and driver-mechanic Trooper John Kelly. As a crew they epitomized the regiment at its best. Madden – 'Dickie' – was textbook LD officer-specification: house captain at school, a good degree in Russian, handsome, clean-cut, a JUO at Sandhurst, the Armourers and Braziers Prize (i.e. top) on his troop leader's course, a hunting man, a fine musician, and a caring officer – 'a very parfit knight'. Ovington – 'Ovi' – a married man, joined up a little later than most. He was from the heart of the recruiting area, Easington, with its mining heritage and manly virtues, and he was textbook too: equally clean-cut and good looking, and a sensitive man, he was a trooper with that little bit extra like so many men who join the cavalry – a talented artist, a glass engraver and a poet. The memorials in the regimental journal describe how he and Richard Madden became an inseparable team. And Kelly – 'Swede' – another textbook Light Dragoon: the Geordie (well, Sunderland) with a twinkle in his eye, the likely lad known by everybody, especially the SSM, who had joined the Junior Leaders' Regiment at sixteen, a natural and devoted mechanic and skilled driver to whom others turned for advice. Their regimental memorial was returned from Bosnia in 2005 and is now proudly placed in the Leases Memorial Garden in Newcastle. Lance-Corporal Anthony Braithwaite, in the Scimitar behind, risked his life trying to save his comrades that day, and was badly burned. He received a Queen's Commendation. The textbook has many pages indeed. Scripture seems apt: *Lovely and pleasant in their lives, and in their death they were not divided* (II Samuel, 1.23).

* * *

Colonels-in-chief are important. They provide an external focus, necessary when a regiment is so busy and inward-looking; they add distinction, occasionally glamour, and sometimes opportunity. The Regiment was both fortunate and unfortunate in equal measure in its first decade: fortunate in those whom Her Majesty appointed, unfortunate in the short time that the princesses were able to occupy the colonelcy. Following the divorce settlement which removed her royal status, in July 1996 Princess Diana decided that she would have to stand-down. With unusual speed, in March 1997 Princess Margaret was appointed in her place. It was, though, really a homecoming (she had been appointed colonel-in-chief of the 15th/19th Hussars in 1958), but not for long, for in February 2002, Her Royal Highness died. There followed two years of – sometimes anxious – waiting until Her Majesty approved a successor. None of The Light Dragoons' antecedents had ever had other than a female colonel-in-chief (an interesting though ultimately fruitless fact on which to ponder) but on 1 July 2003 the Queen appointed His Majesty King Abdullah of Jordan. It is a rare thing for a foreign head of state to be given such a rank, but the King's credentials were, of course, impeccable. He lost no time in visiting his regiment, and his speech on that occasion is illuminating:

> "To be Colonel-in-Chief of any British regiment is a fantastic privilege that is seldom granted. To be Colonel-in-Chief of this regiment is a particular honour. Today I feel I have come home. I hope you will not be surprised to know that I have followed the fortunes of The Light Dragoons with great interest since I was a young troop leader in the Regiment, first commissioned from Sandhurst. Your high reputation within the British armed forces is therefore well known to me and believe it or not I learned a lot as a troop leader in this Regiment. I learned that important jobs are simple… simple jobs are hard… hard jobs are given to The Light Dragoons… and The Light Dragoons will always get the job done!"

* * *

In 2000 the regiment had left Germany for, ironically, the same geological feature in England: the loamy belt that stretches from the *heide* of Soltau-Hohne through the Low Countries to East Anglia. Swanton Morley, in mid-Norfolk, a World War II bomber station (the US Army Air Force's first bombing mission in Europe took place from here), had been an armoured recce barracks only since 1996, and was named after that fine cavalryman 'Trooper-to-Field Marshal' Sir William Robertson. It was well appointed but miles from anywhere. But if anyone thought that this was to be a move to *Blighty* – a long spell of R&R – it could only have been a very passing delusion, for such was the army's overstretch that the actual 'Arms Plot' move took place while B Squadron was still in Bosnia – the Regiment's thirteenth tour.

In Swanton Morley, with an uncertain chain of command but in the knowledge that too much peacekeeping (even the Bosnia sort) can be bad for battle skills, training for warfighting again became the priority. It was *firefighting*, however, that the Regiment was first called out to do. In 2002 nationwide fire brigade strikes saw the re-emergence of the 'Green Goddess' auxiliary fire engines from preservation, and soon after returning from a summer season in Canada at the armour-training area near Calgary – BATUS – (where predictably they left with the accolade 'best battle group on the prairie') The Light Dragoons made an unexpected visit to the recruiting area at the end of unglamorous hosepipes. The reader will probably have guessed, too, that Bosnia roulements continued the while.

But there was unfinished business in Iraq. Following the decision to remove Saddam Hussein, and the brilliantly successful Second Gulf War (20 March – 9 April 2003), there came, and continues, the hard bit: turning Iraq into a functioning democracy. It is not exaggerating to say that this phase was wholly misjudged by the Allied planners: insufficient troops to keep order, inadequate Iraqi bureaucracy and security forces on which to build, and a hopeless infrastructure. From June to October 2003, two independent squadrons (A and B) and RHQ deployed to the Basra region on Operation TELIC, the name for both the fighting and the supposedly post-combat phases, reinforced by seventy-five volunteers from C Squadron just returned from Bosnia (what a band of brothers these!). At this stage the Coalition Provisional Authority had been formed in Baghdad, but the regiment had a sense of operating in a vacuum, exacerbated by the dispersal: RHQ was located in the Basra

Palace overlooking the Shatt-al-Arab waterway, running 'operational support' for 19 (Mechanized) Brigade; A Squadron was based in Al Amara under command 1KOSB, with a troop permanently detached to guard the British Embassy in Baghdad, and others tasked with dominating the Iran/Iraq border; and B Squadron, most unusually (the least pejorative way of putting it) under command of an artillery regiment (40 Field) in Az Zubayr Port, responsible for security of the Iraq/Kuwait border at Safwan (where General Norman Schwarzkopf had received the Iraqi surrender at the end of the First Gulf War). The task included the sexing of sheep, since ewes were not allowed to leave the country.

The Regiment's decade of operational experience was suitably recognized the following year in what may well have been an army 'first' in half a century: two-stars over one from the same regiment – the commander of MND(SE), the Multinational Division South-East (Andrew Stewart), and the brigade commander (David Rutherford-Jones).

Then in May 2005 The Light Dragoons deployed as a unified regiment (RHQ, B, C and HQ squadrons) on Op TELIC 6. The political situation in Iraq had, on paper at least, improved, but security had taken a distinct turn for the worse – and not only in the hard Sunni Moslem areas in which the Americans operated: Shia militias were making south-east Iraq a lethal place for British troops, who at the outset had been hailed as liberators. The regiment deployed a few months after the first national elections for the Iraqi Transitional Government. This time there appears to have been less of a sense of vacuum and more of a focused purpose: helping the Iraqi security forces to be self-reliant, which remains key to the coalition's 'exit strategy'. But the operational situation was, to say the least, fluid, the regiment's deployment and tasking changing half a dozen times during work-up training. In the event, the withdrawal of the Dutch from Iraq at the end of March required a redeployment of forces in the MND(SE) to Al Muthanna province, equidistant between Baghdad and Basra. The regiment was therefore re-assigned, but when they got there they found several hundred newly arrived Australian troops not under command but nevertheless expecting full logistical support. Anyone with experience of a Royal Armoured Corps regiment appreciates the importance of Headquarter Squadron, but the early months of this far-flung deployment almost defy description, with for instance the master chef (or for those more conversant with the soldiering of the earlier chapters, the cook serjeant-major), finding himself with a thousand hungry mouths to feed rather than the expected 450 – in field conditions and in temperatures regularly above 70 degrees.

B Squadron had responsibility for the urban areas, which included the significant towns of As Samawah and Ar Rumaythah, and for helping the Iraqi police run the Provincial Joint Operations Centre (PJOC), a frequent target for rocket attacks. It was in As Samawah that the Regiment sustained its only serious casualty (it was surprising there were not many more) when a night foot patrol came under automatic fire, and Lance-Corporal Anthony Duncan took a bullet in the leg. The patrol commander, fresh out of Sandhurst – as ever – was Second-Lieutenant Jake Rugge-Price, whose grandfather had commanded the squadron on D-Day. Meanwhile C Squadron had the job of helping the Iraqi Border Police control the Iraqi/Saudi-Arabia border, and with security in the desert – a haven for smugglers and criminal gangs. Troops regularly operated on their own over 200 miles from RHQ, not in CVR(T) but in cut-down landrovers, all rather reminiscent of the pre-Alamein Long Range Desert Group; or even perhaps, at the border forts, of Beau Geste. But any idea that this deployment, far away from the hot spots of Basra, was somehow a cushy billet is soon scotched by the fact that the regiment was relieved at the end of October by 2nd Battalion The Parachute Regiment – a measure, too, of how flexible the Regiment's operating drills had had to be.

* * *

In many ways the first dozen years could have been the story of any of the 'Options for Change' amalgamations. Except that what stands out in The Light Dragoons' story is the sense that everything matters. All the training and the operational deployments would have been so much of an army-wide piece had it not been for everything else crammed in: polo in both Germany and England against all the odds; hunter trials at Bredebeck; officers riding the Queen Mother's horses (and their own) in the Grand Military at Sandown (on one occasion the day before taking his squadron to Bosnia); the football team regularly winning the Cavalry Cup (in the last five years alone, 2001, 2003 and 2004); pressing the Australians hard at cricket in 'The Desert Test'; producing the Combined Services ski champion (Lieutenant Nick Binnington) and the Army light-heavyweight boxing champion (Lance-Corporal 'Twinny' Richardson); keeping regimental affiliations and alliances alive; and so much more. The Light Dragoons were chosen to provide the royal guards of honour for the Queen and the Prince of Wales at the Sixtieth Anniversary of the Normandy Landings, bringing accolades for their faultless turnout and drill from veterans and VIPs at the commemoration itself and from countless others who watched on television. There have been further manpower cuts, and rebadging of jobs such as clerks to other corps, all of which put the regimental system under incomprehensible strain. And the regimental band, which was at first 'brigaded' with other hussar bands, will now all but disappear in the latest innovation: two bands for the whole of the Royal Armoured Corps – The Light Cavalry Band, and The Heavy Cavalry Band.

Despite all this, throughout the pages of *The Light Dragoon*, as the new journal is called, there are smiling faces. If soldiering isn't fun, then why do it (it certainly isn't well paid)? This willing, cheerful spirit, which is never without cost, however, is both the manifestation of and the inspiration for the CDS's singular tribute which heads this postscript chapter. Or rather it should be called 'additional' chapter, for the word 'post' has something of finality about it, and the story very much continues. As the second, revised edition of this book goes to press, the regiment, not long returned from Iraq, is beginning to think about its next operational challenge: Afghanistan in 2007, perhaps a squadron as early as November this year – within half the time that the Army Board judges prudent for a regiment to return to active operations. The New World Order: it looks like a *second* decade of operations.

Viret in Aeturnum
Merebimur

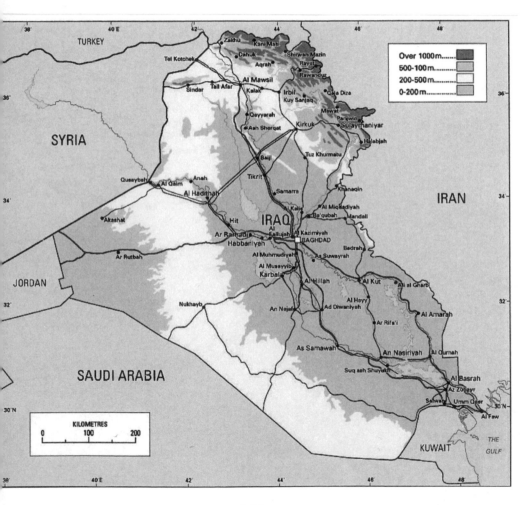

BOSNIA AND HERZEGOVINA

Bibliography

Anglesey, Marquess of, *A History of the British Cavalry* (4 volumes), Leo Cooper

Baden-Powell, Lord, *Lessons from the Varsity of Life*, Pearson

Barnett, Correlli, *Britain and Her Army 1509–1970*, Pelican

Barrett, C.R.B., *History of the XIII Hussars* (2 vols), Blackwood

Bastin, Jeremy, *The History of The 15th/19th The King's Royal Hussars 1945–1980*, Keats House

Biddulph, J., *The Nineteenth and Their Times*, John Murray

Blaxland, Gregory, *Destination Dunkirk*, William Kimber

Bond, Brian, *War and Society in Europe, 1870–1970*, Fontana

Bowling, A.H., *British Hussar Regiments 1804–1914 (Dress)*, Almark Publishing

Briscoe, Diana (Ed), *The Diary of a World War I Cavalry Officer* [Brig-Gen Sir Archibald Home], Costello

Bryant, Sir Arthur, *The Years of Endurance* and *Triumph in the West*, Collins

Burnett, Brig-Gen C.K., *The Memoirs of the 18th (Queen Mary's Own) Royal Hussars 1906–1922*, Warren & Sons

Calvocoressi, Peter, *World Politics Since 1945*, Longman

Carnock, Lord, *The History of the 15th The King's Hussars, 1914–1922*, Crypt House Press

Chandler, David, *Waterloo – The Hundred Days*, George Philip

Churchill, Winston, *The Gathering Storm*, Cassell

Cooper, Bryan, *Ironclads of Cambrai*, Pan Books

Courage, G., *The History of 15/19 The King's Royal Hussars, 1939–1945*, Gale & Polden

Dewar, Michael, *Brush Fire Wars*, Robert Hale

Durand, H. Mortimer, *The Thirteenth Hussars in the Great War*, Blackwood

Ensor, Sir Robert, *History of England 1870–1914*, Oxford University Press

Essame, H., *The 43rd Wessex Division at War 1944–1945*, William Clowes

Farwell, Bryon, *Armies of the Raj*, Viking

Fortescue, Sir John, *A History of the British Army* (13 volumes), Macmillan

Hamilton, Nigel, *Monty – The Making of a General 1887–1942*, Hamish Hamilton

Hastings, Max, *Overlord*, Michael Joseph

Hayter, Tony, *An Eighteenth-Century Secretary at War – The Papers of William, Viscount Barrington*, Army Records Society/The Bodley Head

Haythornthwaite, Philip, *Wellington's Military Machine*, Guild Publishing

Hennessy, Patrick, *Young Man in a Tank*, Self-published

Hibbert, Christopher, *Corunna*, Pan Books

Horrocks, Brian (with Eversley Belfield), *Corps Commander*, Sidgwick & Jackson

Howarth, David, *A Near-Run Thing*, Collins

Kee, Robert, *The World We Fought For*, Hamish Hamilton

Keegan, John, *Six Armies in Normandy*, Pimlico

Lee, Emmanoel, *To the Bitter End* [Boer War], Guild Publishing

Macksey, Kenneth, *A History of the Royal Armoured Corps*, Newtown

Malet, H, *Memoirs of the Eighteenth Princess of Wales' Own Hussars*

Maurice, Sir Frederick, *History of the War in South Africa, 1899–1902*, Hurst and Blackett

Massie, Robert K., *Dreadnought – Britain, Germany, and the Coming of The Great War*, Jonathan Cape

Miller, C. H., *History of the 13th/18th Royal Hussars (Queen Mary's Own), 1922–1947*, Chisman Bradshaw

Montgomery, B.L., *Normandy To The Baltic*, Printing and Stationery Service B.A.O.R.

Moyse-Bartlett, H., *Nolan of Balaklava*, Leo Cooper

Napier, Sir William, *History of the War in the Peninsula*

Naylor, John, *Waterloo*, Pan Books

Norman, C.B., *Battle Honours of the British Army*, David & Charles

North, John, *North-West Europe 1944–5*, H.M.S.O

Oman, Sir Charles, *A History of the Peninsular War* (7 volumes), Oxford University Press

Pemberton, W. Baring, *Battles of the Crimean War*, Pan Books

Pemberton, W. Baring, *Battles of the Boer War*, Pan Books

Rommel, Erwin (Edited by B. H. Liddell Hart), *The Rommel Papers*, Collins

Ryan, Cornelius, *A Bridge Too Far*, Coronet

Sheppard, E. W., *A Short History of the British Army to 1914*, Constable

Strawson, John, *Beggars in Red*, Hutchinson

Strawson, John, *Gentlemen in Khaki*, Secker and Warburg

Taylor, A. J. P., *English History 1914–1945*, Oxford University Press

Terriere, B.de S. La, *Days That Are Gone*, Hutchinson

Terraine, John, *Mons*, Pan Books

Thomas, Donald, *Charge! Hurrah! Hurrah! – A Life of Cardigan of Balaclava*, Routledge & Kegan Paul

Times, The, *History of the War in South Africa 1899–1902*, Sampson, Low, Marston & Co

Ulyatt, Kenneth, *Hussars of the Napoleonic Wars*, Macdonald

Waters, W.H.H., *The German Official Account of the War in South Africa*, John Murray

Watson, J. Steven, *The Reign of George III, 1760–1815*, Oxford University Press

William, Basil, *The Whig Supremacy, 1714–1760*, Oxford University Press

Woodward, Sir Llewellyn, *The Age of Reform, 1815–1870*, Oxford University Press

SERVICE OF THE LIGHT DRAGOONS 1715 – 1922

THIRTEENTH		FIFTEENTH	
1715	Munden's Regt of Dragoons raised		
	First Jacobite Rebellion		
1715–45	England & Ireland		
1745–46	**Second Jacobite Rebellion**: Scotland		
1746–96	England & Ireland	1759	Eliott's Light Horse raised
		1760–63	**Seven Years' War**: Germany
		1763–93	England
		1793–95	**Netherlands**
1796–98	**West Indies**	1795–1808	England
1798–1810	England	1799	**Netherlands**
		1808–09	**Peninsula**: Spain
1810–14	**Peninsula**: Portugal, Spain & France	1809–13	England
		1813–14	**Peninsula**: Portugal, Spain & France
1814–15	England	1814–15	Ireland
1815–16	**Waterloo Campaign:** Belgium & France	1815–16	**Waterloo Campaign:** Belgium & France
1816–18	England		
1819–40	India	1816–39	England, Ireland & Scotland
1840–54	England, Ireland & Scotland	1839–54	India
1854–56	**Crimea**	1854–70	England, Ireland & Scotland
1856–66	England, Ireland & Scotland		
1866–69	Canada		
1869–73	England	1870–81	India: **Afghanistan**
1873–84	India		
		1881–82	South Africa
1884–85	South Africa		
1885–99	England, Scotland & Ireland	1882–99	England, Scotland & Ireland
1899–1902	**Boer War**: S. Africa	1899–1909	India
1902–04	England	1909–13	South Africa
1904–14	India	1913–14	England
	1st World War:		**1st World War:**
1914–16	France & Belgium	1914–18	France & Belgium
1916–19	Mesopotamia		
		1919	Germany
1919–22	England	1919–22	Ireland
1922	Amalgamation with 18th Hussars	1922	Amalgamation with 19th Hussars

SERVICE OF THE LIGHT DRAGOONS 1715 – 1922

EIGHTEENTH		NINETEENTH	
1759	Ireland: Drogheda's Light Horse raised as 19th Light Dragoons	[1759	see EIGHTEENTH]
1759–94	Ireland	1779–83	England: 19th Light Dragoons raised & disbanded
1763	19th Light Dragoons renumbered 18th		
		1781	England: 23rd Light Dragoons raised
1794–98	**West Indies**		
1798–1808	England & Ireland	1782–1806	India: **Mysore Campaigns**
1799	**Netherlands**		
1808–09	**Peninsula**: Spain	1786	23rd Light Dragoons renumbered 19th
1809–13	England		
1813–14	**Peninsula**: Portugal, Spain & France	1807–09	England
		1809–13	Ireland
1814–15	England	1813–17	**War with United States**: Canada
1815–16	**Waterloo Campaign:** Belgium & France		
1818–21	England & Ireland	1817–21	England & Ireland
1821	18th disbanded	1821	19th disbanded
1858	18th re-raised	1858–70	England/India: 1858, 1st Bengal European Light Cavalry raised; 1861 redesignated 19th Hussars
1858–64	England		
1864–75	India	1870–82	England & Ireland
1875–88	England & Ireland	1882–86	**Egypt & Sudan**
		1886–93	England
1888–98	India	1893–99	India
1898–1902	**Boer War**: S. Africa	1899–1902	**Boer War**: S. Africa
1902–14	England & Ireland	1904–14	England & Ireland
	1st World War:		**1st World War:**
1914–18	France & Belgium	1914–18	France & Belgium
1919	Germany	1919	Germany
1919–22	India	1919–22	India
1922	Amalgamation with 13th Hussars	1922	Amalgamation with 15th Hussars

SERVICE OF THE LIGHT DRAGOONS 1922 – 1992

	13th/18th		15th/19th
1922–29	England & Scotland	1922–24	England
1929–31	Egypt	1924–28	Egypt
1931–38	India	1928–34	India
1938–39	England	1934–39	England
1939–40	**2nd World War:** France & Belgium	1939–40	**2nd World War:** France & Belgium
1940–44	**2nd World War:** England	1940–44	**2nd World War:** England
1944–45	**2nd World War:** France, Low Countries, Germany	1944–45	**2nd World War:** France, Low Countries, Germany
1945–48	Germany	1945–47	**Palestine**
1948–50	Cyrenaica and Libya	1947–49	Sudan
1950–53	**Malaya**	1949–54	Germany
1953–58	Germany, 1957–58 **Arabia** (Squadron)	1954–57	**Malaya,** 1957 **Arabia** (Squadron)
1958–61	**Malaya** and Singapore	1957–59	Ireland
1961–67	Germany	1959–61	England
1967–68	England	1961–68	Germany, 1967 Libya (Squadron)
1968–72	Germany	1968–69	England
1972–75	England & **N. Ireland**	1969–74	Germany, including tours in **N. Ireland**
1975–77	Germany	1974–76	**N. Ireland**
1977–79	**N. Ireland**	1976–77	England & Cyprus
1979–83	England & Cyprus	1977–84	Germany & **N. Ireland**
1983–86	Germany	1984–86	England & Cyprus
1986–91	England & Cyprus	1986–92	Germany & Cyprus
1991–92	Germany		
1992	Amalgamation with 15th/19th The King's Royal Hussars	1992	Amalgamation with 13th/18th Royal Hussars (Q.M.O.)

Light Dragoons

1992-2000 Germany, Bosnia & N. Ireland
2000-2006 England, Bosnia & Iraq

TITLES BORNE BY THE REGIMENTS AT DIFFERENT TIMES

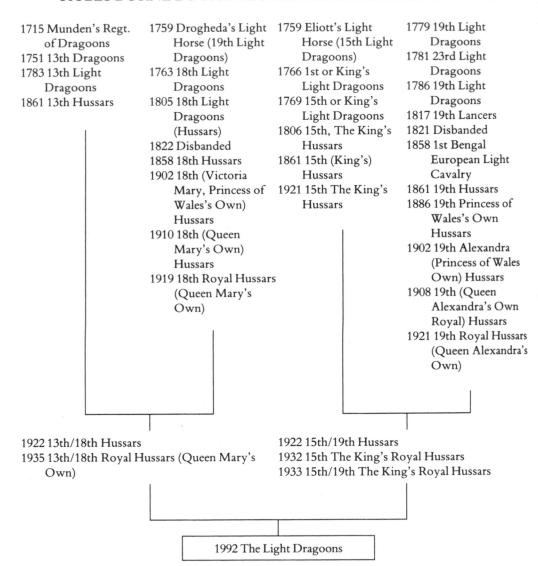

1715 Munden's Regt. of Dragoons
1751 13th Dragoons
1783 13th Light Dragoons
1861 13th Hussars

1759 Drogheda's Light Horse (19th Light Dragoons)
1763 18th Light Dragoons
1805 18th Light Dragoons (Hussars)
1822 Disbanded
1858 18th Hussars
1902 18th (Victoria Mary, Princess of Wales's Own) Hussars
1910 18th (Queen Mary's Own) Hussars
1919 18th Royal Hussars (Queen Mary's Own)

1759 Eliott's Light Horse (15th Light Dragoons)
1766 1st or King's Light Dragoons
1769 15th or King's Light Dragoons
1806 15th, The King's Hussars
1861 15th (King's) Hussars
1921 15th The King's Hussars

1779 19th Light Dragoons
1781 23rd Light Dragoons
1786 19th Light Dragoons
1817 19th Lancers
1821 Disbanded
1858 1st Bengal European Light Cavalry
1861 19th Hussars
1886 19th Princess of Wales's Own Hussars
1902 19th Alexandra (Princess of Wales Own) Hussars
1908 19th (Queen Alexandra's Own Royal) Hussars
1921 19th Royal Hussars (Queen Alexandra's Own)

1922 13th/18th Hussars
1935 13th/18th Royal Hussars (Queen Mary's Own)

1922 15th/19th Hussars
1932 15th The King's Royal Hussars
1933 15th/19th The King's Royal Hussars

1992 The Light Dragoons

INDEX

Chapters 1 to 18

361

Y